Gérard Bodson is a researcher, theologian and scholar. In addition to religion, his areas of expertise include political science and law. He has received degrees from the Institute of Comparative Law and from the European Communities Study Center University of Law. He is the author of several books on geopolitics.

ACKNOWLEDGEMENTS

I would first and foremost like to thank Anne Akrich for her invaluable contribution to this work. Thanks must also go to André Journo for his absolute dedication and for his helpful advice.

CRACKING THE
APOCALYPSE CODE

The shocking secrets of the
Book of Revelation decoded

Gérard Bodson

ELEMENT

Shaftesbury, Dorset • Boston, Massachusetts • Melbourne, Victoria

English edition ©Element Books Limited 2000
Text ©Édition °1 1999

First published as *Les secrets de l'Apocalypse* in France by Édition °1
English translation by Rosetta Translations, London

First published in Great Britain in 2000 by
Element Books Limited
Shaftesbury, Dorset SP7 8BP

Published in the USA in 2000 by
Element Books, Inc.
160 North Washington Street, Boston MA 02114

Published in Australia in 2000 by
Element Books and distributed by Penguin Books Australia Ltd
487 Maroondah Highway, Ringwood, Victoria 3134

Cover design by the Bridgewater Book Company
Designed and Typeset by the Bridgewater Book Company
Printed and bound in the USA by Courier Westford Inc.

British Library Cataloguing in Publication data available

Library of Congress Cataloging in Publication data available

ISBN 1 86204 730 8

CONTENTS

PICTURE CREDITS

The author and publisher would like to thank the following
for kind permission to use copyright material:
Bridgeman Art Library for permission to reproduce plate 2 of 'St John the Evangelist at Patmos',
right wing panel from the *Mystic Marriage of St Catherine Triptych* (1479) by Hans Memling,
Memling Museum, Bruges, Belgium; plate 6 of 'Seven-headed serpent from the Book of Revelation'
from Luther Bible (c.1530), Bible Society, London; and plate 12 of 'The Four Horsemen of the
Apocalypse – Death, Famine, Pestilence and War' from the *Apocalypse* or *The Revelations of St John
the Divine* (pub. 1498) by Albrecht Dürer, private collection.

Hulton Getty of Getty Images for permission to reproduce plate 3 of Hitler; plate 4 of US President
Franklin D Roosevelt addressing the nation on neutrality, October 1939; plate 5 of Joseph Goebbels
(right) saluting a Nazi rally; plate 7 of Panzer tank units of the German Army passing through a
blazing village; plate 8 of D-day landings; plate 9 of Erwin Rommel; plate 10 of Chief Nazis in the
dock during the final stages of the Nuremberg trial; plate 11 of Neville Chamberlain addressing the
crowd on his return from Munich, 30 September 1938; plate 13 of Abraham Lincoln; plate 14 of J
F Kennedy; plate 15 of the first atomic explosion over Hiroshima, Japan.

Magnum Photos for Tanks in Beijing by Stuart Franklin

Prologue

> *Everything of importance that happens to anyone is unexpected and unpredictable. When curiosity is overcome, prudence has to be overcome as well.*

NOTHING COULD SUM up this mad adventure better than these words. This work began with the unexpected and a lack of prudence allowed us to go forward. The small team of investigators who surrounded me for four years consisted of three men and a woman, certainly well qualified in their own fields, but nothing had prepared them for such a work as this. What had seemed at the start a kind of challenge turned progressively into a real passion. And this passion turned our lives upside down, sometimes without our knowing and sometimes with our full awareness.

Even today, I do not know if we have opened a breach in the wall of time; I do not know if what we have glimpsed, in the past and the future, can be written in the book of scientific 'certainties'. All that I know is that for Myriam the theologian, David the computer expert, Jean-Pierre the semiologist, Dimitri the historian, and myself, nothing will be the same again; never again will we look on the world with the same eyes. We have known moments of doubt and of deep discouragement, as well as hours of exaltation near to happiness; our family lives have been upset, our friends have suffered, and more than once we have nearly torn up our work irrevocably. But, here is the book!

When we started, there was never any question in our minds of the possibility of publishing our work, and this was for a particular reason.

In view of the fact that our discoveries concerned the fate of millions of individuals, we did not feel we had the right to plant worries in their minds, to provoke any feelings of anxiety, or even fear.

An event that took place in September 1998 made us question our decision. This event (which will be discussed later) was reported by the international press and it was sufficiently serious to stimulate a debate among us: should we publish or not? Of the five of us, three opted for publication. So what is presented here are the notes that I began collecting from the moment I felt that the enquiry had become more than a mere diversion. At the request of the publisher, the style has been reworked to some extent so that the reader may find it easier and less arduous to read, but the essential parts have been reproduced in their entirety. At the end of the book you will find the original text of the Revelation, as well as a table of the Hebrew alphabet with its numeric correspondences. These have been included to aid clarity. It should be noted that where verses are quoted in the main text, the italics are mine. Unless stated otherwise, chapter and verse numbers refer to the Revelation.

On this point, I should warn readers who may glance through these pages that, like us, they will find some passages harder to understand than others; however, they should not be discouraged. To make this book accessible to everyone, I have tried wherever possible to exclude terms and expressions that would be familiar only to a small group of initiates. But if my desire for clarity has not been achieved system-atically throughout the book, I ask for indulgence for the 'difficult moments'. After all, should not a reader meet the book halfway?

What is the Revelation?

The Revelation,[1] or the Apocalypse (from the Greek *apokalupsis*, 'revelation'), is the last of the books of the New Testament. It is without question the most mysterious, the most disconcerting and the most complicated of all the sixty-six books in the Bible. Few sacred writings have so gripped the imagination, and not without reason: the Revelation holds the secrets of the end of humanity, in the same way that Genesis contains the history of its origins. The violence of the visions expressed, the repeated use of dense and frequently confused symbols, its dramatic atmosphere and grandiose scenes have all contributed to make the Revelation a genuine enigma.

According to the most widespread tradition, it was written in the Greek language in about AD 95 by the apostle John, who had been exiled to the island of Patmos during the reign of Emperor Domitian (81–96). He returned to Ephesus under Nerva (96–8), and died there at the beginning of the reign of Trajan (98–117).

John, the son of Zebedee and Salome, was born in Bethesda and became a fisherman. Before the ministry of Jesus, he had probably been a disciple of John the Baptist. He then became one of the twelve apostles and was one of the inner group of Jesus' disciples. Both before and after the resurrection of Christ, John was often named together with Peter.[2] The College of Jerusalem sent the two apostles to Samaria.[3] In the fourth Gospel, John is referred to as 'the disciple whom Jesus loved', and he was the only one of the twelve to be mentioned at the foot of the cross, at the moment of the death of Jesus.

With a greater or lesser degree of certainty, several works are attributed to John: the fourth Gospel, three Epistles, the Dormition of Mary, and … the Book of Revelation. But at this point it should be made clear that many historians are convinced that John the son of Zebedee was not the author of the Book of Revelation. Even the date of the apostle's death is controversial. Relying on Mark 10:35–47, some people put the martyrdom of John in the year 72 or 70, about thirty years earlier than the date assumed for the writing of the Revelation. Nevertheless, I deliberately chose the 'traditional' version, and it is not my intention here to take part in a debate on the subject, still less on the authorship and dating of the Holy Scriptures. To use the phrase of Gérard Mordillat and Jérôme Prieur, we were all aware that the whole of the Bible is 'a compost heap of controversy'.[4]

THE CONTENTS

What can we learn from the Book of Revelation? Let me say right away that at first sight it as complicated as it is confusing.

On the island of Patmos, in a moment of complete ecstasy, a visionary calling himself John sees the Son of Man. He is the leader of a mission to the Seven Christian Churches of Asia Minor, the main one of which is in the capital, Ephesus. The first part of the book consists of moral exhortations to the Churches in the purest tradition of the oracles of biblical prophets.

Then the visionary sees the Lord in all his glory. He holds a sealed book which is opened by the Lamb. The opening of the seals causes four coloured horses to appear. At the opening of the sixth seal, the prodromes or warning signs of the reign of God appear. At the opening of the seventh seal, seven angels blow their trumpets one after another, further sign of the trials preceding the reign of the elect.

Next an angel appears, carrying a small scroll that the visionary must 'eat' (as Ezekiel had done at the time of his first vision). Like Ezekiel, John is charged with measuring the celestial city. But the seventh trumpet sounds. The sky opens and the visionary sees a struggle between a woman and a dragon. This monster is succeeded by two beasts, the first with seven heads and the second with two horns. The Lamb again appears triumphant. After the reaping and harvesting of blood, John sees the seven plagues of the wrath of God distributed by seven angels holding seven goblets.

Then he sees the punishment of Babylon, the whore. The sky triumphs, with the appearance of a rider on a white horse who captures the beast and chains it up for a thousand years. The martyrs rule. Satan reappears but he is beaten once again; the dead are judged and the New Jerusalem shines forth.

THE FORM AND THE CONTENT

The weight of opinion is that, compared with the Gospels, the Acts of the Apostles and the Epistles, the Revelation represents a completely different literary genre. Its mysterious aspect is reinforced by the contrast that is apparent between the content of the Revelation and the rest of the New Testament. Although certain links with other canonical writings can be identified, in particular with the Epistle to the Hebrews, the 'historic' aspect of the Christian message is almost entirely passed over.

Doubts have been raised about the authenticity of this strange book since the early days of Christianity. It quickly became apparent that it was unlikely that the same person could have been the author of two works so dissimilar in both content and form as the Revelation and the Gospel of St John. In the third century, Denys of Alexandria had already pointed out the differences that separated the two books, making it clear that it was very implausible that the visionary of the Apocalypse could have been an apostle, and in particular the apostle John. Some fathers of the Church such as Cyril of Jerusalem, Gregory of Nazianzus,[5] Theodore and John Chrysostom mocked the doctrine contained in the work or abstained from talking about it. This no doubt explains why the Church rejected the text for over 300 years. Although quoted with admiration by many ancient authors, it was only known to Rome through its opponents, who saw in it the work of a heretic called Cerinthus.[6]

The whole of the Eastern Church also had major reservations about it, to the extent that it was positively excluded from its catalogue of Holy Books. It was not until the Council of Laodicea in 397 that the Book of Revelation found favour in the eyes of the theologians of the time. The Church then trusted the facts provided by Irene of Lyon,[7] whose authority removed any doubts.

1 The number of the beast

The creation signals the end of the world,
just as birth already heralds death ...

IT ALL BEGAN on 24 September 1992 .While reading the official journal of the European Community, I came upon a written question from Mr David Martin. At that time Mr Martin was Vice-President of the European Parliament and a member of the United Kingdom Labour Party. Dated 6 April 1992, the question was addressed to the Commission, as follows:

WRITTEN QUESTION NO 739/92

Is the Commission aware that, in the name of their Christian faith,
some people are opposed to the compulsory application of the symbol
of the Community? Could the Commission draw up a list of the
directives which impose the use of the symbol of the Community,
and specify if exemptions from using this symbol may be authorized
and, if so, in what situations?

And here is the reply given by M. Bangemann, who at that time was Vice-President of the Commission, responsible for the internal market, industrial affairs and relations with the European Parliament.

ON BEHALF OF THE COMMISSION (2 JUNE 1992)

It is true that it has been reported to the Commission that, in the name of their Christian faith, some people are opposed to the compulsory application of the EC mark, which they associate with the mark of the beast in the Book of Revelation, Chapter 13. Today the Council of Ministers has adopted ten directives in the framework of the new approach which foresees the use of the EC mark; these directives are as follows …

A geopolitician by training but always fascinated by religious matters, I remembered that the question referred to a passage in the Revelation of St John. Stopping what I was doing, I grabbed my Bible and found the relevant verse:

… so that no one can buy or sell who does not have the mark, that is, the name of the beast or the number of its name.[1]

What could this mean, other than that some Christians were making an association between this verse and the 'EC' symbol imposed compulsorily on all products sold within the European Community. Naivety? Excessive credulity? Also, how did the initials represent the 'name of the beast or the number of its name'? As we shall see, it was not until much later that this parallel was to take shape and appear in all its clarity. For the time being, I put my Bible back on the shelf and thought no more about it.

Some time later, the Revelation came to mind again.

It was in September 1993. I had gone to my bank to change some money. I was waiting my turn at the counter when my eye fell on the board giving the current exchange rates: Dutch guilders, Swiss francs, yen, dollars, and the Ecu, which has now become the Euro. The exchange rate for the European Currency Unit was fixed at … 6.66 francs. Immediately I recalled another verse, one that is undoubtedly the most striking of all the verses in the Book of Revelation, since it is connected with a very particular number that has inspired a plethora of films dealing with the Devil or the Antichrist: 666.

> *... let anyone with understanding calculate the number of the beast: for it is the number of a man. Its number is six hundred and sixty-six.*[2]

We are indeed in the realms of the trivial, I thought! Although the figure of 6.66 applied in relation to the franc, obviously this exchange rate would not apply to the other currencies in the Community. I smiled to myself that I should be so 'gullible', and the moment passed.

Toward the end of May 1994, I was in Greece defending my candidature in the European elections. Once the political meetings were over, I decided to go somewhere I had a particular liking for: Mount Athos, a holy place of the Greek Orthodox Church, and a magical site if ever there was one.

It was in the tenth century that the first monks were established on this 'holy mountain', to be immediately joined by fellow Christians from the whole of the Orthodox world: Greeks, Georgians, southern Slavs, Russians, Italians and Romanians. Since then, twenty great, virtually independent, monasteries have shared this peninsula, organized in a sort of autonomous federation and frozen outside time.

Often in the past, I have felt the need to retreat to Mount Athos to reflect, meditate and take stock. Over the years I have struck up a friendship with a priest, Father Alexander, a learned man deeply interested in theology who is successfully mastering Hebrew. It was naturally to his monastery that I went right away. I told him about the two 'events' I had come across: the parliamentary question and the exchange rate of the franc to the Ecu. I expected a condescending or even an ironic remark, but what he said was quite the opposite. The monk gravely nodded his head:

'My friend, chance does not exist. It is only the pseudonym of the Lord God when he wants to preserve his anonymity. You can be sure that the key to the Revelation is in *the number of the beast*. Nowhere else. I know this, I who have been trying to find this key for over ten years. As you may imagine, I have been searching in vain.'

'Where does your certainty come from?'

He did not answer my question but said: 'Follow me.'

A moment later we were in front of a lectern on which the priest had put the Book of Revelation.

'Listen closely to me, this is very important,' he said, pointing his finger at chapter 13, verse 18:

... let anyone with understanding calculate the number of the beast, for it is the number of a person. Its number is six hundred and sixty-six.

'You know of course that in both the Hebrew and the Greek languages, as well as in many ancient alphabets, letters have particular numeric values. So, we can use the value of the letters of a word to interpret it, by comparing it with another word which has the same numeric value. For example, if we take the phrase from Genesis 32:5: "I have lived with Laban", the numeric value of Laban is equivalent to 613, which would mean that "during his time with Laban, Jacob kept the 613 commandments".'

He continued: 'The first mention of this procedure is found in an inscription of Sargon II[3] (727–707 BC) describing the construction of a temple whose measurements corresponded to the numerical value of the king's name. Known to the ancient Greeks, it appears in Hebrew literature at the time of the Second Temple and it was frequently used in the Talmud,[4] the midrash[5] and, during the Middle Ages, in the speculations of the Hassidim[6] of Germany.'

He paused before going on. 'Yes, I know, my friend. The explanation that follows may seem arduous and rather tedious, but I have to give it to you, because it is on this that the mechanism depends. Known as "gematria", this method of coding was extremely widespread in the time of John, particularly (indeed essentially) with the cabbalistic Jews[7] who were trying to penetrate the mysteries of the Torah. But when we mention arithmology (commonly known as numerology), we cannot avoid referring to the mathematical/religious genius Pythagoras. To him, all things *were numbers*. Starting perhaps from reflections on musical harmony, which he reduced to a system of mathematical proportion, he arrived at the conclusion that numbers were so to speak the principle, the source and the root of everything. According to this thinking, which makes no distinction between arithmetic, geometry and physics, arithmetical unity is at one with the geometric point. From this kind of speculation came the mathematical discoveries traditionally attributed to Pythagoras.'

The monk was silent for a moment before he continued. 'So far as the Revelation is concerned, John himself refers frequently to gematria. This method of analysis is therefore the only possible one if we want to try and decode the secret meaning that the apostle has concealed in his work. Believe me, this secret meaning does exist.

'According to St John, the number of the Beast is 666. As you may imagine, this strange figure aroused the curiosity of Christian exegetes and learned men who, after the death of St John, spontaneously sought to attribute it to a Roman emperor – a natural step when you consider the suffering to which the Christian church was subjected, particularly during the reigns of Nero and Domitian. I therefore tried – using *Greek numbering* – to find a correlation between a Roman emperor and the number 666.[8] Immediately Emperor Domitian (755) was eliminated. I tried Nero, but "Nero" is equivalent to 1005! The compound name Lord-Caesar was also considered. But "Caesar" (332) and "Lord" (284) come to 616.

'I then tried another compound name "Caesar-Nero". But here again, the sum obtained (332 + 1005 = 1337) did not match.

'In despair I decided to change the method. I took *Hebrew* numeration as a basis rather than Greek, and I found 676. As you can see, this number is imperfect since it still does not correspond to that given by John which is, as we know, 666. But it is the number arrived at using Hebrew numeration. Do you understand me so far?'

To my embarrassment, I had to admit that I had difficulty in following him.

He replied patiently: 'One of the Hebrew letters that makes up Caesar-Nero (קיסר נרון) is none other than Yod (י), which has a value of 10. In arithmancy, 10 represents the figure of the Lord, and the letter Yod, the first of the holy letters, is part of the composition of the divine name. Remember: *Yod, hé, vav, hé* (יהוה) – YHWH or Jehovah – was the name chosen by Elohim when he revealed himself to Moses in the Burning Bush.'

He quoted from memory:

Then said Moses to the Lord: 'So! I am going to find the children of Israel and I say to them: "The Lord of your fathers has sent me to you!" But if they ask what is his name, how shall I reply to them?'
The Lord then said to Moses …

Father Alexander interrupted himself, picked up a pencil and paper, and wrote: יהוה 'Ehyeh, acher, Ehyeh.' I am what I am.[9]

Then he continued speaking. 'The number 10 is therefore necessarily inseparable from God, and God could not in any event be connected with Nero, a pagan emperor if ever there was one. We must therefore deduct the number 10 from the total number. That is how the number 666 is arrived at.'

'And so? What does it all mean?'

This time he made a weary gesture. 'I do not know … The only conclusion I was able to reach was that John could not disregard the fact that in the Greek language the number 666 did not correspond to anything. But, being Jewish, he would have perfectly understood that the same number, calculated according to the Hebrew tradition – that is to say, gematria – would arrive at Caesar-Nero. It nonetheless remains the case that it is absurd to want at all costs to find a connection between a Roman emperor such as Nero and the "number of the beast", since John writes in the first verse of the first chapter:

The revelation of Jesus Christ, which God gave him to show his servants what must soon take place …

'And in 1:19:

Now write what you have seen, what is, and what is to take place *after this.*

'The Revelation, let us remember, was written in AD 95. The great persecution inflicted on the Christians by Nero dates back to about the year 65. Nero himself died in 68. So, what sort of prophecy was it that predicted an event that had already occurred thirty years earlier?'

Deeply confused, I decided to return to France and gather together a group of investigators, with the aim of decoding the strange text of St John. An amazing adventure was about to begin, of whose outcome I was completely unaware.

2 A mind that has wisdom…

A thread drawn in a labyrinth
can restore the skein.

I ADMIT THAT convincing the other members of the team was not an easy task. While some were immediately enthusiastic about the cause, others were more hesitant. It was not that the people in question doubted the logic of Father Alexander's reasoning, but to them the task seemed so vast. There were also more down-to-earth problems. Each of us already had a job; some of us worked in information technology, others in education or, in my own case, in an equally exciting milieu as a political representative in an official body. But ultimately, passion, curiosity and, most of all, the dream itself triumphed.

That is how in the middle of autumn 1994 we came to meet in Paris for a work session. In addition to myself there were four others: Jean-Pierre, a semiologist, and, like me, a Frenchman; David, an English computer specialist and a Protestant; Dimitri, a Greek historian and linguist who was teaching in Paris; and, finally, a brilliant young woman, Myriam, a theologian from Haifa, for whom 'numerology' held no secrets and who spoke French as fluently as Hebrew.[1]

In fact, it was Myriam who first went into more detail about Father Alexander's remarks on gematria: 'Your friend has failed to develop a point that is quite important. It is true that we obtain the number 666 for Caesar-Nero by subtracting 10. But you should also know that we can carry out the same manipulation with the figure 1. I shall explain.

'א (aleph) is the first letter of the Hebrew alphabet and corresponds to the number 1. Like 10, this number represents God in the Science of Numbers, the supreme Unity. And in the same way that the Science of Numbers allows us to subtract 10 from words that express an opposition to the divine, we can do the same with the number 10.

'I should explain that the letter א (aleph) is silent. That is, it does not have its own sound and it cannot be voiced without the help of a vowel.'

She paused with a slight smile on her lips. 'You realize the symbolic importance of this? The Name of God is silent. It is by definition unpronounceable. And for their part, the Muslims forbid any reproduction of his image. No one can pronounce the sacred name, just as the imagination of man is forbidden to represent him in any way at all. But let us return to gematria. See how the mechanism works. It is both subtle and brilliant. 'Take a word like EMETH (אמת). It means Truth. Its value is 441, or 4 + 4 + 1 = 9.

'Since the original sin of Adam, the most perfect human being will never be able to rise above that number. On the other hand, God who is the supreme truth is the only being with a value of 10. In the word "Emeth" the number 1, placed at the end, represents Omega (the end). By adding 1, the value of alpha, the beginning, to the start of the number, we get 1,441, making a total of 10, the absolute truth. The message is clear: without God there is no absolute truth.'

She wrote the four digits on a page and asked: 'Do you notice anything interesting?'

Each of us in turn made a suggestion, but none of them was the right answer.

She laughed at our lack of observation and said jokingly: 'You are only men after all … Look, whether you read from left to right or right to left, you always get 1,441.'

'So what? What is so revealing about that?'

'So the wheel turns full circle. God, the absolute truth, envelops the universe, and whichever way we turn, this truth is omnipresent. On the other hand, if we remove the letter aleph (א) from the word "Emeth" (as if we had removed the E) we are left with "Meth" (מת), which means "death". The message is simple: without the help and support of the divine, man is condemned to nothingness. But I must mention something else as well. Gematria can be taken further by "theosophical reduction", a technique known throughout antiquity that consists in reducing all numbers made up of two or more digits to one-digit numbers by adding them repeatedly until only one digit is left. For example, 378 = 3 + 7 + 8 = 18 = 9. Is that clear to you all?'

The whole group agreed that it was.

Having clarified this matter, our first task was to try and define what Father Alexander called 'the key'.

Looking through the Book of Revelation, one is immediately struck by the fact that the Greek syntax is sometimes incorrect and that the author had not fully mastered the language. There is a reason for this: John was first and foremost a Jew and his native tongue was Hebrew, or more probably Aramaic. So why did he write in a language with which he was unfamiliar when he could have used his own? He did so simply because at that time Greek was the most widespread language in the Mediterranean region. It was therefore natural for John to write in Greek, since he wanted his text to be read by as many people as possible.

On the other hand, the Revelation abounds with recollections, reminders and references to what is commonly called the Old Testament or the Torah. It is evident that the author thinks and reasons in a manner dictated by his Jewish culture and his mother tongue, Hebrew or Aramaic.

The symbols, the numeration and the eschatological character[2] of the text are very Jewish in tone. There is no doubt that the author expresses himself through biblical images and terms borrowed from the Books of Isaiah, Jeremiah and Ezekiel, the Apocalypse of Daniel[3] and the Psalms, in other words from the Old Testament in general. This clearly shows that John was very familiar with the Old Testament in the original Hebrew or Aramaic version. He never quotes from the Greek translation of the Old Testament known as the Septuagint.[4] In addition, the Revelation is full of Aramaic expressions, creating the impression of a typically Hebrew prophecy.

All the symbols and fantastic visions of dragons, angels, candlesticks, stars, lambs, and fights with monstrous animals in which God always came out victorious were familiar to readers of works such as the Books of Baruch and the Books of Enoch.[5] There are also many similarities with the Fourth Book of Esdras. The vision of the little book that John must 'eat' recalls a passage from Ezekiel (2:8):

> But you, mortal, hear what I say to you; do not be rebellious like that rebellious house; open your mouth and eat what I give you.

The various plagues that devastate the earth are naturally reminiscent of the plagues of Egypt, and the list of examples could be continued. But it would be a mistake to interpret the text as a naive transcription of the mystical experience of a visionary. On the contrary, the book has been skilfully conceived and teems with erudite symbols.

Still more decisive is the fact that in its four hundred and five verses the Apocalypse contains *two hundred and eighty-five text quotations from the Old Testament!* This averages out at *five quotations every seven verses,* a far larger number of quotations than there are in all four Gospels together. Also, the Book of Revelation consists of twenty-two chapters representing the twenty-two letters of the Hebrew alphabet.

Sometimes John even leaves passages undeveloped, merely referring to the prophets. An example is the final struggle between Gog and Magog and the Lord God.[6]

Once it is accepted that the work was written in Greek by a Jew, an inevitable conclusion follows. In order to decode its symbolism the work should be 'read' in the language in which its author John was accustomed to think – that is, in Hebrew.

If the Book of Revelation has resisted all attempts at decoding it until now, it is because the various theologians, mainly Catholics, who have studied it have approached it through the Greek language, ignoring essential points such as the mind of the author, his way of thinking, his culture and his roots. As far as Jewish cabbalists are concerned, very few have been interested in a 'Christian' text. But as soon as one becomes interested in the work's esoteric aspects, it is immediately apparent that the text addresses not only Christianity but humanity as a whole. In this lies the most moving and most unexpected message. In his exile, Christ's disciple John, the greatest of the apostles, turned towards the whole world, towards all men and women, whether they were Jewish, Christian or children of Islam.[7]

As our research progressed we had a premonition, without being certain, that something would be revealed to us. This was a disconcerting feeling, bewildering both in its strength and its visionary aspect. Very soon we had to give in to the facts: *the Book of Revelation contained a message*, complex yet surprisingly discreet. Even more disturbingly, it was John himself who was giving us the key to decipher this message. Twice the apostle put us on our guard:

> *This calls for wisdom: let anyone with understanding calculate the*
> *number of the beast, for it is the number of a person. Its number is six*
> *hundred and sixty-six.8*

Then again:

> *This calls for a mind that has wisdom.9*

Obviously it was the first verse, the one mentioned by Father Alexander, that initially caught our attention.

We saw clearly that John had used Hebrew numeration while constructing his sentence in Greek. Why did he use this stratagem? For fun? Or inadvertently? This is a difficult question to answer. In truth, the only plausible reason must be that he wanted to communicate the 'instructions for use' of his Revelation to future readers 'endowed with insight'. By skilful use of the two languages, he sought to convey to us that there were two meanings contained in his writings: the first one 'exoteric' (from the Greek *exōterikos,* from the outside), the other 'esoteric' (*esōterikos*, from the inside, reserved for followers).

The first meaning is the one that has prevailed until now. To the Church, the Book of Revelation is merely about the struggle of Christianity against the beast, symbolizing the Roman Empire. But to restrict oneself to this interpretation – that is, an exclusively 'exoteric' explanation – is to betray the deep meaning contained in John's message. Also, as we have seen, a prophecy that refers to past events is no longer a prophecy.

The number 666 is indeed the keystone to the mechanism that enables the secrets of the Revelation to be deciphered. When John mentions this number, is he not warning us that he is making a transition from Greek to Hebrew? So, if we want to use the key provided by the apostle, we must use the same method he used.

Besides the exoteric meaning, what else could the beast that dominates the Revelation from beginning to end represent? Let us look again at the verse of John:

This calls for wisdom: let anyone with understanding calculate the number of the beast, for it is the number of a person. *Its number is six hundred and sixty-six.*

This clearly gives us three tasks:

1 To find the name of the person.

2 To put further details next to this name, such as 'Caesar' in the case of 'Nero'.

3 To add all the letters together using Hebrew numerology to obtain the number 666.

As one might suspect, the major difficulty lies in the multitude of possible names. To us it seemed an immense, almost insoluble, task, to which it would be necessary to devote several years. We had no choice. The only way of overcoming this difficulty was to call on the computer. This was David's responsibility. Nevertheless, however powerful a computer may be, it is still only a machine. It has neither soul nor intellect. It would be an affront to the human spirit and its genius to imagine that everything could be solved by the single expedient of the computer. After all, it was not the machine that invented man ... So – forgive us – we also used our grey matter.

We were all of us convinced that the beast personified a person of exceptional calibre, someone unique, one of those beings who has left an indelible mark on the existence of humanity. To judge by the descriptions that John made throughout the text, this person could only have been a conqueror:

> ... *the beast that comes up from the abyss will make war on them and conquer them and kill them.*[10]

> *And the beast that I saw was like a leopard, its feet were like a bear's, and its mouth was like a lion's mouth. And the dragon gave it his power and his throne and great authority.*[11]

I will spare the reader the meticulous list of compound names which we made to enter into the computer.

Briefly, this ranged from Genghis-Khan, Genghis-Mongolia, Napoleon-Bonaparte, Julius-Caesar-Rome, Hannibal-Carthage, Alexander-the-Great-Macedonia, to Tamerlane. The program developed by David asked the computer to extract the equivalent numbers from these names, using Hebrew numeration, and to see if the total of these numerical equivalents resulted in the number 666.

That evening, all five of us met again in front of the computer screen, and – dare I admit it? – we were all as excited as a bunch of teenagers, at the same time anxious and burning with impatience. Were we going to discover something that would be worthy of interest? Were we on the right lines? Was this enterprise anything more than a pipe dream?

We did not have to wait long. After a few minutes, a single compound name appeared before our eyes, just one name which met our conditions.

I remember as if it was yesterday the black letters that shone out from a blue background:

ADOLF-HITLER-AUSTRIA

אדולף היטלר אוסטריה

A quick calculation, a double check, served only to confirm the incredible result presented by the computer:

Adolf =   *121*
Hitler =   *254*
Austria =   *291*
Total =   *666*

As may be imagined, we were completely overcome. Was it possible? And what did this information mean?

David cut short our astonishment. 'Just a moment! Myriam clearly explained that in gematria we had to subtract the number 10 or 1 from words or expressions that were in opposition to the divine. Logically, therefore, we must subtract one or other of these two numbers from the total.'

It was Myriam the theologian who replied. 'That's not so. When John quoted 666, which commentators have incorrectly associated with Caesar-Nero, he was, as we have seen, making a prediction of the future, and not of the past. Consequently, in subtracting 10 from Caesar-Nero, which actually makes 676, the number that John proposes to us is, if I may so put it, "pure" a number already reduced by 10.'

A tense silence followed the young woman's explanation. So did the Revelation foresee the advent of the Führer? The Second World War? At this stage there was nothing to support such an assumption. It might perhaps have been a coincidence, an accident. But then again, perhaps it was not just a matter of chance … ?

3 The great city

A giant clamour arose as a prelude to the apocalypse evoking the fear of the end of the world.

'WE MUST TAKE care, not to arrive at too hasty a conclusion, built on shifting sands,' said Jean-Pierre. 'We might be building castles in the air. Let's be careful and try to be as rigorous as possible.'

We could only agree that he was right. If the 'presence' of the Führer had a reason, if it concealed something deeper, we must prove it. But how should we search through the maze without going astray? What route should we follow?

I made a suggestion: 'In assuming that the words Adolf-Hitler-Austria are not the result of a coincidence, would it not be logical to look in that direction?'

'No doubt, but how should we set about it?'

'We must read the text again and again, analyze it, and examine it in the smallest detail to try to discover a connection: some words perhaps or some names that relate to the individual or the period.'

'It would be easier to search for a needle in a haystack … '

Nonetheless, we settled down to the task. Several days passed, fruitless yet exciting. We remained on the alert for an internal thrill, something indefinable that would sustain us in our quest. It was during one of our work sessions that David made a suggestion:

'It seems to me that there is perhaps a clue in these verses:

11:8 And their dead bodies will lie in the street of the Great City that is prophetically called Sodom and Egypt.
16:19 The great city was split into three parts, and the cities of the nations fell. God remembered great Babylon *and gave her the wine-cup of the fury of his wrath.*

He went on: 'What do these verses tell us? Essentially they mention cities and countries: Sodom, Babylon and Egypt.'

'Yes indeed, but where is the link with Hitler?'

'It could be that behind these indications is hidden the name of a German city, probably Berlin, or that of a country, Germany.'

We could only agree.

'To begin with, let us take the first clue of the verse: the great city (העיר הגדולה).' He turned towards Myriam: 'What is its numerical value?'

The theologian calculated for a few seconds and then said: '338.'

'Let's compare it with Germany.'

'Germany (גרמניה) makes 308. False trail.'

'And Sodom?'

Another moment, then Myriam replied: '110. Again no relationship.'

The disappointment began to show on our faces.

'Shall we try Babylon?'

Myriam made her calculations: '34. I think we're on the wrong track.'

'Perhaps we could compare the names of the cities with Berlin?

Myriam sighed. 'Sorry. Berlin makes 292. No correlation with Sodom or Babylon.'

There was a long moment of silence. Obviously, we were going round in circles. Then an idea suddenly came to me:

'Wait a second! Read John's verse again: "The great city was split into three parts." I get the idea that the message is somewhere in these two words: great city.'

Everyone looked in my direction, while I became more specific: 'At the end of the war, and after the defeat of the German forces, Germany was divided into three parts: Berlin, which had a special status; the Soviet zone, known as "Die Zone" by the Germans, which would give birth to the German Democratic Republic; and finally the zone occupied by the Allies, itself divided into three, which would become the Federal Republic of Germany. Do you follow me?'

I repeated: 'Into three parts ... "The great city was divided into three parts".'

This produced some indecision within the group.

'It is certainly possible,' Dimitri conceded. 'But it is only a hypothesis; it remains to be proved.'

I went on: 'The verse tells us: "the *great city* that is prophetically called *Sodom and Egypt*". What this is saying is that the great city is also Egypt.'

I turned towards Myriam, but she had anticipated my question. 'Egypt (מצרים) is equivalent to 380!' She announced the figure as if it was a cry of victory. 'Egypt (מצרים), 380 and Germany (גרמניה), 308. The figures are the same but in a different order!'

'Things are definitely becoming clearer.'

There was another silence. The tension was almost palpable.

'This is encouraging,' said David, 'but it is still not enough. We must go deeper and find other confirmation.'

Still following the direct line of a geopolitical thought, I continued: 'If St John called Germany to mind, it must certainly be implicated in the "final battle".'

'You mean you are talking about Armageddon?' asked Myriam.

'Yes indeed.' And I quoted the verse in question (16:16): ... 'And they assembled them at the place that in Hebrew is called Armageddon ... '[28]

'Armageddon ... ' repeated the young woman. 'Of course, you know that the word is already itself an enigma.' Without waiting for our reply, she went on: 'It is the transition of the Hebrew word *har-megiddōn* (הרמגדון), "the mountain of Megiddo". The place is situated in a plain, and the nearest mountain, Mount Carmel, is over 10 kilometres (6 miles) away. It is quoted a dozen times in the Torah. It is to the south-east of Megiddo, where Saul died, and it was at Mount Carmel, to the north-west of Megiddo, that the prophets of Baal were massacred on the orders of Elijah. In the Book of Judges, chapter 5, verse 20, it is said that at Megiddo: "The stars fought from heaven." Some commentators are certain that the future battle of Armageddon will flare up all over the Middle East.'

'However that may be,' retorted David, 'the apostle also seems to attach great importance to it, since he wrote "they assembled them at the place that in Hebrew is called Armageddon". According to him it is there that the final battle will take place. So it confirms the prophecy of Ezekiel: the battle between Gog and Magog. If Gérard is correct, it could refer to the final battle that ended with the fall of Berlin, on 30 April 1945.'

I became impatient: 'What number does Armageddon make?'

Myriam immersed herself again in her calculations, then looked at us with a troubled expression. 'This time I think we are onto something.'

'What is the numerical value?'

'308 ... '

'308! The same figure as Germany! Are you sure?'

She nodded her head in agreement.

I leapt up from my chair. 'Let us summarize:

1 The great city or Egypt (מצרים) = 380

2 Germany (גרמניה) = 308

3 Armageddon (הרמגדון) = 308

'We have not reached the end of the exercise, but for my part I am more and more reluctant to think that the words "Adolf-Hitler-Austria" were there by chance, and believe that this coincidence is repeated by the numerical equivalents of the words "Germany", "great city" and "Armageddon".'

'No doubt you are right,' David interrupted. 'However, without wanting to play the troublemaker, these clues – which are not insignificant, I admit – still do not prove that the text of the Book of Revelation refers to the Second World War. I mean the whole of it.'

'The opposite would be impossible. If not, why would they be mentioned in the text?'

He raised his arms heavenwards. 'If I had the answer, we would not be here. I repeat: I find these clues not insignificant, but insufficient. I would like us to confirm them.'

No doubt David was right, but we were exhausted. We were certainly not going to find confirmation that night, particularly as Myriam had to return to Israel the next day. We would keep in touch with her through the Internet. (I should point out that in autumn 1994 this means of communication, which has since become so widespread, was only in its infancy in France. In a way we were pioneers.)

About two weeks later, the four of us, David, Dimitri, Jean-Pierre and I, met together again. At each of these gatherings, my flat resembled a caravanserai, littered with extra beds, storage boxes, computers, scanners and so on, the whole interspersed with cups of strong coffee.

Immediately we decided to tackle a direction we found interesting. It involved the same logic that had brought us to the word Armageddon. Had not that word led directly to the final battle? But a battle implies protagonists. Who did the apostle suggest as contestants?

> *20:8 ... the nations at the four corners of the earth, Gog and Magog, in order to gather them for battle; they are as numerous as the sands of the sea.*

As well as in St John, the names Gog and Magog appear in the Books of Ezekiel, Genesis, and Chronicles. What is said about them is extremely confusing. Some cabbalists even suggest that, according to circumstances, Gog could be Magog and vice versa.

Our new approach could be summarized in a few words. If Armageddon really referred to Germany, it was possible that Gog and Magog represented Germany and its conqueror, the United States of America. Our first step was to send the two names to Myriam. Glued to the computer screen, we waited for her reply.

Gog (גוֹג) = 12
Magog (מגוֹג) = 52

We had difficulty in hiding our disappointment. Neither of these numbers corresponded to the numerical value of Germany (308) or America (356). The house of cards was collapsing. What was the answer? We suddenly had the impression that we were slipping into a labyrinth whose exit even the architect himself had been unable to find.

But this was to reckon without intuition. Intuition can be a two-edged sword. I no longer remember who wrote: 'The discoveries of intuition must always be supported by logic. In everyday life as in science, intuition is a powerful but dangerous means of knowledge. It is sometimes difficult to distinguish it from illusion.' We had indeed to avoid the danger of illusion.

The voice of Dimitri, our Greek linguist, brought me out of my reverie. 'Do you remember the remark that Father Alexander made about the apostle's method?'

'What was that?'

'If my memory serves me right, talking to you he said about the number of the beast: "When John spelt out the number, what was he doing if not warning us that he was making a conversion from Greek to Hebrew?"'

'That's right.'

'So might not the apostle have done this in the opposite direction? For the sole pleasure of shuffling the cards.'

Jean-Pierre and I opened our eyes wide.

'You mean to say that a word could also be used in its original language, in Greek?'

'That is a supposition. From all the evidence, we are looking at a man of great learning, and one who is fully aware of what he is doing. He is very familiar with the Old Testament and all the holy texts. He writes in Greek but he thinks in a Jewish way. He scatters his information like so many pebbles. If he is true to his method, which consists of writing in Greek a text coded in Hebrew, it is also possible to envisage the opposite.'

'This would mean that the words Gog and Magog must be calculated in relation to the Greek alphabet and not the Hebrew one.'

'I think so.' He scribbled the two names Gog and Magog on a piece of paper and calculated their values.

'Well?'

He did not reply, but continued writing until at last he laughed hesitantly in a way that could have been provoked either by satisfaction or nervousness, I could not tell which.

'Judge for yourselves,' he said, pointing his index finger at the paper.

Gog (Γωγ) = 806 = 8 + 6 = 14, 1 + 4 = 5

Magog (Μαγωγ) = 847 = 8 + 4 + 7 = 19

Below that he had written:

Germany (גרמניה) = 308 = 3 + 8 = 11, 1+ 1 = 2

America (אמריקה) =356 = 3 + 5 + 6 = 14, 4 +1 = 5

Dimitri continued: 'I was right. Gog has the same value as America: 5.'

Jean-Pierre protested. 'But Magog (847) does not correspond to the word Germany (2). And in any case one cannot separate Gog from Magog. Both sets of names must correspond. One is not enough!'

Another tunnel, another disillusionment. But Dimitri was partly right. We were convinced that there was nothing coincidental about the relationship between Gog and the United States of America. But why, then, was there not an identical link between Magog and Germany? There must be a flaw in our reasoning. What was it?

The answer came to us in the small hours of the morning, when we were about to end the discussion.

I was on the landing waiting for the elevator, when suddenly an image of the war and the adversaries who were fighting each other came to me. On the one hand, in effect, there was the massive strength of the United States, without which it is very probable that Europe would today be German territory. On the other side was Germany, but not Germany alone.

I went back into the room, followed by the others. The computer was still on. I wrote a new e-mail to Myriam and sent it off. There was nothing more to do but cross our fingers and hope …

4 Gog and Magog

THE NEXT DAY at dawn I checked my e-mails. I found Myriam's reply to the questions I had sent her:

Germany (גרמניה) = 308
Japan (יפן) = 140
Italy (איטליה) = 65
Romania (רומניה) = 311
Hungary (הונגריה) = 279
Finland (פינלנד) = 224
Bulgaria (בּלגריה) = 250
Total = 1577, or 20

But actually, as the young theologian Myriam pointed out, the total is really 19. This is because, as explained earlier, one or other of the two sacred numbers (1 and 10) has to be subtracted from the number of anything opposed to the divine.

The numerical value of Magog! Seven countries. The seven heads of the Dragon ... On the one hand we had America and Gog, both equalling 5; on the other, Magog, which came to 19.

In fact, only in this way could the apostle's message be read. Faced with the military power of America, the other side did not consist of

Germany alone; willingly or not, a coalition of seven countries were on the side of the Third Reich.

When Germany invaded Soviet Russia, Romania joined it in order to recover Bessarabia. It crossed the Dnieper and annexed Odessa. This event influenced the war against Great Britain and the United States.

As for the Hungarian government, having achieved a revision of the Treaty of Trianon it then allied itself with the cause of the Reich. This enabled it to recapture Koflice and recover part of Transylvania. In return it was compelled to enter the war against the Soviet Union, taking part in the operations on the Russian front without enthusiasm.

On the Finnish side, discreet meetings at a high level had been taking place with German emissaries since the summer of 1940. These meetings continued for several months. In April 1941 the German–Finnish pact was signed and on 25 June 1941 Finland officially entered the war, following the bombing of Helsinki by Soviet aircraft. In the early days the armies of Mannerheim won some significant successes. In autumn 1941, they attacked the city of Petroskoi, but they did not take part directly in the siege of Leningrad.

Under the nationalist officers of the Zveno group, Bulgaria had been moving towards authoritarian government since 1935. The drift of internal politics towards fascism was accompanied by a similar development in foreign policy: Bulgaria's political affinities were with the Axis countries, but it also adhered to a system of exchange that seemed then to offer the only possible solution to the economic crisis. During the Second World War, the Filov government took the side of Nazi Germany and, in March 1941, opened Bulgarian territory to German troops on their way to invade Greece and Yugoslavia. As a reward, Bulgaria was allowed to occupy Macedonia and Thrace, territory that it had long coveted.

The work session that followed could not have been stormier. Two of us did not support the predominant role of America: Jean-Pierre, who was an eternal sceptic, and David, who, as a good Anglo-Saxon, quite rightly refused to allow the role played by Britain to be diminished.

David was the first to protest: 'You give an essential role to the United States, but you do so in a purely subjective way! If the Battle of Britain had not been won by Churchill, Britain would have been conquered and the whole of Europe would have become Nazi. Moreover, it was also the British who stopped the advance of Rommel at El-Alamein.'

Jean-Pierre raised the bid: 'And it was the Russians who broke the Wehrmacht, with the loss of millions of lives, at Moscow, at Stalingrad and at Kursk. These were the ones who literally exhausted the German forces!'

I replied: 'I would be rude if I contradicted you. It would be stupid, if not absurd, to want to diminish the role of the Allies, but it nonetheless remains a fact that, without American intervention, the history of the war would have been turned upside down! The United States only entered the war in December 1941, after the disaster of Pearl Harbor, and from that moment only its participation increased. The US role was mostly against the Japanese, a vital task after the Normandy invasion. This is the role that the apostle seems to be indicating to us. Nothing more. On the other hand, if we think carefully, isn't it reasonable to imagine that the winner of this war was nonetheless the United States? Europe emerged from it bled white, and the former USSR was virtually wiped out.'

'I still maintain that you are giving much too much importance to the United States ... '

I interrupted: 'It is not me who decides this, but the text of John! Also, the word Gog does not correspond to Britain, or to France, or to the Soviet Union! So it was John who showed us this!'

'All right then, prove it! Prove it to us clearly and objectively, without ambiguity, and without preconceptions! Find some other information for us to support your opinion!'

I remained silent, short of arguments.

Irritated and tense, we thought it better to defer our meeting until later.

I don't remember how many days I spent thinking about this new obstacle erected before me, which had all the appearance of a challenge. How could the dominant position that I had attributed to the United States be confirmed? Nonetheless we made progress.

I made a list summarizing our findings:

The Beast: Adolf-Hitler-Austria = 666
Germany: = 308 = great city or Egypt, 380, or Armageddon, 308
Magog:
Germany = 308
Japan = 40
Italy =65
Romania = 311
Hungary = 279
Finland = 224
Bulgaria = 250
Total = 1577, or 19
Gog = 5
America = 5

Supported by Dimitri, who agreed with my hypothesis, I had pored over the texts for days on end without finding the confirmation demanded by David and Jean-Pierre. But, curiously, when we met again,

I saw that the attitude of the two 'critics' had developed a little. Better still, a certain serenity emanated from them, as if they had suddenly been reassured. They had lost the scathing tone that had predominated during our last exchanges. I showed my surprise and Jean-Pierre replied, with some embarrassment:

'I was too harsh, and I apologize. Meanwhile I have thought a lot about the problem. You are right. The predominant status of the Americans is confirmed.'

I stared at him, disconcerted.

He went on: 'Who was in charge of the United States at that time?'

'Roosevelt, of course.'

'So we have Roosevelt and his opposite number Hitler.'

I agreed.

He turned to David: 'Show him the e-mail from Myriam.'

David did so.

I read the text transmitted by the theologian and I swear I thought that I was going to faint from the shock of the emotion.

Hitler (היטלר) = 254

Roosevelt (רוזבלט) = 254

These numbers, identical in all respects, symbolized the absolute duality of the struggle of opposites: $254 = 2 + 5 + 4 = 11$ and $1 + 1 = 2$.

Myriam attached a document for information. This was a copy of the speech made by Hitler on 11 December 1941 at the Reichstag:

I understand only too well that a world-wide distance separates Roosevelt's ideas and my ideas. Roosevelt comes from a rich family and belongs to the class whose path is smoothed in the democracies. I was only the child of a small, poor family and had to fight my way by work and industry. When the Great War came Roosevelt occupied a position where he got to know only its pleasant consequences, enjoyed by those who do business while others bleed. I was only one of those who carried out orders as an ordinary soldier, and naturally returned from the war just as poor as I was in the autumn of 1914. I shared the fate of millions, and Franklin Roosevelt only the fate of the so-called Upper Ten Thousand.

After the war Roosevelt tried his hand at financial specula-tions. He made profits out of inflation, out of the misery of others, while I... lay in a hospital...

On reading this text, a shiver went down my spine. But there was another document in Myriam's e-mail. In glancing at it I thought I was dreaming. I quote its exact words:

Do you remember the first verse of the fifth chapter? It has always intrigued me: 'Then I saw in the right hand of the one seated on the throne a *scroll* written on the inside and on the back, sealed with seven seals.'
Following the discovery of the parallel between Roosevelt and Hitler, I became interested in this scroll and its numeric value. Here is what I found:

Scroll (מגולל ספר) = 452

This contains exactly the same numbers as the two heads of state (254), but in reverse order. To me that says only one thing: the destiny of these two men was sealed in the Book, since the dawn of time. Neither of the two could have modified a single letter of his future. The one was the antithesis of the other. It remains to be seen what followed.

'What do you think?' asked Jean-Pierre.

Dimitri frowned. 'One point worries me. Why Roosevelt and not Churchill?'

Without knowing it, he had raised a point that had already been tormenting me for some time.

I replied: 'I have no idea. I realize that in our decoding there exist some hiatuses. Some gaps. And I have no explanation.'

'I do,' retorted Jean-Pierre. 'And it risks offending your ego. Mine too. But I believe that it is time that we tackled the problem and that we should lance the abscess.'

He paused for a moment before continuing: 'We do not find Churchill, but nor do we find Mussolini or Stalin. And there are all the opportunities that these gaps have wasted. Why? Because we are incapable of filling them for the moment. The formidable energy with which we have thrown ourselves into this adventure sometimes triggers the unknown. Decoding the Revelation ... that is a whole life's work ... no, the work of several lifetimes. That is the amount of time that would be needed to lift completely the veil that covers the text. Several lifetimes. What were you thinking? That it would be enough just to bend down and pick it up? Stalin, Roosevelt, Truman and the others? Come, a little modesty. Let us accept that we are only pioneers. Who knows, others may walk in our footsteps and they may have the good fortune to do better and go further than us. We can only touch on this sacred account which, I would remind you, has remained sealed for nearly two thousand years. Let us accept once and for all the idea that we are not geniuses in the pure state and that none of us possesses innate knowledge. It would be so much more "practical" to find Churchill and the others … '

He shook his head several times: 'No, I'm sorry. We will not be able to decipher everything systematically, all the time. That is a matter of moral integrity.'

There was a short silence, then he concluded: 'The beast, Adolf-Hitler-Austria, Germany, America, Hitler and Roosevelt, to which is grafted this message as a form of confirmation: "The scroll". It would in any case be ungracious of us to deny these clues. It is no longer a matter of simple coincidences. The Revelation deals well with the advent of the Führer and the Second World War.'

It was at this moment that David intervened, a certain gravity in his voice: 'If this is really so, we are not talking about just a single passage of the Revelation because, referring to the text, St John describes not one but *two* beasts:

13:1 And I saw a beast rising out of the sea, having ten horns and seven heads; and on its horns were ten diadems, and on its heads were blasphemous names.

'Theoretically, this verse relates to Hitler. On the other hand, St John also wrote:

17:3 So he carried me away in the spirit into a wilderness, and I saw a woman sitting on a scarlet beast that was full of blasphemous names, and it had seven heads and ten horns.

'This second Beast is literally the image of the first, with seven heads and ten horns, but with one small difference. John describes it as "scarlet".'

I was confused: 'So there were two Revelations?'

'Skilfully linked; yes, I am sure.'

He was right. Moreover the future would confirm his analysis.

We know that the apostle's text presents a certain number of similar passages, and breaks in passages apparently out of context. Evidently most commentators have tried to explain these anomalies, and they have done so in a variety of ways: for instance, they have said that they arise as the result of compilation from different sources, or the accidental displacement of some passages or chapters. Some have let it be understood that the prophetic part (chapters 4 to 22) consists of *two distinct Revelations*, written by the same author at different dates then merged into a single collection by another hand. As for the 'Letters to the Seven Churches', they would have existed originally in the form of a separate text.

In reality, there are not two Revelations merged into a single text, one repeating the other, but two Revelations referring to *two different periods*, represented by the two beasts. The role of the dragon and Satan is consistent in both Revelations.

Also, like the Koran, it is immediately apparent that the verses are not written in chronological order. The whole has therefore to be looked at as an enormous puzzle, not as a traditional composition founded on a unity of time and place. The elements of this puzzle are mostly scattered throughout the verses. Hence the difficulty consists in gathering them together to extract a homogenous and above all a consistent text.

In conclusion, we were certain that one of the Revelations directly concerned the history of the Third Reich. As for the other, it had to forecast another longer-lasting cataclysm, a Third World War. In autumn

1994, something deep within us suggested that this war to come would undoubtedly be far more terrifying and infinitely more horrendous than all the atrocities committed by mankind to date.

We were preparing to go our separate ways when Jean-Pierre, who had remained silent until then, remarked: 'I can tell you that there are not two beasts, but three.'

'What's that you're saying?

He quoted:

13:11 Then I saw another beast that rose out of the earth; it had two horns like a lamb and it spoke like a dragon.

Seeing my doubtful look, he hastened to reassure us: 'Don't worry, it is not the new unlocking of a third Revelation, nor the advent of a "third Hitler". No, this beast has nothing in common with the other two. You need only compare the descriptions. While this one has only two horns, the others have seven heads and ten horns.'

'But what does this mean?'

'Good question. We are still at the beginning of our journey … '

But would we ever reach the end?

5 The false prophet

Propaganda and torture are the direct means of bringing about disintegration.
Albert Camus, *L'Homme révolté* (The Rebel)

CHRISTMAS WAS UPON us. Paris was resplendent with Christmas trees and garlands, but, looking at the people squeezing into the shops, I couldn't help wondering about the paradoxes of existence. The birth of Christ that the world has learnt to celebrate: was it not directly connected to the Revelation? But what a contrast there was this evening in my soul between this festive atmosphere, this apparent unconcern, and the troubled, tortured aspect of the verses that we were uncovering! I was aware that a certain anxiety had seized us all to a greater or lesser extent. Was it possible that a book written two thousand years ago could contain such an accurate description of the future? Would the text of the visionary of Patmos really open a breach in the wall of time?

The first clues seemed to confirm our intuition: part of Revelation related to the Second World War. But being neither jurors nor in a tribunal where private conviction is enough to absolve or condemn another, we had need of more proofs and yet more certainties.

16:13 And I saw three foul spirits like frogs coming from the mouth of the dragon, from the mouth of the beast, and from the mouth of the false prophet.

19:20 And the beast was captured, and with it the false prophet *who had performed in its presence the signs by which he deceived those who had received the mark of the beast and those who worshipped its image.*

20:10 And the devil who had deceived them was thrown into the lake of fire and sulphur, where the beast and the false prophet *were, and they will be tormented day and night for ever and ever.*

I admit that, thanks to my geopolitical studies, I have a good understanding of the Second World War in general, and of the Third Reich in particular. This was why I became interested in this 'false prophet' before my colleagues did. What was a false prophet if not a person who manipulated information, who disguised it, indeed who made everything up? And if there was one man who could be defined by this term, someone without a hint of a soul, and a past master of deception, it was Joseph Paul Goebbels. I put this hypothesis to the team. The response was unanimous. It was certainly so, without any doubt. If a link existed between Hitler and this condemned soul, it would need to be obvious, direct and flawless.

Strangely, once convinced of this, the next stage was disarmingly easy. Judge for yourself:

Adolf Hitler (אדולף היטלר) = 375
or 3 + 7 + 5 = 15, 1 + 5 = 6

We saw before us the first figure of the number of the Beast.

Joseph Paul Goebbels (יוֹסֵף פּוּל נבלס) = 357 (after subtracting 10)
or 3 + 5 + 7 = 15, 1 + 5 = 6

It was also noticed that the numerical value of the Führer (375) had the same figures as that of his Minister of Propaganda, but differently arranged (357). And finally:

False prophet (נביא שֶׁקֶר) = 663
or 6 + 6 + 3 = 15, 1 + 5 = 6

Here again the number of the Beast appeared: 666. This time it was clearer still. What more was there to add?

In 1929 Goebbels was named chief of propaganda for the National Socialist Party, and given the task of spreading the ideas of his master by all necessary means. In this he succeeded beyond Hitler's greatest hopes. It was thanks to Goebbels that the Party achieved spectacular success in the elections of 1930. There was a record number of voters – 35 million, 400,000 more than in 1928 – and the Nazis received more than 18 per cent of the total votes cast and increased their representation from 12 to 107 seats.

On 30 January 1933, Hitler became Chancellor of the Reich, and on 11 March 1933 a Ministry of Information and Propaganda was created, which Goebbels took control of on 14 March.

On his arrival at this post, this little man (he was barely 1.5 metres/ 5 feet tall) who walked with a limp perfected the system that would subsequently be instituted in the occupied countries. It involved closing the frontiers to all sources of foreign information and keeping a heavy hand on all internal organs of information, extending into every field, whether intellectual or cultural: the press, publishing, cinema, theatre and radio, all of which Joseph Goebbels knew how to manipulate effectively in order to influence the masses. This was the Nazification of culture, which began with a massive burning of books that were judged contrary to the national spirit. The Nazis muzzled literature, stifled art and controlled education. Those who resisted or were apathetic were eliminated, and, as in the Spain of the Inquisition, so were the racially impure.

Singing too became an instrument of propaganda and school children were taught to pay homage to the Führer:

> Adolf Hitler is our saviour, our hero,
> The noblest being in the whole world,
> For Hitler we live,
> For Hitler we die,
> Our Hitler is our Saviour
> Who rules a wonderful new world.[1]

For twelve years, the German population lived under the remorseless weight of Goebbels' propaganda. The history of mankind has rarely seen so talented a 'false prophet'.

Discovering Goebbels also brought us the answer to the question that Jean-Pierre had raised in the previous chapter. We had listed the three beasts and we had identified two of them. The first heralded Hitler:

> *And I saw a Beast rising out of the sea, having* ten horns and seven heads; *and on its horns were ten diadems.*[2]

The second forecast a Führer to come:

> *And I saw a woman sitting on a scarlet beast that was full of blasphemous names, and it has* seven heads and ten horns.[3]

Only the last beast presented a problem. Already we had an answer:

> *Then I saw another beast that rose out of the earth; it had two horns like a lamb and it spoke like a dragon.*[4]

This last two-horned beast was none other than Joseph Paul Goebbels, the false prophet. It was sufficient to read the reconstructed verses to be convinced:

> *13:12 It exercises all the authority of the first beast on its behalf, and it makes the earth and its inhabitants worship the first beast ...*
> *13:14 and by the signs that it is allowed to perform on behalf of the beast, it deceives the inhabitants of earth, telling them to make an image for the beast ...*
> *13:15 and it was allowed to give breath to the image of the beast, so that the image of the beast could even speak and cause those who would not worship the image of the beast to be killed.*

If the Führer and Goebbels were so intimately close, to the point of having the same numerical value, it must be possible to find in the destiny of the two men other ways in which they were similar.

• Hitler committed suicide on 30 April.

• Goebbels, on 1 May, was shot in the neck (at his request) by an SS man.

At the end of the research we met to discover yet another element. John had written, still about the false prophet:

> *13:15 and it was allowed to give breath to the image of the beast ...*

How could one not be reminded of the extraordinary invention that is cinema? Surely this is nothing other than an animated image? If we calculate the value of the word 'image' (תמונה), we obtain 501, 5 + 1 = 6. And the word 'cinema' (הקולנוע), gives us 267, 2 + 6 + 7 = 15, 1 + 5 = 6.

In 1934, a great rally of the Party was organized at Nuremberg to celebrate its anniversary. Hitler chose Albert Speer as stage manager. He removed the temporary tiers of the Zeppelin airfield and, inspired by the altars of Pergamon, built a stone structure more than 400 metres (1,300 feet) long and over 20 metres (66 feet) high. An enormous eagle with a wingspan of 30 metres (100 feet) crowned the stadium and on all sides thousands of swastika banners waved in the wind. The area was surrounded by 130 air force searchlights with a range of 7,000 metres (23,000 feet). But what use would these rallies have been if they did not become engraved in the memory of men, for ever? It was at this point that, at the instigation of Goebbels, the services of Leni Reifenstahl, a well-known actress and film-maker were called upon. At first she refused, but yielded under pressure. She was a very talented woman whose skills were much appreciated by the Führer.

Reifenstahl worked for six days, in the course of which she made a film completely devoted to the glory of the Party, with a crew of 120 people, 16 of them cameramen. *The Triumph of the Will* won the First of May cultural prize for best film of the year. Afterwards it became universally known as one of the most important documentaries ever made, and won a gold medal at the 1937 Paris Universal Exhibition for its artistic qualities. Among other things, the film showed a frenzied crowd yelling 'Sieg Heil!' (Victory!). This was heady, exciting stuff, but for those who did not find themselves under the charm of the beast, this chant made their blood run cold. To quote one witness, it was like a 'wild animal's roar, the shout of cavemen'.[5]

Chapter 19, verse 20 offers an unexpectedly striking conclusion:

And the beast was captured, and with it the false prophet who had performed in its presence the signs by which he deceived those who had received the mark of the beast and those who worshipped its image. These two were thrown alive into the lake of fire that burns with sulphur.

The remains of Hitler and his minister were soaked with petrol and burnt. It should be noted that before committing suicide, Goebbels had poisoned his 6 children ... As you can see, the figure 6 becomes a leitmotiv, echoing like a knell throughout the text of St John.

After confirming the parallel between the Führer and Goebbels, we needed to ask ourselves about the philosophical aspects of this affair. Only one of us could really qualify as a believer, in the absolute meaning of the word: our friend Myriam. Jean-Pierre, David and Dimitri were in the 'lukewarm' camp. As for me, although I had faith, although all my life I had been fascinated by holy texts and was a lover of spiritual matters, it was not because of my relations with the Church. I did not regularly attend Mass on Sunday. Rightly or wrongly, this was my way of steering clear of the Princes of the Vatican whom I considered – perhaps too strongly – anachronistic characters. Paradoxically, at the same time my faith in Christ and his message never changed. I judged, but I did not condemn. In short, I had 'fallen out of love' with the Church. As someone close to me complained, I was a musician who loved music but was reluctant to play an instrument.

Nonetheless, for some time, or to be precise since the day when we had begun to interest ourselves in the Book of Revelation, a certain anxiety had arisen within us. Without any of us having said so openly, we sensed that a tiny invisible seed had been sown in our divinely Cartesian brains, and that it was in the process of growing, insidiously and imperceptibly. I repeat, Myriam alone remained unperturbed. To her, these 'discoveries' were in no way surprising. Ultimately, she did not understand our excitement and repeated amazement. To her, John was a prophet, like Isaiah, Ezekiel and others. And everything was written in the great book of life: that is, the Bible. In the genes of the young woman were two thousand years of quests and reflections, the studies undertaken by the first cabbalists, the amoraim[6] sages, the Talmudists and the rest, in whose eyes there was not a word in the Torah, not a letter, that did not have a hidden meaning. Not only had our decoding sessions been nothing extraordinary to her, but she found it natural that through the power of perseverance the unfathomable would become transparent. It was she who pointed out to us another verse in which the number of the beast appeared yet again.

The holiday period was over and we returned to the task with renewed enthusiasm. That morning, in a gesture that had become almost mechanical, I switched on my computer to check my e-mail. I found a few words from Myriam, expressed in the form of a riddle:

Hi you goys! To tease your brains I am sending a little rebus, which may make you swallow some aspirins to start the new year.

And, below it, the young woman wrote:

So the four angels were released, who had been held ready for the hour, the day, the month, and year, to kill a third of humankind.

The number of the troops of cavalry was two hundred million. I heard their number. A third of humankind was killed.

Good luck!

Evidently she had found the answer and was gently mocking us. It did not take us long to notice that this text, which seemed to form a whole, was actually made up of verses 15, 16 and 18 of chapter 9. A third of humankind? Cavalry troops of 200 million?

Having been stumped for several days, we decided to send the verses to Dimitri in Athens. Perhaps, as with Gog and Magog, a Greek approach would reveal the solution, because this time, the Hebrew method seemed to reveal nothing of interest. We had a text with very precise numbers. Translating them into Hebrew would have revealed nothing special. Dimitri quickly threw in the towel.

As a last resort, we swallowed our pride and asked our theologian to be so kind as to show leniency and take pity on the simple souls that we were, by telling us her interpretation of the verses. There was no reply. It was Friday, the eve of the Sabbath. We could be sure that she would not reappear before the end of the ritual.

We were fidgeting with impatience and, in my heart of hearts, I cursed these traditions, Christian, Jewish or Islamic, which immobilize men in a yoke. But it was not the time for polemic, especially with someone as religious as Myriam. Once the Sabbath was over, the reply came at last. As soon as I saw the first lines I remember experiencing a certain frustration, combined with anger. It was the same for David and Jean-Pierre, sitting beside me. How had we not thought of carrying out so infantile a calculation?

The theologian had repeated the verses in their entirety:

9:15 So the four angels were released, who had been held ready for the hour, the day, the month, and the year, to kill a third of humankind.
9:16 The number of the troops of cavalry was two hundred million; *I heard their number.*
9:18 A third of humankind *was killed.*

A question followed: 'What is one-third of 200?' And below it: 'Mazel Tov!' (Congratulations!)

That was all. But the answer was indeed there. In a few seconds the calculation was done: one-third of 200 million was: 66,666,666 ... With disarming simplicity, our friend had told us (through St John) the number of people killed in the Second World War, including Asia: 66 million. Let me say at once that today it is not possible to determine *with absolute certainty* the exact number who died in this conflict. It was between 35 and 40 million for Europe and the United States, but, if we add to this the millions who died in Asia, we reach a total of between 65 and 70 million victims, which enables us to respect the figure forecast by the apostle.

I could not help thinking back over the past weeks, in particular to my conversations with Father Alexander on Mount Athos. His voice echoed within me, moving and insistent. Never before had the advice, and the assertions that he had pronounced at our meetings assumed such portent: 'Be sure that the key to the Revelation is in the number of the beast. Nothing else.'

Did he then doubt the importance of his reflections? In telling me about them, was he aware of their consequences? Chance is the pseudonym of God ... , he had said. What part did God play in this affair? Would it be his initials that would be revealed at the bottom of the page?

Adolf-Hitler-Austria

Germany

America

Gog and Magog

The rolled-up book

Roosevelt/Hitler

Goebbels, the false prophet, the moving picture

66 million dead

But where was the signature of chance?

6 Babylon the great, mother of whores

> *So God created humankind in his image, in the image of God he created them; male and female he created them.*
>
> Genesis 1:27

OUR INITIAL RELUCTANCE had been swept away by these first findings, which we looked upon – rightly or wrongly – as signs of encouragement. All the same, before going any further it was necessary to 'clean up' the text to try and see it a little more clearly. Myriam had come to spend a few days in Paris, and once again all five of us were reunited for the start of this new stage.

Who were the 'characters' we would endlessly find throughout John's work? Which verses held real meaning? Analyzing the work carefully, we could not help noticing that many verses were there for their form rather than their content. They play a literary rather than a 'pragmatic' role, as in the following examples:

> *1:3 Blessed is the one who reads aloud the words of the prophecy, and blessed are those who hear and who keep what is written in it; for the time is near.*

Or again:

> *1:5 and from Jesus Christ, the faithful witness, the firstborn of the dead, and the ruler of the kings of the earth. To him who loves us and freed us from our sins by his blood,*

1:6 and made us to be a kingdom, priests serving his God and Father, to him be glory and dominion for ever and ever. Amen.

1:7 Look! He is coming with the clouds; every eye will see him, even those who pierced him; and on his account all the tribes of the earth will wail. So it is to be. Amen.

We therefore had to reduce the Revelation to its essentials, initially by extracting the dominant and, above all, recurrent characters. We found there were four of these: the Lamb, the beast, the dragon and Satan. This was the cast of the Revelation.

Today, all commentators restrict themselves to a single explanation: for them, the Lamb can only be the Church of Christ. Moreover, it cannot be dissociated from the beast. The two are therefore complementary. And if we depart from the principle that the hidden meaning of the Revelation concerns not only Christians but the whole of humanity, then 'the Lamb and the beast' are clothed in a completely different meaning.

As was already the custom, Myrian devoted herself to analyzing the numerical values of the two words:

Beast (חיה) = 23
Lamb (גדיה) = 22
Total = 45

'To a non-believer, this number does not mean very much. But once an explanation is found, an apparently insignificant number becomes clothed with a sense as unexpected as it is moving. In Hebrew, the number 45 symbolizes the first man, that is, Adam (אדם).[1]

'How could one fail to deduce that the beast and the Lamb are one and the same being, expressing man's fight against man, the struggle between good and evil: the two faces that have confronted each other in every human being since the dawn of time, and that will continue to confront each other until the Last Judgement. Furthermore, John clearly says: *"the number of the beast, it is the number of a person."*

'Without wanting to be provocative, but weighing everything up, might not one ask what use God and the devil would be if they did not have man to fight over?'

'And woman?' Myriam quickly asked.

'What's that? What do you mean?'

'My question is simply logical. We have just talked about Adam. But Eve was there too.' She seized the Revelation and pointed at a succession of verses:

12:1 A great portent appeared in heaven: a woman clothed with the sun, with the moon under her feet, and on her head a crown of twelve stars;

'That is not all. The apostle describes a second woman:

17:3 So he carried me away in the spirit into a wilderness, and I saw a woman sitting on a scarlet beast that was full of blasphemous names, and it had seven heads and ten horns.

'You can see that woman was not forgotten. It hardly needs a trained theologian to point out that the two individuals have nothing in common; least of all in appearance. One seems to symbolize the beautiful, the good; and the other, horror and decay.

'What does this mean? We have been led to assume that the beast and the Lamb were one and the same person: Adam, standing for the struggle between the man-lie and the man-truth. And would this not be the same for a woman?

'To begin with, Eve (חוה) has a numerical value of 19. That is 1 + 9 = 10. In Hebrew tradition, this number is the symbol of *absolute truth*. But once a sinner, Eve is no more than a woman. The numerical value of the word "woman" is 306; that is, 9. Remember, the numerical value of Adam is 45 and 4 + 5 = 9. At the risk of displeasing the misogynists, woman is quite equal to man in this quest for truth!'

We could but agree.

'But then, who is the second woman, representing the abominations and the stains of prostitution?'

Two more of St John's verses were more specific:

17:1 Then one of the seven angels who had the seven bowls came and said to me, Come, I will show you the judgement of the great whore who is seated on many waters,
17:3 So he carried me away in the spirit into a wilderness, and I saw a woman sitting on a scarlet beast that was full of blasphemous names, and it had seven heads and ten horns.

And the apostle added:

17:5 and on her forehead was written a name, a mystery: 'Babylon the great, mother of whores and of earth's abominations.'

Babylon, which means 'Gateway of God' or 'babel' in Hebrew, enjoyed its time of glory between 1894 and 301 BC. A strong symbolic value was attached to this capital, which so impressed the people of the Bible with its imposing monuments. Herodotus wrote that Babylon was so magnificent that there was no other city in the world with which it could be compared. Its enclosing walls with their hanging gardens were among the seven wonders of the world.

A story in Genesis places the Tower of Babel, the symbol of human pride, there. Babylon is the antithesis of the celestial Jerusalem and Paradise. Behind this 'Gateway of God' lay a perverted world, ruled by the instincts of domination and luxury. Babylon symbolized not a magnificence condemned for its beauty, but a tainted magnificence that condemned itself by turning man away from his spiritual vocation. When Nebuchadnezzar sacked the Temple of Jerusalem in 587, the prophets called Babylon the 'Great Whore', the agent of evil, and predicted its destruction:

And Babylon, the glory of kingdoms, the splendour and pride of the Chaldeans, will be like Sodom and Gomorrah when God overthrew them.[2]

But Babylon lost its glory long ago. Its decline goes back to the time of Cyrus, who seized the city in 539 BC. In that case, why would St John have bracketed its name with that of the second woman, unless it was to make us understand that, like Babylon the whore, it represented absolute evil?

What biblical person is the ill-fated reflection of Eve? All the writings indicate Lilith. Moreover, she was well known to the Babylonian world under the name *lilù* or *lilitù* in Akkadian, and she personified the devil. She is only mentioned once in the Bible, in Isaiah:

34:14 Wildcats shall meet with hyenas, goat-demons shall call
to each other; there too Lilith shall repose, and find a place to rest.

Who was Lilith? In cabbalistic tradition, she was the woman whom God created before Eve and at the same time as Adam. Like Adam, she was drawn from the clay of the earth. Proclaiming her equality loud and strong, she confronted her companion and then left Paradise in a great fury to devote herself to a devilish career. From that day, she became the enemy of Eve, the instigator of illegitimate love affairs, the breaker of the marital bed. She lived in the depths of the sea, from where with her admonishments she continued to trouble the lives of men and women on earth.

Like a woman supplanted or abandoned, Lilith represents the hatred of couples and children. She was also the nocturnal temptress who tried to seduce Adam. It was she who begat the ghostly creatures of the desert. She has been compared to the black side of the unconscious, to dark urges.

And what is the numerical value of Lilith (לִּלִת)? 460, and $4 + 6 = 10$. This value is exactly the same as that of Eve: 10. But there is a difference: one personifies absolute truth, the other absolute evil.

So here we have a new confirmation of the extraordinary subtlety of the text of St John. Quite clearly nothing has been disregarded. The most subtle details have been included in a desire for balance and absolute wisdom. The only question that tormented us at that moment was whether we would have enough energy and clearsightedness to reach the end of our quest.

7 The dragon

> *For from the fruit of the snake will come forth an*
> *adder, and its fruit will be a flying fiery serpent.*
>
> Isaiah 14:29

THAT NIGHT IT was unbelievably cold. I do not remember so icy a February. Or maybe it was the nervous tension and the exhaustion of hours of wakefulness that made us all suddenly vulnerable. Moreover, a vital clue was appearing, a taut but infinitely fragile thread that we were beginnning to glimpse. Myriam's presence in Paris for twenty-four hours was the occasion for another working meeting.

Since we had begun to interest ourselves in the 'recurrent figures' of the Revelation, we could but continue in that direction. We had listed six:

1 The Lamb
2 The beast
3 Eve
4 Lilith
5 The dragon
6 Satan

We already knew that the Lamb and the beast, like Eve and Lilith, symbolized the struggle of man against man; truth against falsehood; evil against good. But who was the dragon? In ancient texts, the word is generally used for a fabulous monster, depicted as a living reptile of the sea. It can also be compared to Leviathan, another sea monster with seven heads, whom the Lord had fought against triumphantly from the primordial chaos.

> *On that day the Lord with his cruel and great and strong sword will punish Leviathan the fleeing serpent,* Leviathan *the twisting serpent, and he will kill the dragon that is in the sea.*[1]

But was this not the role taken by the dragon that St John described? It appears for the first time in chapter 12, verse 3:

> *Then another portent appeared in heaven: a great red* dragon, *with* seven heads and ten horns ...

And it continues to appear forcefully throughout the book.

David pointed his finger at the Revelation. 'Miriam has calculated the value of the dragon (דרקון) as 360. The words "Lamb" and "beast" have revealed their symbolism easily, yet the meaning of the "dragon" seems to be unfathomable.'

I spoke as follows: 'Patience. We now have the proof that there exists a logical approach in the development of the text of John; I was going to say it was "arithmetical". What did we notice at the very beginning? The description that the apostle gives us of the dragon is exactly the same as that which he gave of the two beasts: seven heads and ten horns. The appearance of the third beast is different and, as we have shown, it relates to Goebbels, the false prophet.'

'What conclusion should we draw?'

'I put one question to you. Why else would the apostle have drawn a twin portrait of the two beasts and the dragon if it was not because he wanted us to understand that the two creatures are, if I dare say so, the same?'

There was a moment of reflection. Then David suggested that we draw up a list of verses where the word 'dragon' is mentioned. There were eleven altogether.[2] We examined them minutely in the hours that followed. All described the same scenario: devastation, destruction and battles, all at the instigation of the dragon.

We tried to compare the numerical value of the dragon with each of the elements we had listed: Hitler, Führer, Germany, Goebbels, Roosevelt, Berlin, Eve, Lilith, Babylon, etc. Not a single one corresponded. We were certain that the key must be there, hidden between the lines. But in which of the eleven verses? After I don't know how many re-readings, Jean-Pierre proposed verse 9 of chapter 12:

The great dragon was thrown down, that ancient serpent, who is called the Devil and Satan, the deceiver of the whole world – he was thrown down to the earth, and his angels were thrown down with him.

'Look at this passage. John gave himself over to a comparison that he reiterated in chapter 20, verse 2.'

He seized the dragon, that ancient serpent, who is the Devil and Satan …

Jean-Pierre repeated the words, separating them: 'The enormous dragon … the ancient serpent … who is the Devil and Satan. Do you see what I'm getting at?'

'I think so,' replied David. 'If I interpret your thinking correctly, this would be a repetition of the comparative system used by the apostle with Babylon and Lilith.'

'Exactly so. St John constructs enigmas and provides answers by analogies. If we read the verses carefully, we notice that the dragon and the Devil are made one.'

'What is the numerical value of "Satan"?'

'359,' Miriam replied.

'And the dragon, 360. No correspondence.'

'You are mistaken,' said Miriam. '359 is the numerical value, but it does not correspond to the Jewish tradition. With us, the true value of the Devil is 364. There is a good reason for this. To Christians, Satan is a fallen angel acting with complete freedom in the final pit of hell. To the Jews, on the other hand, he is found by the side of the All-Powerful, and can intervene only with the All-Powerful's approval. In this context, the prologue of the Book of Job is very revealing. Let me quote it.'

One day the heavenly beings came to present themselves before the Lord, and Satan also came among them. The Lord said to Satan, 'Where have you come from?' Satan answered the Lord, 'From going to and fro on the earth, and from walking up and down on it.' The Lord said to Satan, 'Have you considered my servant Job? There is no one like him on the earth, a blameless and upright man who fears God and turns away from evil.' Then Satan answered the Lord, 'Does Job fear God for nothing? Have you not put a fence around him and his house and all that he has, on every side? You have blessed the work of his hands, and his possessions have increased in the land. But stretch out your hand now and touch all that he has, and he will curse you to your face.' The Lord said to Satan, 'Very well, all that he has is in your power; only do not stretch out your hand against him!' So Satan went out from the presence of the Lord.

She paused before going on. 'You will have noticed that the Lord authorizes Satan to intervene.'

I asked: 'But why is he given the numerical value of 364?'

'Because the Eternal is keen to let him tempt men every day of the year, except one: the day of Yom Kippur, the day of Atonement.'

I turned to the others. 'If we adopt this version, that would mean that the word "dragon" would have the value 364 and not 360. Let us spell it out: "The dragon is the Devil".'

It was at this point that a rather stormy debate took place to decide the direction to follow next. We had found the proof that the number of the beast, 666, related to Adolf Hitler and, through him, to the Second World War; and subsequently we had decoded Goebbels, Roosevelt, Germany, America, and so on. Following this, some of us thought it would be logical to restrict our researches to this very specific period of history. But Dimitri and I thought the opposite. 'Scientifically speaking' it seemed more rigorous to us to extend the area of debate.

Let me say at once that of the five, it was Dimitri and I who were wrong. To have enlarged the debate to cover all periods and events in the history of humanity would have been absurd, completely fantastic. It would also have meant that among so many events our discoveries would be simply 'coincidences' devoid of foundation, and therefore of no account. That is why, at the end of the argument, we were persuaded to maintain our course and persevere in the direction described by the first words we had deciphered: the Second World War, and nothing else.

As we have already explained, our last resort for analysis was the computer. Without getting bogged down in a technical discussion, the situation was that David had loaded the computer with a multitude of references to the Third Reich: terms, doctrines, armaments, and names of people and places. He had also added the twenty-two letters of the Hebrew alphabet and their numerical correspondences. Unfortunately, this program, so cleverly developed, was unable to suggest a solution. The screen remained hopelessly empty.

David sought to defend his data-processing universe, but without much conviction. 'After all, a computer can only give out what has been entered into it. Reasoning and deduction are the kind of behaviour that it ignores.'

'Fine,' retorted Myriam. 'In this case we are working "logically". Let us ask simple questions. What are the characteristics of the dragon? John sometimes defines it as a devourer of infants, as a seducer, as a power capable of transmitting power, who leaves combat to the children of God. Whether you admit it or not, all these descriptions make me think that it represents an ideology, a philosophical representation rather than a physical "material" entity. To me, the dragon is not a person, it is an idea.'

'That is a point of view,' David admitted. 'It still has to be proved.'

And so the debate broke up. As a last resort we launched into a study of another verse. I no longer remember when Myriam decided to return to the attack. I can only recall the word that she abruptly launched: 'Fascism!'

I stared at her, taken aback. I was not alone. 'Fascism?'

'Yes indeed! Is not fascism directly linked to the Third Reich? In Italy under the Duce, and in Spain under the Caudillo? Was it not the ideology that was responsible for all the atrocities committed? The central key of this tragedy? In a word: the dragon. And I can prove it to you.'

She rapidly carried out a series of calculations on a piece of paper and handed it to us.

Fascism (פשיזם) = 436

Quickly she continued: 'Intellectual integrity obliges me to explain that we obtain this number by subtracting the number 1. That is to say, 437 *minus* one. This is still in accordance with the fundamental principles of gematria. Remember, at the very start of our researches, I explained to you that 1 is the first letter of the Hebrew alphabet, and that it represents the Lord, the Supreme Being. This allows us to subtract it (in the same way that we can with the number 10) from any words that are opposed to the divine. Can you imagine fascism as a divine ideal? Dragon-Satan is 364, and fascism 436. Do you understand?'

Although not very convinced, we could not refute her deduction. As in the case of Egypt (מצרים), 380, and Germany (גרמניה), 308, the digits are the same but in different order. The result was not uninteresting. But – and this time we were in perfect agreement – we decided that it was essential to look further into the reasoning.

'What conclusion is to be drawn from this information, except that Satan, the dragon and fascism share the same value?' asked Dimitri.

David was amazed: 'Your question is ridiculous! The dragon is the inspiration, the manipulator of everything. What does verse 2 of chapter 13 tell us?

> ... and the Dragon gave [the beast] his power and his throne and great authority.

'And chapter 13, verse 4:

> They worshipped the dragon, for he had given his authority to the beast, and they worshipped the beast, saying "Who is like the beast, and who can fight against it?"

'It is clear. Fascism (the dragon) gives its destructive power to the beast (Hitler).'

Myriam, still immersed in her mathematical calculations, agreed: 'During your discussion, I was devoting myself to theosophical reduction. The result is even more convincing:

Fascism = 436 = 4 + 3 + 6 = 13
Dragon = 364 = 3 + 6 + 4 = 13

'I maintain that the dragon well and truly represents fascism. But there is another thing. Decide for yourself:

666 = 6 + 6 + 6 = 18 (the beast)
3 + 6 + 4 = 13 (the dragon)
4 + 3 + 6 = 13 (fascism)

'These three numbers, 18, 13 and 13, are found in Revelation, chapter 13 verse 18 ... '

At this point, I should explain that the expression 'fascism' is taken not in the sense of 'political doctrine', but in a deeper meaning, that is: the denial of man in all that he represents that is noble, beautiful, divine or worthy. Taken in the literal sense, the term describes the movement founded in Italy in 1919 and the political system set up in 1922 after Benito Mussolini, the head of the movement, came to power. But, in fact, the doctrines of fascism were defined by the rejection of the principles of traditional liberalism, a systematic rejection of the political, economic and social order that had been progressively instituted during the nineteenth century in most Western societies, and whose essential characteristics were parliamentary government, multilateralism, and the guarantee of rights and liberties. Every fascist party was driven by the will to conquer the state and to fashion it in its image; consequently, its ideology became the ideology of the state, and by the same token the ideology of the community as a whole. One could also associate this doctrine with communism.

When Stalin launched his purges in the years 1935-6, he promulgated some appalling laws, including one which provided for the death penalty for children over twelve. Between 1937 and 1938, he had killed three marshals out of five; 60 generals out of 85; 136 major-generals out of 199 and about 35,000 officers out of 70,000; and under the aegis of Beria more than 7 million citizens were arrested, of whom more than half were coldly murdered. This too can only be described as the denial of man.

It was late. We were on the verge of collapse. I don't know if my friends were able to sleep, but as far as I was concerned, my brain was in turmoil. A jumble of figures was jostling in my head. It was like a hellish merry-go-round, an obsessional tangle of words and images.

A few hours later I half-opened my eyes, with the clear impression that I had never closed them. I got up and found a note from Myriam with some sheets of paper on the kitchen table.

> My aeroplane leaves soon … Here are some notes that may support my hypothesis:
>
> First: the sacred tetragram that, you will remember, is formed of the four letters Yod, hé, vav, hé,[3] and works out at 26. Half of this is 13.
>
> Second: 13 in the Hebrew tradition represents the 'face of the Lord' (פני יהוה). This is equivalent to 166, or 13. Therefore it would be natural to imagine that the number 13 representing

fascism and the dragon represents the 'back' of the Lord and Darkness.

I have examined verse 2 of chapter 13:

... and the dragon gave it his power and his throne *and* great authority.

It is interesting to see that the value of the word 'throne' is equivalent to 576; that is, $5 + 7 + 6 = 18 = 9$. The words 'great authority' are equivalent to 234; that is, $2 + 3 + 4 = 9$. And the Führer is equivalent to 496; that is, $4 + 9 + 5 = 18$, and $1 + 8 = 9$

That being so, although you have not said so openly, but my feminine instinct clearly tells me that you will find my interpretation 'dragon equals fascism' a little ... shaky. You are partly right. There, I have made myself the Devil's advocate. It is true that nothing proves a direct relationship between the dragon and the two beasts mentioned in the Revelation, the one announcing Hitler and the other foreseeing his successor. It is not enough that dragon-Satan has a value of 364 and fascism 436. What is needed is an immediate and unanswerable correlation between the two elements, namely Adolf-Hitler-Austria = 666 and the word dragon.

I then turned to verse 3 of chapter 12:

Then another portent appeared in heaven: a great red dragon, with seven heads and ten horns, and seven diadems on his heads.

What do the words hold? A dragon, of course. Seven heads and ten horns.

No need to rush into complicated calculations. $1 + 7 + 10 = 18$, or $6 + 6 + 6$.

Here is the first verse of chapter 13, the one which evokes the first beast, Adolf Hitler.

And I saw a beast rising out of the sea, having ten horns and seven heads … and on its heads were blasphemous names.

Here too, the figures speak for themselves: one beast, seven heads, ten horns. Again, $1 + 7 + 10 = 18$, or $6 + 6 + 6$.

And finally, here is the verse relating to the second beast, since we know that there are two linked Revelations, and that this verse foretells the appearance of another lunatic at some time in the future …

17:3 … And I saw a woman sitting on a scarlet beast that was full of blasphemous names, and it had seven heads and ten horns.

One beast, seven heads, ten horns. Yet again totalling 18, or $6+6+6$. The numerical aspect of the two beasts (seven heads, ten horns) is therefore exactly the same as that of the dragon!

Demonstration over. Do you still doubt my hypothesis about the dragon and fascism?

Permit me this aside: seeing that the Eternal had conceived 'man in his own image', what would Satan do other than try hard to tear out the image of the Lord that is in man. That is to say, in each of us. Since Genesis, original sin and the murder of Abel, has not the Prince of Darkness worked inexorably towards this end? And, to destroy man, what can he do except serve man, to whom he entrusts the greatest powers … powers that enable him to do battle with the rest of the earth, against humanity empowered by faith; whether that faith is founded on Judaism, Christianity or Islam. Hitler was his instrument. The next one too will become like him …

Best regards. Myriam.

That morning, reading Myriam's notes, we had the impression that we were making progress, but we were aware that we were at the start of a path that could lead either to light or to the abyss; none of us could be certain which.

Also, without our knowledge, a selfish desire was insinuating itself into each of our beings, which none of us wanted to admit to – and would not admit to it until later, much later.

There were five of us. We were little different from the majority of people. Two Catholics, one Greek Orthodox, one Protestant and one Jew. However much each of us wanted to be a person who was universal, impartial and tolerant, sometimes there would shine forth the sterile flame that Kant called 'the transcendental unity of me' – more commonly called the Ego. Unconsciously, each of us was entertaining the secret hope of finding his own Revelation in the text of John, the one that fitted in best with his personal convictions. It would probably be the same if our work saw the light of day. Certain ill-humoured spirits would perhaps say that it was blasphemous or inopportune to interpret a book of the New Testament on the basis of Hebrew traditions; others would condemn us for using gematria, the sacred tool of the cabbalists, to decode the text of a disciple of Christ.

Someone once said of Jerusalem that there was only one way of settling the difference of opinion that faced the three religions that belonged to this holy city: amnesia. So far as we were concerned, we needed a good dose of amnesia to get to the end of our investigation.

More than a month passed before we were able to resume our work sessions. Although the Revelation had become the centre of our preoccupations, the fact remained that daily life had to go on; we had our private lives, our concerns, our families. And we wanted to manage everything. The task was not easy, far from it.

At the end of the day, our work sessions were transformed into a ritual. Although apart, we each followed our own researches. When reunited, we revealed our results, which were then rejected or debated if we thought a point seemed worth following up.

On this particular day, verse 5 of chapter 13 was at the centre of our discussions. I had suggested it, knowing its importance and, as I said, I had already 'decoded' its content.

The beast was given a mouth uttering haughty and blasphemous *words, and it was allowed to* exercise authority *for* forty-two months …

'What interpretation do you suggest?'

'Before answering you, I would like to be sure of one thing: should we continue on this course or not? I will explain. Are you still convinced that we should restrict ourselves to everything connected with the Second World War?'

The general feeling was that we should.

'In that case, I see no other interpretation of this verse than this. In the first place, what could the "haughty and blasphemous words" imply if not the incendiary speeches of the Führer?'

No one made any comment. I continued.

'By "exercise authority", one should understand "conquer, transform". Indeed, in its literal meaning, to act means "to carry out an activity that changes the existing situation".'

Still everyone was silent.

'I now move on to the phrase "forty-two months". This caused me the most diffculty. I have spent hours meticulously analyzing Hitler's triumphant career, without finding any particular association between the dates and the events of his life with the number 42. It was only this morning that the answer came to me.'

I stopped for a moment to gather my thoughts. Then I asked: 'In your opinion, when did Hitler's triumphant career begin? I mean in a military sense.'

Dimitri was the first to reply: 'In my view, on the day when Hindenburg, who was then President of the Reich, appointed Hitler to the position of Chancellor. That was in January 1933, I think.'

'Yes, the 30th to be exact. But I'm sorry, Dimitri, I said in a military sense, not a political one.'

'In that case,' suggested David, 'it must refer to the Anschluss, in February 1938, when Hitler entered Vienna.'

I corrected him: 'It was in March, not February. And this entry was carried out without meeting any opposition. It took place after the resignation of the hapless Austrian Chancellor, Schuschnigg. Because the Austrian people were broken by the slump and economic misery and had nothing else to lose, they welcomed the Führer's intervention. Objectively, one cannot really consider this event as the first of a series of military victories.'

'What about the annexation of Sudetenland in 1938? And of Bohemia and Moravia in 1939?'

'As you say, these were annexations, not victories.'

Jean-Pierre became impatient. 'All right then, can we get get the point?'

'In my opinion, it all really began with the signing of the German-Russian non-aggression pact – on 23 August 1939. This pact, we now know, was accompanied by a secret protocol that established the respective zones of influence of the signatories. Finland, Estonia and Latvia fell within the Russian sphere and Lithuania the German; Poland was to be divided along the line of the Vistula, Narew and San rivers. The

German army then "exercised authority" and won a series of impressive victories on all fronts. Poland was conquered in three weeks. In the following spring, France fell in the same way. In April 1941 the Wehrmacht overran Yugoslavia and Greece, while the Afrika Korps surged across North Africa alongside Italian troops.'

'So at what date do you place the end of the "triumphant career"?'

'31 January 1943. The surrender at Stalingrad.' I continued. 'It was there, in the former city of Tsaritsyn on the banks of the Volga, that the mad dreams of the one-time corporal were shattered. Let me remind you of the circumstances. The decisive battle started at the beginning of September 1942. Being inferior still in terms of aircraft and motorized troops, the Soviets used heavy tanks and artillery barrages. As winter came, they fought in Stalingrad, whose conquest would have immense symbolic value for either side. General Paulus wanted to retreat, but Hitler ordered him to remain in position. His army had extended its advance towards the east and its flanks were vulnerable to enemy counter-attack, particularly as Russian troops were concentrated on either side of the salient of Stalingrad. They also held the bridgeheads on the right bank of the river. Although the Wehrmacht had some success, it did not achieve its main objective. The German front extended over more than 2,000 kilometres (1,200 miles) and supplying the troops became an ever slower and more difficult task. This was ultimately their undoing. The Wehrmacht was defeated.

'This defeat had immense repercussions all over the world. As a result of it, hope was reborn in all the countries occupied or conquered by the Axis powers. It ended the myth of the Wehrmacht's invincibility. In this terrible campaign the German army lost nearly 250,000 men – 150,000 killed, wounded, or frozen to death, and 94,000 taken prisoner, of whom only 6,000 returned to Germany.

'Like his illustrious predecessor Napoleon Bonaparte, who was also a martyr to his pride, Hitler had too great an ambition. In ordering the taking of Stalingrad and the march on Baku at the same time, he dissipated his forces. His spirit was permanently broken. Read the verse of St John again:

> *The beast was given a mouth uttering haughty and blasphemous words, and it was allowed to exercise authority for* forty-two months ...

'Between the signature of the German-Russian non-aggression pact and the siege of Stalingrad, there were exactly forty-two months.'

I waited for a response to my dissertation, a criticism, but there was none. There was no need to question my friends; it was obvious that what at the beginning had been merely a vague intuition had now taken a more final form. And although intellectual rigour still demanded doubt and awareness of us, as it always did, we felt more and more confident of our interpetation of the text. The points we had clarified so far could no longer be dismissed as simply coincidental. But we were still at the dawn of our adventure and this was by no means the last of the surprises we would encounter.

8 Two witnesses

You shall speak my words to them, whether they hear or refuse to hear; for they are a rebellious house.

Ezekiel 2:7

IT WAS THE beginning of summer. We had decoded the main characters of the Revelation: The Lamb and the beast, who are one and the same entity, representing the struggle of man against man; the dragon, representing fascism and Satan; the two women. It was already more than two weeks since I had sent our first results to Father Alexander. I thought it quite natural that I should keep him informed of our progress because, after all, he had in a way been the instigator of our enterprise. I was looking forward to hearing from him, but in vain.

The priest eventually made contact towards the middle of June. The telephone rang. As soon as I heard his voice I could tell that something was wrong. His voice sounded weary and feeble, the voice of a sick man. He explained that he had had an operation; nothing serious, he assured me with his usual modesty, but at his age the slightest ailment took on serious proportions. Then he suddenly changed the subject and started talking about the notes I had sent him. 'There is no doubt you are on the right track. But you are mistaken on one point.' 'Which one is that?' I asked at once. 'You have not considered two protagonists who, I believe, play an important part.' And he added: '*The two witnesses.*' There was a moment of silence. I did not have time to remember the verse in question because he was already quoting it:

'And I will grant my two witnesses authority to prophesy for one thousand two hundred and fifty days, wearing sackcloth.'[1]

'You are probably right,' I replied, 'but these two witnesses play a secondary role; in any case, they are only quoted once.'

I thought he was going to choke with annoyance. 'Read the text again, my friend. Read it again very carefully. You will see how wrong you are.' He suddenly had a coughing fit and said, 'You must excuse me now but I must leave you'. And he put the phone down.

I remained motionless for a moment or two, the phone still in my hand, more worried by the priest's health than by the advice he had just given me. For many years there had been an occult link between Father Alexander and myself. I have always believed that each one of us has a role to play. Often such a role merely involves being someone who inspires, sometimes someone who instigates. Sometimes we are sent into someone's life at the very moment when that person is at a particular crossroads. Whether deliberately or not, we influence their choice. This person will opt for one or the other direction and their whole future will be transformed by it. This was the role Father Alexander was playing in my life. But he never knew it.

Once this moment of sadness had passed, I communicated the priest's suggestions to my friends. Our brain cells were faced with a new challenge. What did these witnesses represent?

Myriam opened the discussion: 'The first mention of the word "witness" is in Exodus, chapter 22, verse 10:

When someone delivers to another a donkey, ox, sheep, or any other animal for safekeeping, and it dies or is injured or is carried off, without witnesses ...

'You know that the ancient law required two, or sometimes even three, witnesses to validate an accusation. One alone was not enough.

> *If anyone kills another, the murderer shall be put to death on*
> *the evidence of witnesses; but no one shall be put to death on the*
> *testimony of a single witness.*[2]

But what does this information tell us? Nothing. We are definitely on the wrong track.'

We had to agree. All verses mentioning the word 'witness' were then carefully analyzed. Having read through the Old Testament we turned to the New Testament. Finally our attention was drawn to a passage in Luke:

> *24:46 and he said to them, 'Thus it is written, that the Messiah*
> *is to suffer and to rise from the dead on the third day,*
> *24:47 and that repentance and forgiveness of sins is to be proclaimed*
> *in his name to all nations, beginning from Jerusalem.*
> *24:48 You are witnesses of these things.'*

Here the word had only a 'legal' meaning. What else could the text mean but that Christ was meeting people (in this instance the pilgrims on the road to Emmaus) who were witnesses of his resurrection, and that he promised them eternal grace? Who were these two pilgrims? All that is known about them is that one of them was called Cleopas and that they were both Jews – Jews who would bring the news of their encounter with Christ to the twelve apostles. Was there not a contradiction here?

Myriam immediately began to calculate the numerical value of the 'two witnesses'. She had by now acquired the ability to calculate at a speed that was very impressive. The result she obtained was 484 and, after theosophical reduction, 7 (4 + 8 + 4 = 16, 1 + 6 = 7).

'We are not much further on,' she sighed. 'The number 7 has always been recognized. It is the sacred number par excellence. It occurs forty times in Revelation: there are seven seals, trumpets, bowls, visions, and so on.'

I cannot remember how long it was before 'grace' deigned to descend upon us, or rather on our Greek friend Dimitri.

'I believe I have the beginning of an answer. Do you remember Gog and Magog?'

'But ... '

'How did we proceed? Have we not inverted the process?'

Dimitri was right. To solve the enigma of Gog and Magog we had used Greek numeration rather than Hebraic. Immediately I asked: 'Do you think we should use the same method for the two witnesses?'

He nodded: 'I would go even further. It is John himself who is imposing this method on us.'

The group seemed uncertain.

He continued, unperturbed: 'In Greek, in this context and in this declension, (μαρτυσιν), "witnesses" does not have the same meaning as it does in French. It means "martyrs".'

This information left us speechless. 'Martyrs,' Dimitri repeated and nodded with a smile. 'Now do you understand?'

'Is it possible?' Myriam whispered.

'I think we are very close,' Jean-Pierre added. 'Who were the martyrs offered up in the holocaust by the beast, who were his main targets if not the Jews and the Christians?'

Myriam cried out: 'As far as the Shoah is concerned, it is obvious, but Hitler was Catholic! How can you … '

This time I decided to interject: 'Dimitri is right. We must refer to history to understand him better. In fact, John spelt it out in chapter 13, verse 6: "It opened its mouth to utter blasphemies against God, blaspheming his name and his dwelling." Hitler was a Catholic of course, but only in name. Very few people knew his real policy towards Christianity. Listen … In order to keep in the good graces of the Catholic Church, Hitler signed the Vatican Concordat on 20 July 1933. But almost immediately afterwards he dissolved the League of Catholic Youth and decreed a law on sterilization that shocked the Catholic Church. During the purge of 30 June 1934, he ordered the assassination of Erich Klausener, leader of the Catholic Action, and in the years that followed he arrested and imprisoned many priests and nuns. In his encyclical letter of 14 March 1937, *Mit Brennender Sorge* (With Burning Concern), Pius XII accused the Nazi government of sowing "the tares of suspicion, discord, hatred and calumny, and a fundamental hostility, both secret and open, to Christ and his Church". But it did not stop there. After the war, in a speech he made on 2 June 1945, Pius XII described National Socialism as "an arrogant apostasy of the religion of Jesus Christ, the negation of His doctrine and His work of redemption, a cult of violence, an idolatry of race and blood, and the destruction of freedom and human dignity". Also … '

David stopped me in my flow: 'And what about the Protestant Churches?'

'They were in exactly the same situation. In July 1934 a Church of the Reich was created and "One People, one Reich, one Faith" was proclaimed. Any opponents were arrested en masse in 1935. That's not all … Please hear me out.' I walked over to my bookcase and took out a book from which I read as follows:

> In February 1937 Dr Hans Kerrl, who had been appointed
> Minister of Churches in July 1935, declared: 'The Party believes in
> the principle of Positive Christianity, and Positive Christianity is
> National Socialism! National Socialism is the will of God! The will
> of God is revealed in German blood. Dr Zoellner of the Protestant
> Church and Count Galen, Catholic Bishop of Münster, have tried
> to explain that Christianity lies in faith in Christ, the Son of God.
> That makes me laugh … No. Christianity is not based on the
> symbol of the Apostles. True Christianity is represented by the
> Party, and today the German people are called by the Party, and
> especially by the Führer, to practise true Christianity … The
> Führer is the herald of a new revelation.[3]

I turned the pages and continued: 'Let me read you a few of the thirty
articles that made up the "religious" programme of the Third Reich:

> Article 1 – The National Church of the German Reich categori-
> cally demands the exclusive right and the exclusive power of
> control over all the churches within the boundaries of the Reich.
> It declares these churches the national churches of the German
> Reich.
> Article 5 – The National Church is determined to exterminate
> irrevocably foreign Christian cults introduced into Germany in
> the sad year 800.
> Article 7 – The National Church has neither scribes, nor
> ministers, nor chaplains, nor priests, but only orators of the Reich
> who will speak in her name.

Article 13 – The National Church demands that the publication and distribution of the Bible in Germany shall cease immediately.

Article 14 – The National Church declares that for her, and therefore also for the German nation, it has been decided that *Mein Kampf* is the greatest of all texts. It not only defines but also embodies the purest and truest ethics of our nation, as much in the present as in the future.

Article 18 – The National Church will set itself apart from altars and crucifixes, Bibles and images of saints.

Article 19 – There must be nothing on the altars apart from *Mein Kampf* – the most sacred of all books to every German and therefore also to God – and on the left of the altar, a sword.

Article 30 – On the day this comes into effect, the Christian cross must be removed from all churches, cathedrals and chapels and replaced by the only invincible symbol, the swastika.

Article … '

Myriam gestured towards me asking me to stop: 'That's enough, Gérard … I was ignoring all this. Excuse me, I feel sick … '

She rose quickly and left the table. I just had time to notice that she had tears in her eyes. It was not so much the content of what I had been reading that had upset her as the horrifying memories the text had brought back to her. Her family had been exterminated in the concentration camps. The sealed carriages, sectarianism, the barking of the dogs at the foot of the watch towers in the camps, she had been told all these stories.

I could not help thinking of those stupid people who try to reduce the number of Jews exterminated in this terrifying war of man against man. 'Come on!' They say, 'the figures are clearly exaggerated. There were not 6 million dead but 4, or 3, or 2 million … ' It is a little as if you, dear reader, were asked 'Why are you crying? Your mother, your father and your child have been murdered, but your uncle and your cousin are still alive … '

A heavy silence hung over us. We waited for the young woman to return, then Dimitri continued: 'Let us go back to the Revelation … If the two witnesses are Judaism and Christianity, we must prove it with numbers. Up to now we have only expressed our subjective opinion – because of my interpretation of the word martyr, I admit.'

'It's easy,' said Myriam. 'Let us work out the numerical value of the words Jew and Christian. If we are right, the two numbers should correspond.'

She wrote on a piece of paper:

Jew (יהודי) =35
Christian (כריסטין)= 359

For a moment we thought we were wrong again. Then we applied the theosophical method once more:

Jew = 3 + 5 = 8
Christian = 3 + 5 + 9 = 17, and 1 + 7 = 8

The two numbers were absolutely identical! We were beginning to feel optimistic again when Jean-Pierre coldly asked: 'What is the connection between the "two witnesses"? Perhaps by this you are proving that Jews and Christians are bearers of the same divine message. That's all. But you are not proving that they are the two witnesses mentioned by John.' He turned to Dimitri: 'What is the Greek numerical value of the expression "two witnesses"?'

'1765. I had checked it already.'

'And in Hebrew?'

Myriam answered: '484. And after the theosophical reduction we obtain the number 7.'

Jean-Pierre slammed the table with the flat of his hand. 'You see! On the one hand we have "Jew" and "Christian", which both have a value of 8. On the other, we have "two witnesses" which has a value of 7. Your hypothesis does not stand up.'

Had a freezing wind suddenly blown into the room it could not have had a greater effect than this statement. Just when utter despondency was forcing us to bring our meeting to an end, Myriam suddenly uttered a cry of triumph, or perhaps of relief.

'We have misled ourselves! We failed to take our own conclusions into account. The two witnesses are indeed Judaism and Christianity and correspond perfectly with the apostle's verse.' She wrote in large letters:

Two witnesses = 484 = 4 + 8 + 4 = 16, 1 + 6 = 7

Christian = 359

Jew = 35

And then:

Christian + Jew = 359 + 35 = 394, 3 + 9 + 4 = 16, 1 + 6 = 7

The theologian was right. The expression 'two witnesses' was effectively in phase with the words 'Christian' and 'Jew'. Exhausted as we were, we had forgotten the most important thing: not to separate the Jews from the Christians, but rather to bring them together as John demanded. There was a whole message, a whole way of thinking in this realization.

What was there to say? Nothing, except that at that moment we felt something akin to what one feels when a task has been completed. However, even though I was satisfied with this development, I was not entirely happy about it, although I was careful not to say this at the time. We had indeed decoded the meaning of the 'two witnesses', but the interpretation of the verse was still incomplete. This was because the visionary of Patmos had actually said, 'And I will grant my two witnesses authority to prophesy for one thousand two hundred and sixty days, wearing sackcloth.' What did these 'one thousand two hundred and sixty days' correspond to, and why 'wearing sackcloth'? I would have hated to be such a killjoy as to mention this. After all, tomorrow was another day …

9 Twenty-four elders

When you hear of wars and insurrections, do not be terrified;
for these things must take place first,
but the end will not follow immediately.
Luke 21:9

THE FOLLOWING MORNING we were hard at work again. I started the debate with the points that had worried me the previous day.

'I think it is vital that we should look again at the three verses referring to the "two witnesses". We cannot dissociate them as if they were meaningless. Either they will confirm our interpretation, or they will invalidate it. What do you think?'

Everybody agreed.

'Let us look again at those verses in question:

11:1 Then I was given a measuring rod like a staff, and I was told, 'Come and measure the Temple of God and the altar and those who worship there,
11:2 but do not measure the court outside the temple; leave that out, for it is given over to the Gentiles, and they will trample over the holy city for forty-two months.
11:3 And I will grant my two witnesses authority to prophesy for one thousand two hundred and sixty days, wearing sackcloth.'

'To use one of Myriam's expressions, let us try and work "logically". What are the words we should concentrate on?

1 Temple of God
2 outside court
_ 3 holy city
4 forty-two months
5 Two witnesses
6 one thousand two hundred and sixty days
7 Sackcloth

'And their numerical value?'

As usual the young theologian quickly did the calculations:

1 Temple of God (מקדש יהוה) = 470, 4 + 7 = 11, 1 + 1 = 2
2 Court outside (כיכר חיצונית) = 824, 8 + 2 + 4 = 14,
   = 1 + 4 = 5
3 Holy city (עיר קדושה) = 695, 6 + 9 + 5 = 20 = 2

She thought it wise to explain: 'It may surprise you, but you should realize that "holy city" and "Jerusalem" have exactly the same value. "Jerusalem" (ירושלים) is equivalent to 596. In other words, 5 + 9 + 6 = 20, that is, 2. It is the same as the "holy city", although the digits are reversed.' She paused for a moment and looked at us mischievously: 'Here is something else rather surprising. The word "Bible" (תנך) also works out at the same value as "Jerusalem" and the "holy city". It is equivalent to 470, that is, 4 + 7 = 11, or 2. What do you make of that?'

'Coincidences ... ' I continued to think aloud: 'We have already decoded the meaning of the "forty-two months" and the "two witnesses".

The meaning of one thousand two hundred and sixty days is understood since it is the same as forty-two months. But we still have the "sackcloth". Does anyone have any suggestions?

'You are going to get annoyed with me soon,' said Myriam jokingly. 'But I am the only one who knows the meaning of the word. It is very simple. In the Jewish religion, when disaster strikes, you must fast, wear sackcloth and cover your head with ashes. Indeed John emphasized this when he wrote in chapter 18, verse 19: "And they threw dust on their heads, as they wept and mourned, crying out … "'

'So is it the symbol of mourning?'

'Of disaster, of terror. Sackcloth gives us 450, or 9. And disaster gives 117, or 9 as well.'

This decoding session was beginning to feel like a game, almost as if someone up there – perhaps John himself – was enjoying our little discoveries. I now teased Myriam with this question: 'You who know so much, explain to us what "court outside" means. How should we interpret that?'

She threw up her arms and cried out: 'You are asking me too much now!' She looked at me ironically. 'After all, I am only a woman … '

I turned towards Jean-Pierre, our semiologist, looking for an answer. He looked uncertain.

'Literally, the word used for "court" means "Space situated in front of a church and generally surrounded by a balustrade or portico".'

'In that case, why does God tell John: "but do not measure the court outside the temple," adding: "leave that out, for it is given over to the Gentiles". Also, his words contain a pleonasm because a "court" is by definition "outside". It is therefore the outside that John has been asked not to measure.'

David replied: 'There could be a thousand answers to this. If the

Lord asks John not to measure it, it is probably because it would be useless to do so "for it is given over to the Gentiles" ... Gentiles being the opposite of believers or monotheists. This leads to another question. What is the place occupied by the "outside", by those who do not practise the religions of the Book? Would it not refer to "the rest of ... the earth?" Could you check that, Myriam?'

The young woman did the calculations: ' "Court outside" has a value of 5. "The rest of the earth" (שאר הארץ) is equivalent to: 797, or 7 + 9 + 7 = 23, and 2 + 3 = 5.'

So I said: 'Let us recapitulate ...

1 Temple of God = 2
2 Holy city = 2
3 Jerusalem = 2
4 Bible = 2
5 Court outside = 5
6 The rest of the earth = 5
7 Sackcloth (שקים) = 9
8 Disaster (אסון) = 9

'This is how I understand the verse. "Get up, count the children who have remained faithful to the Bible ('Come and measure the temple of God'). Leave the rest of the earth to the Gentiles ('but do not measure the court outside the temple; leave that out for it is given over to the Gentiles'), for forty-two months. But I will give to the Christians and Jews ('to my two witnesses') the power to continue preserving their faith in this world for these forty-two months, in spite of the great disaster ('sackcloth') that befalls them."

'To conclude: the two witnesses are certainly Christianity

and Judaism who, oppressed and persecuted, will be reborn from their ashes at the end of the forty-two months of Hitler's reign.'

There would have been a hint of hope in this conclusion had we not had a horrible foreboding that the tragedy that had already taken place would recur ... Later ... But when? At what hour? On what day? In what year?

Jean-Pierre poured himself another cup of black coffee. 'Since the last indications seem to revolve around the victims of this war, we should look again at the verses or expressions that deal with the subject. There are two words that interest me in verses 13 and 14 of chapter 7.'

'We're listening ... '

The semiologist picked up the text of Revelation and read:

Then one of the elders addressed me, saying, 'Who are these, robed in white, and where have they come from?' I said to him, 'Sir, you are the one that knows.' Then he said to me, 'These are they who have come out of the great ordeal; they have washed their robes and made them white in the blood of the Lamb.'

'There are two words in this passage that trouble me. "Great ordeal" ... Does that remind you of anything?'

I shook my head.

Jean-Pierre looked at Myriam: 'I could not help noticing how distressed you were when listening to the Articles of the Church of the Reich ... A few moments earlier you had mentioned the word "Shoah". We all know what this word means. All the horror it represents. Is it not possible that the "great ordeal" refers to the tragedy suffered by the Jews and also by people of all races judged undesirable under the Third Reich? I use the words "all races" intentionally.'

'That's interesting,' said Dimitri. 'But do go on and explain what you are getting at.'

'Earlier on in chapter 7, verse 9, we read: "After this I looked, and there was a great multitude that no one could count, *from every nation, from all tribes and peoples and languages*" ... Is it not possible to imagine that through the words "great ordeal" John is trying to add to the information he has given us about the "two witnesses"? When he speaks of a great multitude, is he not implying that, besides the Jews and Christians, there were also "people of all races and nations" who suffered?'

'That seems to make sense to me. But I still feel that the "great ordeal" refers in particular to the Shoah, to the extermination of gypsies and communists, and to the death camps in general, where representatives of the "two witnesses" were exterminated.'

We turned first to the science of numbers for help. 'Great ordeal' gave us a value of 143, or 8. We then turned to the computer program for help, in the hope that this time it would provide a clue. We were not disappointed. The following names connected with the Second World War all have the number 8 in common. I should add here that the list is by no means complete. Only a few of the more striking ones have been selected:

Buchenwald (בוכנוואלד) = 125 (8)
Auschwitz (אושוויץ) = 413 (8)
Jew = 35 (8)
Christian = 359 (8)
Of all nations (מכל האומות) = 548 (8)
Crystal Night (ליל הבדולח) = 125 (8)
Munich (מינכן) = 170 (8)

Daladier (רלדיה) = 53 (8)

Chamberlain (צ'מברלין) = 422 (8)

Eight! The number of death! (Meth = 440 = 4 + 4 = 8.) They had an appointment with death!

As can be seen, the most disturbing aspect of this list is the three names 'Munich, Daladier and Chamberlain'. It was in Munich on 29 September 1938 that these two men signed an agreement that presented the Czechs with a fait accompli. An area of 28,000 square kilometres (11,000 square miles) of their country was annexed to Germany, together with almost 3 million Sudeten inhabitants. The announcement of this agreement was hailed with enthusiasm in France and England and the threat of war seemed to recede. Like Daladier, Chamberlain was welcomed home as a hero. We all know the rest of the story ...

We decided to take a break. A rare sun was shining over Paris and the bright day seemed such a contrast to the heavy atmosphere in which the Revelation had plunged us. Joy returned to the five of us as we ate lunch on the terrace of a restaurant. It was almost as if we were discovering life again. Life and light. We had lived with darkness and death for several months now, and all the fire, brimstone and bloodshed had left a bitter taste in our mouths and created a kind of vertigo in our minds. A child walked past our table. A very young child, no more than five or six. Where would he be in half a century? What would become of him?

If what we had glimpsed in the Revelation was to occur not in a thousand years but tomorrow or very soon, then the fate of this child was sealed, like that of many others. Because of one individual, the earth would again be in flames and innocents would pay the price to the beast with their blood. But it is always the innocents who pay for the madness of the guilty.

Man has finally loaded the dice. He has introduced an aspect into his quest that had not been included at the start: the ability to sterilize his own existence and to eliminate himself by an means of invisible force. One day, one of my close friends was explaining the dangers of nuclear power and its destructive potential to his young son. And the child replied with sublime wisdom: 'I see. It is as if insects had invented pesticides … '

Humanity had invented its own pesticide.

We did not work much after lunch. Perhaps we were tired, perhaps we were beginning to feel like Sisyphus, condemned endlessly to push our rock to the top of the hill.

We resumed work only three days later. Without having consulted each other, we knew that we had to start where we had left off, at chapter 7, verse 13: the verse that mentioned the words 'elders' and 'great ordeal'.

> *7:13 Then one of the elders addressed me, saying, 'Who are these, robed in white, and where have they come from?'*
> *7:14 I said to him, 'Sir, you are the one that knows.' Then he said to me, 'These are they who have come out of the great ordeal.'*

Why the presence of these 'elders'? The word 'elders' had already caught our eye when we were trying to decode the meaning of the 'great ordeal'.

David spoke. 'I expect you know this is not the first time that John mentions these characters. He describes them in chapter 4, verse 4: "Around the throne are twenty-four thrones, and seated on the thrones are twenty-four elders, dressed in white robes, with golden crowns on their heads."

I joined in: 'It would interesting to know the interpretation of the exegetists. What do they say about it?

'Everything and nothing. Some claim that these elders represent the twelve sons of Jacob who gave birth to the twelve tribes of Israel. Some say they are angels or celestial armies. Others say that they represent all the redeemed of the old and new alliance, rewarded and crowned. Some say that they play a sacerdotal or royal role, and are there to praise and adore God, to offer the prayers of the faithful. Others again see them as assisting God in governing the world, and their number would correspond to the twenty-four sacerdotal orders mentioned in the Torah.'

'Sacerdotal orders?'

Myriam explained: 'It means the order of the priests. They are listed in the First Book of Chronicles.[1] There, twenty-four men from twenty-four families were chosen by drawing lots to serve Yahweh.'

I nodded.

'This explains why the exegetists describe the elders of the Revelation as God's "assistants" ... '

'That makes sense, don't you think?'

'Absolutely, in an esoteric context. But that is not the context we are interested in. We are looking in the opposite direction since we are searching for an explanation that will be readily understood by anyone ... '

'You are right,' said Jean-Pierre.

'In that case,' Myriam suggested, 'why not look for an inverted interpretation, one that is diametrically opposed to that provided by religious scholars?'

'Which would mean?'

'A mirror image. Did not John help us establish that Lilith was none other than Eve's negative twin?'

'Exactly … '

'Would it not be possible to imagine that the twenty-four elders who represent good would also have their evil doubles?'

This led to general consternation … Myriam's reasoning seemed logical in a way, but how could it be put into practice? As usual we went round in circles for hours. Not one of the ideas we were putting forward at random was leading anywhere. This time we were really stuck with no possible way out. After midnight, we decided to give up and abandon the twenty-four elders to their secret for the time being.

10 A woman clothed in sun

The crimes of the Hitler régime, among them the massacre of the Jews, are without precedent in history because history gives no other example of a doctrine of such total destruction being able to seize the levers of command of a civilized nation.
Albert Camus, *L'Homme révolté (The Rebel)*

'I HAVE BEEN thinking about it all week. Or rather, I have thinking about what Myriam said when she thought that these twenty-four elders were a reflection of evil, not of good. Then I suddenly had a brainwave, quite mad really.'

'Quite normal,' Myriam replied jokingly. 'Isn't everything about this whole adventure mad?'

A few days earlier, I had bought a blackboard which we placed in the centre of the sitting room. Like that, everyone could jot down their ideas and the rest of us could benefit from them. I picked up a piece of chalk and wrote:

ADOLF HITLER

And I explained: 'If we start from the premise that these twenty-four elders do not serve God but the Devil or the dragon, they would be the Führer's servants or assistants. Does that make sense to you?

My four friends agreed more or less enthusiastically.

I added: 'Who were Hitler's assistants? At what moment of history did they get together?'

No one was able to give me an answer, so I wrote on the blackboard:

NUREMBERG

'The trial?'

'Exactly. After the Second World War the Allies set out to try the members and leaders of the National Socialist Party of the Third Reich for crimes against humanity. An international military tribunal was set up in the town of Nuremberg, between 20 November 1945 and 1 October 1946. There was Lord Justice Lawrence, representing British justice, Francis Biddle, representing the United States, Major-General Nikitchenko for the USSR, and Donnedieu de Vabre and Robert Fales for France. It was American attorney Robert Jackson who gave the trial its true dimension when he declared: "The real plaintiff at this bar is civilization." Do you remember the number of Nazis accused in this trial?

'Twenty-four?' David asked rather hesitantly.

'You are quite right ... Let us check anyway.' I picked up a book dealing with the Nuremberg trial. I found the page listing all the Nazis accused at the trial and I read aloud:

1 Doenitz
2 Fritzsche
3 Goering
4 Hesse
5 Jodl
6 Hans Frank

7 Frick

8 Funk

9 Keitel

10 Neurath

11 Raeder

12 Ribbentrop

13 Rosenberg

14 Sauckel

15 Schacht

16 Schirach

17 Seyss-Inquart

18 Speer

19 Streicher

20 Von Papen

21 Walther Funk

'That's strange,' Jean-Pierre remarked, 'there are only twenty-one names ... '

'Of course,' I replied. 'Himmler,[1] Goebbels and Heydrich[2] are missing. The first two committed suicide and the third was murdered.'

'So they would be the twenty-four elders of the Revelation,' said Dimitri. 'But ... '

He did not have time to finish his sentence. Myriam had rushed to the blackboard. The chalk made a grating noise as she rapidly wrote:

Trial (משפט) = 429, or 4 + 2 + 9 = 15, 1 + 5 = 6

Nuremberg (נורמברג) = 501, or 5 + 1 = 6

Adolf Hitler = 375, or 3 + 7 + 5 = 15, 1 + 5 = 6

666

And lower down:

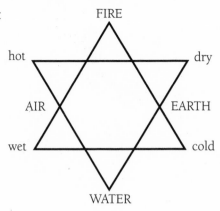

Then she turned towards us, suddenly rather excited: 'I shall not insult you by asking you if you know what this hexagon in a six-pointed star shape means. Some call it Solomon's seal, others the Maggen David or David's shield, or the Star of David. It is a motif that had been shared by many people, both in Europe and in the Middle East, as early as the Bronze Age. Its first manifestation as a Jewish symbol dates from the eighth century BC. Amazingly, archaeologists have discovered a representation of this seal in the synagogue of Capernaum, dating from the third century. Another sign was engraved next to it.'

Under the Maggen David she drew:

'Yes, indeed, it is a swastika ... In fact, there is nothing surprising about that at all. In Sanskrit, the word "swastika" is derived from *su* (well) and *asti* (he is). So it means "that that leads to well-being". Hindus use the swastika to mark the pages of their account books, the threshold of their homes, their doors and their offerings. But I am only explaining this to you so that you understand that this duality suggested by John exists even with the Maggen David. Good is the reverse of evil. Look at the seal. On one side darkness, on the other light. In the Revelation, the Devil uses the same weapons as God and the Antichrist transforms Christ's instruments into stratagems. Therefore, why should we not believe in the perverted vocation of the twenty-four elders?'

'Shall we sum up what we have up to now?' I suggested.

I turned to the blackboard, rubbed out what Myriam had written, and wrote:

666 = Adolf Hitler Austria

Large city or Egypt or Armageddon = Germany

Gog = America

Magog = Germany-Japan-Italy-Romania-Hungary-Finland-Bulgaria

Hitler

Roosevelt

False prophet = Joseph Paul Goebbels

Image = the cinema

66 million dead

Lamb + beast = Adam

1st woman = Eve

2nd woman = Lilith

Dragon = fascism

42 months = timespan between the signature of the
            Germano-Russian pact and Stalingrad

Two witnesses = Judaism and Christianity

Temple of God = the Bible

Court outside = the rest of the non-monotheistic world

The great ordeal = the Shoah and the victims of all nations
and all races
The 24 elders = the Nazi leaders

'Have we forgotten anything?'

'Lots of things, probably,' David replied. 'The pieces relating to the Second World War are beginning to fit together but the puzzle is far from being completed.' He brandished a note he had made and continued: 'Look. Here's an example. When we decided to list the protagonists, we forgot four of them ... and quite important ones.'

Dimitri was the first to reply to this: 'I already know which ones you mean: the four horsemen.'

'Precisely. But there are still many other gaps. We have spoken about the two women. Although our interpretation seems complete and adequate in the case of Lilith, whom John compares to Babylon, this is not true in the case of the first woman; Eve. Read the two verses again.

12.1 A great portent appeared in heaven: a woman clothed with the sun, with the moon under her feet, and on her head a crown of twelve stars.
12.2 She was pregnant and was crying out in birth pangs ...

'One question remains, and it is an important one. Who is this woman about to give birth to? What is the meaning of the crown of twelve stars on her head?'

I pointed out: 'You are aware that most commentators see the Virgin Mary, the mother of Christ, in this description. I have also seen an exegesis that seems to imply that she could also represent the People of God or the Church.'

'There might be an interpretation,' Myriam suddenly cried out. She made a few quick notes and thought for a long time before continuing: 'This is only a proposition. But as you will see, it is a rather interesting one … especially for you Christians. If we calculate the values of "Eve" and of the word "Church", we get respectively 19 or 1, and 145 or 1. Curious, isn't it? How can we bring the twelve stars and twelve Apostles together? The "twelve stars" have a value of 1,068 or 6, and "the twelve Apostles" 1,383 or 6. What does the verse say? "A great portent appeared in heaven: a woman clothed with the sun, with the moon under her feet, and on her head a crown of twelve stars." The word "sun" is equal to 640 or 1. The same as the word "Emeth", 1,441 or 1, which indicates supreme Truth. The "moon" is worth 6 – the number 6 that in numerology represents the opposition of the Creature to the Creator. It is the number of the trial between good and evil … We have seen it with 666.'

I asked her: 'So how should we interpret the verse?'

'Like this. On the one hand is the Church-truth, crowned by the twelve Apostles; and on the other, under her feet, the temptation of lies, conflict, and opposition to the Creator.'

I protested with a smile: 'Don't you think there is an iconoclastic side to your "vision" of the verse?

She shook her head. 'Not at all. But I did warn you, it was only a proposition. However, if you look more closely at the history of the Church, you must admit that it did not always reflect the teachings of Christ. As far as I know, the Inquisition was not an example of man's tolerance and love towards his fellow beings. Nor was the silence of Pius XII during the Second World War, or the condemnation of Galileo and Copernicus.'

'Never mind!' David interrupted. 'I suggest that we postpone the analysis of the verse, because there are still many unexplained points.'

'The locusts, among other things,' added Myriam. 'They are mentioned in chapter 9, verse 3: "Then from the smoke came locusts on the earth."'

'The least that can be said is that we have discovered very little compared to what we still have to do ...

Dimitri made a suggestion: 'Perhaps we could try and decode the four horsemen? After all, they have been the subject of so many interpretations and inspired so many films. In addition, there is one piece of information linked to one of the riders that is rather interesting.' And he quoted in a clear voice: ' "I looked, and there was a white horse! Its rider had a bow; a crown was given to him, and he came out conquering and to conquer."[3] What intrigues me here is the word "bow".'

'Why?' Myriam asked.

'I'll tell you. Some explain this verse by saying that the Parthians were the sworn enemies of Rome, and from it they infer that the Christians hoped that one day the Parthians would destroy the beast, namely the Roman Empire.'

'But what do we really know about these famous Parthians?

'Everything and nothing really. It was during the first half of the third century BC that the Scythian tribes arrived in Iran. Called Parnes or Aparnes by historians, these tribes are thought to have emigrated from the region near the Aral Sea to settle in Parthia. These nomads then built up an empire by capturing vast regions to the west, and it appeared that for five centuries they dominated what we call today the Iranian plateau. Unfortunately, because they appeared to dislike writing, preferring the oral tradition, we know very little about them. All the information we have comes from their enemies, among others the Greeks. Did they create a real civilization? We are unable to answer this question. On the other hand, they were powerful enough to pose a serious military threat to Rome. In fact, if we wanted to caricature the situation, we could say that the Parthians were to Rome what the former Soviet Union was to the United States: the enemy that had to be destroyed.'

I completed my Greek friend's exposé: 'And because history is unpredictable. The fall of the Roman Empire was caused by Barbarian invasions, by the Huns in particular, which no one expected.' Then I asked Dimitri, 'Why are you interested in the word "bow"?'

'Bows and arrows were the weapons used by the Parthians. Their warriors were said to be able to shoot from any position, even over their shoulder while retreating, and still hit their target. You may find me illogical, but what is engraved on five- and ten-dollar coins, whether gold or silver?'

No one could answer the question.

He replied slowly: 'An Indian. A Sioux Indian.'

'So what?'

'The bow and arrow … '

Myriam's reply was immediate: 'You are indeed illogical!'

'And the crown,' I asked. 'What does it represent? Because John did indeed say "a crown was given to him".'

'Since you are accusing me of being illogical, I shall be completely so. The Statue of Liberty is wearing a crown.'

His statement was met with loud cries of protest. Dimitri tried to silence the noise by waving his hand. Finally, he almost shouted: 'All right! Calculate the value of the words "white horse" and "United States"!'

At first Myriam seemed rather reluctant, but seeing the historian's insistence, she gave in. When she had completed her calculation, she looked at us, her face now expressing surprise rather than scepticism. In a subdued voice she said, ' "White horse" is equivalent to 208. "United States" … comes to … 208.'

Dimitri was jubilant: 'Furthermore, John also emphasized "and he came out conquering and to conquer". Surely that refers to the intervention by the United States, who transformed defeat into victory?'

There was a moment of silence. But what was the significance of this unexpected correlation? Once again it was Dimitri who suggested an answer: 'If I am not mistaken, one of the three other riders probably represents Germany.'

Myriam did some more calculations before announcing: 'I'm afraid none of the three riders has a value of 308 or 380, which I remind you are the figures attributed to Germany. "Black horse" has a value of 640, "red horse" 177, and "green horse" 436.'

Someone whispered for the benefit of our Greek friend: 'This is where the Athenians neared their end … '

11 Locusts

WE ALL WENT our separate ways for the summer holidays. One to Greece, one to Italy, another to Brittany or some such place. I was the only one staying in Paris. On the one hand, I hate being idle and spending hours wasting time – as I rightly or wrongly think of a holiday – and on the other, I have always thought that a beautiful landscape becomes even more beautiful when you enjoy it with someone. Not having anyone with whom to share such pleasant moments, I preferred to bury myself in work, meditation and the delights (or torments) of solitude. But the misfortune of loners is that somehow – through no fault of their own – they are seldom alone. This was certainly my situation. If I am not opening my door to a friend in need of comfort, it is to a lost dog without a collar. Such is Fate …

Naturally the Revelation was my constant companion. At night, it lay on my bedside table and I never went to sleep without delving into its mysterious depths. It was during one of those nights that I suddenly woke with a start. For some time now, four horses – one black, one white, one red, one green – had been fighting in my sleep. That night I sat up, the figure 436 flashing in my mind. It was the numerical value Myriam had given to the green, or pale-green, horse. But how could the significance of such valuable information have escaped us? And yet it was so clear. So very obvious. We were trying to prove that one of the riders of the Apocalypse was Germany, and this proof was right under my nose:

Green horse (סוס ירק) = 436
Dragon/fascism (פשיזם) = 436

I turned on my bedside light and began to study the verse in question:

I looked and there was a pale green horse! Its rider's name was Death, and Hades followed with him; they were given authority over a fourth of the earth, to kill with sword, famine, and pestilence, and by the wild animals of the earth.[1]

Almost at the same time I remembered the words often used to describe 'Nazism: the brown pestilence', referring to the brown shirts[2] worn by the storm troopers of the SA, the Sturmabteilung or assault division. This verse mentioned pestilence, and, moreover, the apostle gave this horse the greenish colour typical of the decomposing corpses resulting from bubonic plague. So the green horse did indeed represent Germany. The white horse stood for the United States. Dimitri had been right to insist.

I ran to the telephone and, disregarding the fact that it was night time, I called my four friends to tell them about my discovery. As expected, the most enthusiastic among them was Dimitri. I heard him scream something in Greek that sounded like a cry of victory and a curse combined.

We had to wait until September until the four of us could meet up again (Myriam had returned to Israel for work reasons). That day, seeing the piles of notes on my desk, I realized that my friends had also continued their investigations in an attempt to unravel the mysteries of the visionary of Patmos.

Jean-Pierre started by reviewing our approach to the task: 'You remember the results of our analysis when we first became interested in the Revelation? We concluded that the verses, like the Koran, were not written in chronological order, and that we should consider the whole as a puzzle and not like a traditional composition based on a unit of time and place. Furthermore, we also agreed that the pieces of the puzzle were – most of the time – scattered throughout the verses. For instance, a sentence of verse X of chapter Y might very well complement another sentence in another verse in a different chapter. Do we still agree with this principle?'

'If you ask the question,' said David, 'it must be because you have something in mind … '

The semiologist agreed: 'You know as well as I do that the words that raise questions are those with a "double meaning". Words like head, face, trumpet or sky are not particularly interesting, but ones like 666, dragon, false prophet, court outside, or witness appear to have a much deeper, hidden meaning. I myself feel that "locust" is one of those words. This is what verse 3 in chapter 9 says:

> *Then from the smoke came* locusts *on the earth, and they were given authority like the authority of scorpions of the earth.*

'Further down, in verse 7, still in chapter 9, John continues his description:

> *In appearance the* locusts *were like horses equipped for battle. On their heads were what looked like crowns of gold; their faces were like human faces …*

'And further, in verse 9:

> *… they had scales like iron breastplates, and the noise of their wings was like the noise of many chariots with horses rushing into battle.*

'Don't these descriptions remind you of something?'

David was the first to answer: 'The first image that comes to mind is that of an army. A marching army … '

Jean-Pierre smiled and looked pleased. 'The same image came to my mind. It is indeed quite striking. How could one not think of armoured divisions and battalions when reading expressions such as "horses equipped for battle", "scales like iron breastplates" and "the noise of many chariots".

I decided to join the discussion: 'I have also tried to analyze this passage; it is the word "locust" that fascinates me. I have therefore counted how often it occurs in the Bible, and the answer is thirty-eight times: in the plural twenty-nine times and in the singular nine times. Most of the verses in which the word "locust" occurs concern war.

'For instance in Exodus:

> *For if you refuse to let my people go, tomorrow I will bring* locusts *into your country.*
> *The Lord said to Moses, 'Stretch out your hand over the land of Egypt, so that the* locusts *may come upon it and eat every plant in the land, all that the hail has left.'*[3]

'In Judges:

> *For they and their livestock would come up, and they would even bring*

their tents, as thick as locusts; *neither they nor their camels could be counted; so they wasted the land as they came in.*[4]

'But the verse that interested me most was definitely verse 13 in chapter 7 of 2 Chronicles:

When I shut up the heavens so that there is no rain, or command the locust *to devour the land, or send* pestilence *among my people.*

'Pestilence,' whispered David.

'Yes … pestilence. And since we know that the green horse is linked to fascism and therefore also Germany, the word "pestilence" takes on a very particular dimension.'

There were a few moments of silence before Jean-Pierre spoke: 'So this is purely and simply a description of the Wehrmacht.'

I nodded . 'All the more because John speaks of the "noise of many chariots". Is it possible to dissociate this description from battle tanks or *Panzerdivisionen*, especially when we know that the Panzers were the spearhead of the Wehrmacht?'

Dimitri got up and began to think aloud, pacing the room: 'All this seems very coherent, but only in theory. As always we must prove what we are proposing. Otherwise our theories are mere conjectures.'

We could only agree.

'I would like to go back to the concordances of the word "locusts". There is a chapter in the Book of Joel describing the plague of locusts, which says among other things:

For a nation has invaded my land, powerful and innumerable; its teeth are lions' teeth, and it has the fangs of a lioness. [5]

'And in chapter 2, verses 4 and 5:

> *They have the appearance of horses, and like warhorses they charge.*
> *As with the rumbling of chariots, they leap on the tops of the mountains,*
> *like the crackling of a flame of fire, devouring the stubble, like a powerful*
> *army drawn up for battle.*

'Now let us look again at the passages written by John:[6]

> *In appearance the locusts were like horses equipped for battle … their*
> *faces were like human faces … their teeth like lions' teeth … they had*
> *scales like iron breastplates, and the noise of their wings was like the*
> *noise of many chariots with horses rushing into battle.*

'And the apostle further added in verse 11 of this same chapter 9:

> *They have as king over them the angel of the abyss; his name*
> *in Hebrew is Abaddon, and in Greek he is called 'Apollyon'.*

'I suggest we now draw up a list of all the words and expressions that are capable of having a double meaning.'

An hour later the blackboard was covered with the following words or parts of sentences:

Locusts
Horses, or *the* horses
Scales, or *their* scales
Breastplates, or *the* breastplates

Combat, or *in* combat
Teeth, or *their* teeth
King
Apollyon or Abaddon

'Now we no longer have a choice.'

I turned towards David: 'Please send this list to Myriam. Who knows, the results of her calculations might clarify things a little.'

It was at this precise moment that everything toppled over ... I remember as if it was yesterday the terrible pain that felt as if my head was being crushed. It was as if rats were gnawing away at my brain. Nausea, perspiration, and the feeling that the ground was disappearing under my feet ... I lay down on the sofa. In a daze, I heard Jean-Pierre's voice – or it might have been Dimitri's – shouting, 'Quickly, call an ambulance!' And then nothing ... complete darkness.

How long did it last? I have no idea at all. I can only remember fragmented images with faces I did not know. Strange noises, sounding as if they came from a deep well. I was dying. It was as simple as that. It might have been at that moment, that day, that night, or a week later, that I heard a voice whispering to me: 'Courage, this is your last chance, go and meet death like a soldier so that your wasted life at least ends well. No one will sing your praises, no one will call you a hero or anything like that, but just for that very reason, it is worth it.' I knew those words. I had read them somewhere, long ago, but where? Why did I remember them now?

My delving into the mysteries of the Revelation was suddenly taking me to the very edge of nothingness, where nothing matters any longer except for one last question: 'What is the purpose of life?'

I did not die … obviously, since I am sitting at my keyboard. But I was very frightened. The greater our unawareness of death, the greater our fear when we do suddenly become aware of it. Until then I had always lived without thinking of death; I even smiled rather patronizingly when someone admitted their fear of dying one day. But now I believe that to live without thinking of death is to miss out on a wonderful source of energy: the energy of despair that, contrary to received ideas, is not a sinister energy but a power that rouses amazing forces within one; the sensation of urgency that drives one to a greater intensity of living beyond that soulless feeling of half-heartedness. And above all, the thought of death denies you a futile right – that of putting something off until the next day. Tomorrow becomes automatically synonymous with the improbable.

When I opened my eyes in my hospital room in Neuilly-sur-Seine, the first sensation I experienced was a 'non-sensation'. My entire right side was lifeless. This absence of sensation also affected part of my face. However hard I tried to move my limbs, they refused to obey. It was as if they no longer belonged to me.

After the doctor came to see me, I only remembered one word: hemiplegia … I was half paralyzed. I was suddenly seized by the irresistible urge to pray; not to complain or to lament my fate, but to come to some agreement with the 'divine watchmaker'. Either he would let the illness take its course to the end or he would give me back the full use of my limbs. I found the thought of being paralyzed, and thus dependent on others, completely unbearable.

You may believe or disbelieve the power of prayer, but three days later I had regained full use of my limbs …

As the author Georges Duhamel wrote: 'One day scholars, my colleagues, will discover that a certain tension in the mind can be felt from afar and alter the course of events, the fate of humanity, and perhaps even the structure of the material world. Nothing must be rejected: we have seen people go back on almost all their denials … '[7] Perhaps it was this 'tension of the mind' that I believed in, with all my strength.

12 Abaddon and Apollyon

From the fig tree learn its lesson: as soon as its branch becomes tender and puts forth its leaves, you know that summer is near.

Matthew 24:32

BECAUSE OF MY convalescence, we were only able to resume work at the beginning of December 1996. Strangely, it was much easier than I had thought. Such an experience as I had would change anyone but a completely insensitive person. My brush with death had brought me even closer to the Holy Scripture. I found it a great source of strength that reinforced my faith – not the faith of a bigot but of someone who is increasingly certain that there is 'something else'.

Our first task was to study the notes that Myriam had sent from Israel but that, in view of my circumstances, my comrades had not had the heart to look at without me. Here they are:

The locusts (חגבים) = 63 = 9

Powerful people (עם חזק) = 225 = 9

The iron breastplates (שריונות ברזל) = 1211 = 5

King (מלך) = 90 = 9

In combat (לקרב) = 332 = 8

Their scales (חזיהם) = 70 = 7

Their teeth (שיניהם) = 415 = 1

Apollyon (אפוליון) = 183 = 3

'And now?' asked David. 'What shall we do with these numbers?'

Jean-Pierre replied without hesitation: 'Apply them to our hypothesis, because the verses they come from have a direct link with the German army.'

'Easy to say … But how do we go about it?'

So I said: 'Let's proceed logically, as we always do. We already know that "the locusts" are a powerful people. And if we refer back to the verse of 2 Chronicles: " … or I command the locust to devour the land, or send pestilence among my people," the word "pestilence" implies that this refers to the Wehrmacht.'

'At the risk of repeating myself,' David objected, 'that still remains to be proved … The allusion suggested in the verse in Chronicles is not enough.'

I nodded in agreement as I dialled Myriam's number. It was not very late, yet the voice that answered sounded sleepy. 'Were you already in bed?'

'Shouldn't I have been?' She quickly went on: 'What word?'

'Wehrmacht … '

A moment of silence, then: '495.'

Through theosophical reduction we arrived at the figure 9. I leant towards my friends and said: 'Locusts = 9. Powerful people = 9. Wehrmacht = 9. Any comments?'

Dimitri said: 'Ask her the numerical value of "panzers".'

I passed on his question.

'392,' Myriam replied. 'But why that word?'

'I assume Dimitri is looking for a correlation with "the iron breastplates" that John describes.'

'In that case he is wrong. It is not "panzers" but "the panzers" that you must evaluate, because John refers to "the iron breastplates."

I was agreeing with this when Myriam further added: 'Panzers equals 392, or 5. And if my memory does not fail me ... '

I interrupted her. 'Thank you ... go back to sleep.' And I put the phone down. 'You heard?[5]. The same value as "the iron breastplates".'

The idea that we were dealing with a description of the army, and more especially the panzer divisions, was become increasingly certain.

Several minutes passed before Dimitri asked another question: 'There is something I do not understand. Let us look at the main points in the respective verses.' He wrote on the blackboard:

Then from the smoke came locusts on the earth; they have as king over them the angel of the abyss; his name in Hebrew is Abaddon, and in Greek he is called Apollyon. In appearance the locusts were like horses equipped for battle, on their heads were what looked like crowns of gold, their faces were like human faces, they had scales like iron breastplates, and the noise of their wings was like the noise of many chariots with horses rushing into battle.

'Why should the apostle bother to give us simply a military description? For what purpose? If we look at all the information he has given us, it is apparent that everything contains a specific message, about Adam and the beast – the battle of the man-lie against the man-truth; the dragon (fascism); the false prophet (Goebbels); the great ordeal (the Shoah); and so on. It is therefore unlikely that this is merely a military description, even if it is directly connected with Germany and the Third Reich. What do you think?'

David was the first to reply: 'It is true that it feels as if something is still missing. But that could be due to the fact that we have not completed our work on the verses in question.' He pointed to the blackboard: 'Here for instance … Who is Abaddon or Apollyon?'

'John has told us he is the king leading this army.'

I said abruptly: 'A general … ?'

'Why not?' asked David. 'A general is quite conceivable … '

I hesitated for a moment and called Myriam again. 'You are going to hate us … '

'Too late … I already do. So much so that I could not go back to sleep. I was surrounded by locusts … You too, I suppose?'

'Yes, we were too. And we can see their king. Can you tell us his value again?'

'9.'

'And if he was a general?'

Silence.

'It would also be 9 … '

'Is it?'

'What do you think?'

I could hardly contain myself: 'Myriam, please answer!'

'9 of course. Like the word "king".'

I told my friends: ' "King" and "general" have the same numerical value. I then asked Myriam: 'And Apollyon?' I heard the sound of her pen on the paper.

'It does not work any more … I get 183, or 3 through theosophical reduction.'

I remained silent, perplexed, as I tried to make sense of it all. John was trying to tell us about the presence of a general. But not just any general, because he also mentioned "iron breastplates', thus panzers. Therefore he must be referring to a general commanding one or more armoured divisions.

'Hello? Are you still there?'

Myriam's voice made me jump. 'Yes, I am still here. Be an angel and be patient. I think we are onto something important.' I asked David: 'Could you get me David Chandler's book,[1] which is in the library. Open it at Kursk.'

'Kursk?'

'Yes ... '

He did as I asked him.

'Kursk ... here it is ... '

'What was the name of the general in charge of the panzers during the battle?'

'Von Manstein ... but I also have Model and Guderian and ... '

'No! Guderian was not in Russia. He was an adviser, like General Model in fact.' I was about to ask Myriam: 'Tell me ... '

'Don't bother, I understand ... Von Manstein, is that it?'

I did not have time to reply.

'Yes, you are right ... Von Manstein is Abbadon ... the same numerical value. 531 for the first, or 9, 63 for the second, or 9 too. And they have the same numerical value as the word "king". Also, "locusts" too has the same value as Abbadon, 63 – which confirms that it is indeed his army ... '

I could hardly contain my feverish excitement. 'And ... Apollyon?' I asked nervously, like a child hoping for a last present.

'You are right again ... Apollyon gives 183 or 3. Guderian makes 273 or 3. Can I go back to sleep now?

'Good night, Myriam. I promise I won't bother you again. Not tonight ... ' I had hardly put the phone down when everyone started asking questions.

'How about telling us what all this is about?' I gestured to my three friends to calm down. 'Be patient … You'll soon understand it all.' I wrote in big letters on the blackboard:

KURSK

'So?' muttered David.

'Please, be patient!' I took a deep breath and began reading:

Following their defeat at Stalingrad, the Germans had largely lost the initiative. No doubt this was why, at the end of the month of May 1943, some generals proposed to the Führer the ambitious plan of a great encircling operation with two wings, so as to surround and cut off the Russian forces holding the salient of the city of Kursk.

Many high-ranking advisers, including Model and Guderian, strongly opposed this, arguing that it would be madness to launch such an offensive, considering the state of the Wehrmacht. But, after hesitating, Hitler decided that the operation should be tried. This was the 'Citadel' plan.

As soon as the operation had been launched, at the beginning of July, the 2nd German Army came into contact with the west flank of the salient, to distract the attention of the Russians. But the Soviets were not to be taken by surprise. Their 'Lucie' network of agents in Switzerland warned them in time of what was afoot, and the Russian General Zhukov was able to prepare his defence in the most detailed manner.

Within the salient, the engineers and infantry were working hard to lay eight successive minefields and anti-tank defences. 1,300,000 soldiers, 20,000 artillery pieces and 3,600 tanks were

125

deployed, as well as 2,400 aircraft of the Soviet air force.

On the German side were 900,000 men – 38 divisions, of which 17 were armoured.

A battle of titans was about to take place: in fact, the greatest tank battle in history to date.

One of the most important generals involved in this battle was called Von Manstein. As for General Guderian, he has gone down in history as one of the greatest tank theorists and strategists. Among other things, he revived military art by developing all the opportunities offered to modern warfare through the use of "engine and armour". After the debacle of Stalingrad, it was he who was responsible for the task of rebuilding the German tank divisions by giving them new Tiger and Panther V tanks.

I stopped reading and wrote on the blackboard:

King (מלך) = 90 = 9
General (אלוף) = 9

Abbadon (אבדון) = 63 = 9
Von Manstein (ון מנשטיין) = 531 = 9
Apollyon (אפּוליון) = 183 = 12 = 3
Guderian (גודרין) = 273 = 12 = 3

The locusts (חגבים) = 63 = 9
Wehrmacht (ויירמרכט) = 495 = 18 = 9
The iron breastplates (שריונות ברזל) = 1211 = 5
The panzers (הפּנזרים) = 392 = 14 = 5

Just as I was going to speak again, the telephone rang. It was Myriam. David handed me the telephone.

'Can you switch on the loudspeaker?' she asked without giving any explanation.

'Yes, I've done it.'

The theologian's clear voice rang through the room: 'As you probably guessed I could not get back to sleep. I have been glued to chapter 9 since Gérard's first call. Obviously we have discovered Kursk. But I do not suppose that you have found the word in the text of the verses. I don't know if you will agree with my findings, but I shall tell you anyway. John wrote: "the noise of many chariots with horses rushing into battle".' She paused briefly and continued: 'Numerical value of "into battle"? 332 or 8. Numerical value of "Kursk"? 566 or 17 or 8. And that's not all. "Their teeth" equals 415 or 1; we could replace this with "their power" (עוצמה שלהם), value 586 or 19, which makes 1. Come on, you goys, think about all this! And now I am disconnecting my telephone … '

We looked at each other, completely dazed.

I vaguely heard Jean-Pierre saying: 'Then from the smoke came locusts on the earth; they have as king over them the angel of the abyss; his name in Hebrew is Abaddon, and in Greek he is called Apollyon. In appearance the locusts were like horses equipped for battle; on their heads were what looked like crowns of gold; their faces were like human faces; they had scales like iron breastplates, and the noise of their wings was like the noise of many rushing chariots with horses into battle.'

And Dimitri continued: 'And like a powerful people, the Wehrmacht deployed its men. Its strength and, its power were those of a lion. Its weapons: panzers. At their head: General Von Manstein and the angel of the abyss, Guderian, rushing to attack Kursk …

13 Sands of the sea

That which is, already has been;
that which is to be, already is.
Ecclesiastes 3:15

BECAUSE OF OUR respective obligations, we could not go on meeting, but this did not mean that we stopped working. Far from it. I think that we worked harder than ever and with greater enthusiasm – although separately. But in spite of all our efforts, the Revelation was proving extremely unwilling to reveal its secrets. Chapters and verses gave the impression of suddenly being reluctant to yield further secrets. It was as if a stone slab had slipped over the text, sealing its contents forever.

However hard we tried, however imaginative or crazy our attempts, the result was always nothing. And yet, there had to be so much more. We began to wonder whether we had worked for nothing during all these months. For if we could not discover the missing links, if the events relating to the Second World War stopped here, our theories and hypotheses would be useless.

This went on for almost three months, three fruitless months during which we worked ceaselessly without being able to extract the slightest piece of concrete information. Neither the many books on the Revelation (and there are an amazing number of them) nor the comments of the exegetists were of any help. In the end it was fate once more that helped us move in the right direction.

In April 1997, I decided to accept Myriam's invitation to Israel.

We had mutual friends there whom I had not seen for a long time, and in any case it was a wonderful opportunity to revisit a country I had not been to for many years.

It was a very special time, especially in Jerusalem. There, perhaps, in the dry, suffocating heat of summer, amid the heady fragrance of pine trees, one feels closer to the sky than anywhere else in the world. Some Muslims are thought to have calculated that the distance separating us from the sky is precisely eighteen miles!

The City of David is a city torn apart, coveted by so many for so many centuries, a city of the one God, yet claimed with such violence and bitterness, as if it were an object that belonged just to one single section of humanity. The air is heavy with an indescribable, divine atmosphere, from the Holy Sepulchre to the Wailing Wall, from the Dome to the Via Dolorosa. Everywhere God's presence, the Eternal's presence, can be felt. Allah is sleeping at the foot of an olive tree, exhausted by the sun. These three who have always been one and the same entity amuse or irritate each other depending on the mood of the moment, determined by the degree of people's temporary stupidity.

For two weeks I roamed the countryside, absorbing the dry yet fertile landscape, intoxicated by the heady fragrances, my eyes shedding the salt tears of the Dead Sea and the Lake of Tiberias. And throughout my long peregrinations, moved by the sweetness of Galilee and the harshness of the Negev Desert, I felt St John's presence following me like a faithful shadow.

At Ben-Gurion airport, as we were saying goodbye, Myriam said as a joke, like a reproach to a faithful friend who is going and leaving her behind: 'Here I am in the middle of this dry, arid desert ... ' And she added: 'Ezekiel ... '

Ezekiel ... To kill time, I began reading Ezekiel, the third Book of the section of the Last Prophets of the Torah. Written in the first person, the book comprises no fewer than 48 chapters and 1,273 verses. The content is quite similar to that of the Revelation of St John the Divine. In the first chapters, Ezekiel paints a sombre portrait of the history of Israel, full of innumerable sins and rebellions against God. The prophet then recalls the oracles of condemnation of the nations. He finally concludes with promises of comfort.

Strangely enough, like Revelation, the Book of Ezekiel troubled the rabbis for a long time because of its divergences, and they only accepted the book within the canon after numerous debates. Today, it is traditionally considered the holiest book in the Bible after the Pentateuch.

I never stopped thinking about it during the days that followed. It was at the beginning of May that I understood why I had thought it so important. Myriam was back in Paris, working on a project for a conference. As countless times before, I picked up the Book of Revelation and began reading. I knew it so well that I could recite whole passages by heart. When I got to chapter 20, verse 8, I was startled by the following words:

… they are as numerous as the sands of the sea.

I had read a passage in the Book of Ezekiel that was very reminiscent of this verse in Revelation. I quickly found the chapter and verse, Ezekiel 39:6:

I will send fire on Magog and on those who live securely in the coastlands …

So it was the word 'coastlands' which had reminded me of 'sands of the sea'. Perhaps they had the same value?

I asked Myriam.

'"The sands" … come to 455, or 5. "Coastlands" … make 149, or 5.'

I said to her: 'That is strange, is it not? And then there is this reference to Germany again with Magog: "I will send fire on Magog … "

Myriam laughed: 'As far as I know the Third Reich was not famous for its beaches … '

'But why this parallel? Do you think it is entirely coincidental?'

She replied in a rather stern manner: 'Since we are working on the Revelation, you should know that the word "coincidental" is not part of our vocabulary.'

'I agree. But then, I'll ask you again: why? It is not the first time that John alludes to verses in the Torah. We have seen it a hundred times. Therefore, if the numerical concordance between "sands of the sea" and "coastlands" is not simply a matter of chance, it must be for a reason.'

'Probably … '

We were unable to go any further.

We all met again two days later. Naturally, I informed my friends of the bizarre correlation between the verse in the Book of Ezekiel and that in St John.

'Coastlands? Sands of the sea?' Jean-Pierre repeated, wrapped in thought. 'It would be amazing … '

'What would be?'

He waved his arm in a discouraging manner: 'Nothing, it would ridiculous … '

'Tell me … '

He continued stubbornly: 'I'm telling you, it's stupid! Please, drop it.'

Dimitri asked: 'Have you tried the word "sea"?'

'Yes, its numerical value is 50, or 5.'

'Interesting … we have here three similar numbers: the beaches

5, the sands 5, and the sea 5.

Suddenly, Jean-Pierre joined in the conversation and asked Myriam: '6 June! Can you give me the numerical value of 6 June?'

There was a moment of silence.

'698 ... '

'That is ... '

'6 + 9 + 8 = 5. But ... '

I now understood my friend's reasoning.

'It's the date of the Normandy landings ... I suppose that those were the words you did not dare to pronounce?'

He nodded in agreement.

'It is impossible,' David muttered.

I repeated slowly: 'The coastlands, the sands, the sea, 6 June ... ' And I remembered automatically: 'The preparations for the Normandy landing started towards the end of 1943. The flotilla of boats gathered for this amounted to over 6,000 vessels of every kind, and 156,000 soldiers: "they are as numerous as the sands of the sea ... " Delayed at first because of unfavourable weather conditions – with the boats that had already set off having to sail in circles – the operation was set to take place on 6 June, in spite of the fact that weather conditions had not improved. During the night, frogmen first cut the barbed wire placed in the sea by the Germans; at 2 o'clock, the airborne troops were dropped; at 3 o'clock bombing from the air began; at 5.30 the naval bombardment started; at 6 o'clock the first assault troops and tanks were landed on the beaches. The beaches were undoubtedly the place where the most dramatic events took place ... Omaha, Gold, Juno, Sword ... Moreover ... '

I took a quick breath and continued: '666. The number of the Beast occurs in the day, the month and the time of the landing. On 6 June, the sixth month, at 6 o'clock ... '

Myriam said in a quiet voice: 'Those who live securely in the coast-lands [Magog] … And I will send fire on Magog … ' She got up and wrote on the blackboard:

The coastlands (החופים) = 149 = 5
The sands (החולות) = 455 = 5
Sea (ים) = 50 = 5
6 June (השישה ביוני) = 698 = 5

Then she turned towards us and added: 'Here are a few more "coincidences"' and she wrote:

Europe (אירופה) = 302 = 5
Normandy (נורמנדיה) = 365 = 5
France (צרפת) = 770 = 5

Jean-Pierre joined in: 'I am sure you remember the details of the battle of Kursk, and that we located the two most important generals of this offensive, Von Manstein and Guderian. Who were the most important people during the June landing? Who was in charge of Operation Overlord? Dwight Eisenhower. And on the German side: Erwin Rommel. Could it be possible that … '

Myriam picked up the chalk again and wrote down on the blackboard:

Erwin Rommel (אירוין רומל) = 553 = 4
Dwight Eisenhower (דרייט אהייזנהואור) = 346 = 4

Paradoxically, instead of reassuring us, this new information extracted from St John's writings renewed our doubts. It was David who spoke first.

133

'I don't know what you're thinking at this moment, but for my part, while recognizing the interest of our discoveries, I am wondering whether we are really looking at the truth. In fact, I was going to say "integrity".'

'Are you not questioning our method of working by saying this?'

'Absolutely not. But there is something that does worry me. Read chapter 22, verse 10:

And he said to me, 'Do not seal up the words of the prophecy of
this book ...'

'The warning is completely unambiguous, isn't it? God is telling John: "Make sure that these prophetic words are not encoded, so that they may be read and understood." This instruction is the opposite of the one God gave to the prophet Daniel, to whom he revealed a vision of the end of the world:

8:19 He said, 'Listen, and I will tell you what will take place later
in the period of wrath; for it refers to the appointed time of the end.'

'And the Lord ordered as follows:

12:9 'Go your way, Daniel, for the words are to remain secret and
sealed until the time of the end.'

'Now, the least one can say of the text of Revelation is that it is rather inaccessible. So did John disregard the advice of the All-Powerful? Unless ... '

I encouraged him to finish.

'Unless there is no code, that there has never been any, that it is merely an allegorical text, a kind of epic poem written by a visionary.'

Jean-Pierre shook his head in disapproval: 'You are wrong there. Pythagoras said "everything is number". I would add that in the Bible "everything is code". Rather than meaning that the text has to remain inde-cipherable for most people, it means that it was conceived in such a way as to be understood – at least at the beginning – by a select number of initiates. But the word "initiates" is probably not the right one here. I would prefer to replace it with a metaphor, such as "the beginners". Indeed, what does the word "initiate" mean, if not "begin" or "start"? These initiates or beginners would consist of a small group of people who could understand the true message, which would then be passed on to others. Jesus himself spent years preaching in code. Indeed, are not parables coded texts *par excellence*? There is in fact a passage which confirms what I have just said."

He opened the New Testament, leafed through until he found the passage and began to read:

'Matthew, chapter 13 …

That same day Jesus went out of the house and sat beside the sea. Such great crowds gathered around him that he got into a boat and sat there, while the whole crowd sat on the beach. And he told them many things in parables.

'And in verse 10 we read:

Then the disciples came and asked him, 'Why do you speak to them in parables?' He answered, 'To you it has been given to know the secrets of the kingdom of heaven, but to them it has not been given. For to those who have, more will be given, and they will have an abundance; but from those who have nothing, even what they have will be taken away. The reason I speak to them in parables is that "seeing they do not perceive, and hearing they do not listen, nor do they understand". With them indeed is fulfilled the prophecy of Isaiah that says: "You will indeed listen, but never understand, and you will indeed look, but never perceive."'

'In spite of appearances there is no deliberate discrimination in Christ's words. He is only trying to convey the fact that it is not enough to bend down by the side of the road and gather up truth and knowledge. These two treasures must be deserved. You must go and search for them because they will not come to you. You must earn knowledge. It is only given to those who make the effort to find it. Those people are the initiates.'

He paused before going on: 'Again I am telling you that everything in the Holy Scripture is code. Gérald Messadié devoted a large part of his life to the study of the New Testament, and he quoted the dialogue between Jesus and the woman of Samaria in one of his books.[1] I am repeating it here from memory:

Jesus: Give me something to drink.
The woman of Samaria: What! You a Jew, you are asking a Samaritan for a drink?
Jesus: If you knew who you were addressing, it would be you who would have asked me for the water of life.
The woman of Samaria: You have no bucket and this well is deep. Are you taller than Jacob our ancestor who gave us this well?
Jesus: Those who drink from this well will be thirsty again, but those who drink the water I shall give them will never be thirsty again.

'And the author interprets the true meaning of this dialogue, proving his case:

Jesus: Tell me something of your teachings.

The woman of Samaria: What! You a Jew, you are interested in schism?

Jesus: If you knew who I was it would be you who would ask me about my teachings.

The woman of Samaria: You have no power and no knowledge, and religion has great depth. Do you claim to be a prophet?

Jesus: Your rhetoric is empty and contains nothing of interest, it is I who hold the Revelation.

And Jean-Pierre concluded: 'It is just one example ... There are many others if we look at the ambiguous content of the sacred books. It is interesting to know that this system of coded messages is also used in the Koran. Like Jesus and Isaiah, the Prophet also speaks in metaphors when he says: "They have hearts with which they understand nothing; they have eyes with which they see nothing; they have ears with which they hear nothing."[2] And when you take this verse that announces the end of the world, do you believe that it would not be encoded or concealed? I quote: "That which is breaking! So what is it that is breaking? How can one know what it is that is breaking? It will be the Day when men are like scattered butterflies and mountains are like strands of carded wool."[3]

'And this other verse: "The day when the children will be like old men, and before that the sky will split and the prophecy will be accomplished."[4]

Hardly had Jean-Pierre finished his dissertation than I recalled a passage from the *Hadith*, the traditions of the prophet reported by his disciples. It was one asking him what signs would announce the end of the world, to which Mahomet replied: 'That will be when the servant gives birth to her mistress; when men erect buildings that appear on the surface of the clouds, and when shepherds live in the cities.' There was also a reference to children. To the prophet that would mean: 'When the children, left to themselves, will impose the law on their parents.' There was material there for reflection. There too there was a code.

With our feebleness and our doubts, we were only 'beginners'.

14 Fire from heaven

IT WAS NOW the end of June 1997. Through a combination of circumstances, but for different reasons, Dimitri, Myriam and I found ourselves in Amsterdam for three days. It is a magical city, with little doll's houses along the water's edge. I did not expect for a moment that we would discover anything about the new 'revelation' here, of all places. That evening we had planned to dine in one of those wonderful Indonesian restaurants that abound in Amsterdam. While waiting for my friends in the hotel lobby, I read the e-mail Jean-Pierre had sent me a few minutes earlier. This is what it said:

When we studied the verse referring to the false prophet, Goebbels, we failed to pursue the interpretation to the end. Remember the verse in question:

Then I saw another beast that rose out of the earth; it had two horns like a lamb and it spoke like a dragon.[1]

But in the next verse, St John states:

It exercises all the authority of the first beast on its behalf, and it makes the earth and its inhabitants worship the first beast, whose mortal wound had been healed.[2]

As far as this 'healed mortal wound' is concerned, I have deduced – possibly wrongly – that the expression referred to 'Nazi Germany healed from the humiliation it suffered after its defeat in the First World War'. Remember how that country was 'mortally wounded' in the contest.

However, what really intrigues me is the following passage:

It [the beast] performs great signs, even making fire come down from heaven to earth in the sight of all.'[3]

As you can see, we have failed to decode this information. Our interpretation is incomplete. And yet, what the apostle says seems as important as it is impressive: 'making fire come down from heaven to earth'. Naturally, I immediately thought of the bombing of London. It was a most terrifying ordeal for the inhabitants of that city. But nevertheless, isn't there an underlying detail that has escaped us? With the help of the table Myriam gave me – I am referring to the Hebrew alphabet and its numerical correspondences – I have tried to find a connection between 'bombing' and 'London', but without much success. The only small progress I made was to discover that the 'the fire' has a numerical value of 9 (306), and that 'bombs' has an identical value of 9 (666).

To sum up:

The fire = 9

Bombs = 9

But now I am stuck, although I am certain that the verse in question refers to this episode of the war. See what you can come up with. Love to all three …

Perhaps Jean-Pierre was right. But he was definitely right to mention our failure to complete the interpretation of this verse. When Myriam and Dimitri joined me I mentioned Jean-Pierre's findings.

Bombs = 666. How could we remain indifferent to the recurrence of the number of the Beast, 666? We now knew that each recurrence referred to an important event: Fascism = 666; Adolf Hitler-Austria = 666; Adolf Hitler + Joseph Paul Goebbels + false prophet = 666;[4] trial + Nuremberg + Hitler = 666;[5] The landing at 6 o'clock on 6 June = 666.[6]

We continued our discussion during the meal in the hope of clarifying the verse, but without much success. The question we were asking ourselves was as follows: Should we accept Jean-Pierre's interpretation as correct – that the fire coming from heaven to earth = bombs? Or should we continue to delve into the secret meaning of the verse to discover a more complex, deeper meaning? Discouraged by our failure to make any headway, we concentrated on our other professional duties, momentarily abandoning the Revelation.

Then fate suddenly knocked at the door; indeed, fate was always with us. I was not there at the time, nor was Myriam. It was Dimitri who reported to us what had happened while he was driving on the motorway near Breda, south of Amsterdam, on his way to a business meeting in Utrecht.

I still can still see the feverish expression on his face when he rushed into the hotel foyer where Myriam and I were waiting for him.

'Listen to me,' he said. And he added with typical Mediterranean emphasis: 'Antwerp!'

Seeing our blank faces, he explained: 'It was on my way to Utrecht that I noticed the sign ... Antwerp. Antwerp! The fire from the sky!'

For a second I thought he had gone mad. I asked him to sit down. 'Do you think you could explain?

He flopped into the armchair and launched into a detailed explanation: 'When Europe had been conquered, all hope rested on Britain, the only remaining contestant in the battle. Hitler could not invade England, nor could he persuade it to surrender. Churchill's resolve was unshakeable: "I have nothing to offer but blood, toil, sweat and tears," he told Parliament. "We shall never surrender." When pre-parations for an invasion were abandoned, the task was entrusted to the air force, whose certain victory was trumpeted everywhere by Hermann Goering. As you know, the Battle of Britain was a complete disaster for the Luftwaffe. So Hitler decided to try and weaken Britain by demoral-izing its people through frequent night bombings, against which the country was unable to protect itself at the time. But that was not enough. Unable to conquer the island, he determined to annihilate it. The Führer sought the help of a certain Wernher von Braun. Passionate about rocket propulsion since an early age, this brilliant scientist had been noticed by General Dornberger, who was then in charge of research into new weapons. He appointed von Braun head of a team whose task was to study the military application of rockets. Von Braun built a large base at Peenemünde, on the Baltic, where he could carry out his experiments, backed by substantial funds, materials and staff (20,000 men). His task was to carry out research into the development of a "vengeance weapon", research that finally led to the development of the V-1, a pilotless rocket-propelled missile. The prototype V-1 was launched on 3 October 1942 and it became operational in 1944. The first V-1 hit London on 13 June 1944, marking the beginning of a deadly campaign that caused much greater losses than the bombing of 1940/41.[7] It was truly terrifying.'

Myriam and I were lapping up what our friend was saying. 'But what is the connection with Antwerp?' I asked.

'Not many people know this, but although about 1,250 V-2s fell on London, many more fell on Antwerp: 1,750 to be exact. The V-2 causing the most damage fell on the Rex cinema, killing some 600 people. Now do you understand why I made a connection between this town and the V-2, and then with John's verse: "making fire come down from heaven to earth"!'

In the hotel in Amsterdam, we could not stop thinking about these horrifying scenes and the panic caused by these flying bombs, falling unexpectedly from the sky, destroying whole districts in an instant.

'What should we make of this?' Myriam asked me.

Dimitri replied with a question: 'What is the value of V-2?'

'426 or 3. And then?'

'What follows is connected with Wernher von Braun. Was he not the father of these engines of death?'

After three years of working together we no longer needed to go into every detail. We understood each other. And Myriam no longer needed to consult her alphabetical table.

She suddenly said in a trembling voice: 'Wernher von Braun = 777. Equals 3.

'And V-2 also has a value of 3."

Did we feel a frisson of anxiety, a vague feeling of something like abnegation, as if we were fearful of discovering something else? We decided not to pursue the matter and instead went off for a trip on a 'bateau-mouche' and behaved like tourists.

It was the following day, just before returning to Paris, that we discovered what we had refused to check ourselves. There was a new e-mail from Jean-Pierre.

Good morning or good evening, my friends,

I think you are going to be surprised – my hunch was correct.

By reflecting on the terms 'fire and bombs' I have made a connection – which will not surprise you – with the V-1 and V-2. But I went further than that.

I remind you of the verse:

' ... *even making fire come down from heaven to earth in the sight of all.*'

My conclusions:

The fire = 306 or 9
Bombs = 666 or 9
V-1 = 29 or 2
V-2 = 426 or 3

But I also discovered:

On the earth = 155 or 2
London = 146 or 2

Which corresponds to V-1 (2).

Unfortunately I do not see what number 3 (which represents V-2) corresponds to. Do you have any ideas?

Lots of love, J.-P.

We stood staring at the screen, speechless.

By late morning we were back at Roissy-Charles-de-Gaulle airport, where Myriam was taking a plane to Israel.

I then shared a taxi with Dimitri and returned home.

Dimitri and I met up with Jean-Pierre and David at the weekend. Naturally, the discovery of the V-2 was our main topic of conversation. We all made various suggestions about how to pursue our work. From the very start we had been interested in a verse referring to the coming of the second beast:

> So he carried me away in the spirit into a wilderness, and I saw a
> woman sitting on a scarlet beast that was full of blasphemous names,
> and it had seven heads and ten horns.[8]

What should we do? Should we not try and locate the passages referring to this next 'Führer' instead of continuing our search in the direction of the Second World War? Why continue investigating past events when we could open a window onto the future?

Dimitri interrupted our discussions: 'Whatever path we follow we should not ignore a verse that seems to me very important. I do not know why, but I wonder if it is not linked to an event that is still connected with the Second World War.'

'Which one?'

'Chapter 8, verse 7:

> The first angel blew his trumpet , and there came hail and fire, mixed
> with blood, and they were hurled to the earth; and a third of the earth
> was burned up, and a third of the trees were burned up, and all green
> grass was burned up.

Jean-Pierre disagreed: 'I do not see that this verse is particularly interesting. It is obviously linked to the bombings that punctuated the Second World War, and of course to the V-1 and V-2 missiles … '

Dimitri nodded. 'Do not be fooled. Its meaning goes way beyond that … If you read verses 10 and 11 in chapter 8 you will notice a word that challenges any form of Cartesian thinking. Listen carefully:

The third angel blew his trumpet, and a great star fell from heaven, blazing like a torch, and it fell on a third of the rivers and on the springs of water. The name of the star is Wormwood. A third of the waters became wormwood, and many died from the water, because it was made bitter.'

'Which word is the one you are referring to?' asked Jean-Pierre.

'The word "wormwood".'

I said: 'At first sight "wormwood" does not seem to imply anything in particular. All the doctors in antiquity prescribed wormwood with indications that are largely confirmed by modern science. It was the "Holy Herb" of medieval empiricists and it was an important ingredient of many remedies that apothecaries prescribed as miracle cures as late as the eighteenth century. In the nineteenth century it was used to make the alcoholic drink absinthe. Its fame and popularity was such that it was known as the "green fairy".'

Jean-Pierre agreed while completing my explanation: 'That is the positive aspect. But there is another negative aspect. Indeed, wormwood contains among its various components a very toxic alcohol: thujone. This substance is a terrifying poison, capable of seriously damaging the nervous system and provoking epileptic fits. In fact, the absinthe drink served in French cafés in the time of Baudelaire and

Zola also contained aniseed essence and was a cocktail of poisons that caused serious delirium tremens. This is why absinthe was made illegal in 1915.'

Dimitri who had remained silent during this conversation suddenly said: 'Chernobyl … '

We thought that we had misheard.

'What did you say?

He repeated calmly: 'Chernobyl. The Ukrainian for wormwood is "chernobyl". You can check.'

'You can't be serious!' David cried out.

'Indeed I am. Take a Ukrainian-French dictionary, or any dictionary of Ukrainian and any other language, and you will find that what I am saying is true. I did not invent this.'

We were completely stunned. After a moment I asked: 'So John's verse would refer to nuclear power?'

'Read it again:

'*… It fell on a third of the rivers and on the springs of water. The name of the star is Wormwood. A third of the waters became wormwood, and many died from the water, because it was made bitter.*

A long silence followed. We no longer knew which way to turn.

I got up and picked up a book entitled *La Supplication*.[9] I opened it at the first page and read:

On 26 April 1986, at 1.23 am, a series of explosions destroyed the reactor and buildings of the fourth section of the nuclear power station of Chernobyl. This accident has become the greatest technological catastrophe of the twentieth century.

147

For a small country such as Belarus with its 10 million inhabitants, it was a national disaster. During the Second World War, the Nazis destroyed 619 villages within Belarus territory and exterminated the inhabitants. After Chernobyl the country lost 485 more. Seventy of them were buried for ever. The war killed one in four Belarus inhabitants; today one in five lives in a contaminated area. This affects 2.1 million people, including 700,000 children. Radiation is the most deadly danger facing these people. In the regions of Gomel and Moguilev (which have suffered most from this tragedy) the death rate exceeds the birth rate by 20 per cent.

At the time of the catastrophe, 70 per cent of the 50 million radionuclides propelled into the atmosphere fell back on to Belarus soil; as far as caesium 137 is concerned, 23 per cent of Belarus territory is contaminated by a quantity of radioactive nuclides equal or superior to 37 billion becquerels (Bq) per square kilometre. For your information, 4.8 per cent of Ukrainian and 0. 5 per cent of Russian territory are affected. The area of agricultural land where contamination equals or exceeds 37 x 109 Bq/km² is over 1.8 million hectares. Meanwhile, the land irradiated by a quantity of strontium 90 equal to or greater than 11 x 109 Bq/km² amounts to about half a million hectares. Agriculture is completely forbidden in some 264 hectares of land. Belarus is a woodland country, but 26 per cent of its forests and over half the pastures situated in the flood plains of the Pripiat, Dniepr and Soj rivers are situated in the zone of radioactive contamination.

Because of constant contamination by small doses of radiation, the number of people in Belarus suffering from cancer, mental retardation, nervous and psychological disorders as well as genetic mutations is increasing every year.

According to observations, a high level of radiation was recorded on 29 April 1986 in Poland, Germany, Austria and Romania; on 30 April in Switzerland and northern Italy; on 1 and 2 May in France, Belgium, the Netherlands, Great Britain and northern Greece; and on 3 May in Israel, Kuwait and Turkey.

The gaseous, volatile substances were propelled to a very high altitude and then dispersed all over the world. On 2 May high levels of radiation were recorded in Japan; on 4 May in China; on 5 May in India; on 5 and 6 May in the United States and Canada.

This spoke for itself.

Finally, David suggested hesitantly: 'And what if, with the word "wormwood", John wanted to attract our attention to another nuclear catastrophe – not Chernobyl but … Hiroshima?'

'That is a possibility. Remind me what the previous verse said.'

Jean-Pierre read:

The first angel blew his trumpet, and there came hail and fire, mixed with blood, and they were hurled to the earth; and a third of the earth was burned up, and a third of the trees were burned up, and all green grass was burned up.

I turned to David. 'Could the computer expert check the concordances of the word "hail" in the Bible?'

'Yes, of course.' He consulted his computer and a few minutes later came up with the figure: 'The word "hail" occurs thirty-two times, in Exodus, Leviticus, Psalms, Isaiah and the Wisdom of Solomon.

The predominant meaning is always synonymous with military weapons. For example, in Ecclesiasticus:

Fire and hail and famine and pestilence, all these have been created for vengeance.[10]

Or in the Psalms:

Fire and hail, snow and frost, stormy wind fulfilling his command.[11]

'I see ...' I grabbed the table of correspondences of the Hebrew alphabet. 'I think we have reached a point where we no longer need to call Myriam automatically. Let us list the words that we believe have a double meaning and calculate their numerical value.'

My three friends approved. A moment later we had drawn up our list:

Hail = 206 or 8
The earth = 296 or 8
Fire mixed with blood = 665 or 8
The trees = 215 or 8

David was the first to speak: 'We already have a common denominator: the figure 8.'

'Should we not also calculate the value of the words "atomic bomb"?'

It took us slightly longer than our theologian would have taken: 'Atomic bomb = 710 or ... 8.'

'It would be impossible not to infer from this that "hail" refers to the "atomic bomb".

'There is no way we could do otherwise ... '

Jean-Pierre suddenly leapt from his seat. 'It's mad! Completely mad!'

We looked at him in total consternation.

'It's mad!' he repeated, holding his head as if it was going to explode. 'But what?

He tried to control himself and then began: 'Number 8 represents cosmic equilibrium and a lot of other symbolic signs. But that is not the problem. To hell with the world of symbols! We are looking at a reality. It is much more haunting than all the dreams put together. Listen carefully. Since time immemorial, Japan has been known to its inhabitants as – wait for it – *Eight Large Islands*.[12] Did you hear me? Eight Large Islands. The eight most important islands of Japan and, by extension, Japan itself. In fact, it is the figure that often occurs in the most ancient Shinto writings with the sense of "multiple". In Shinto mythology, a legendary dragon with eight heads and eight tails lived in the province of Izumo. Some believe that this dragon symbolizes a river, while others believe it represents eight kuini (kingdoms).

'But that is not all. In Yokohama in 1932, a national centre for spiritual education was founded by Adachi Kenzo[13], a Japanese statesman. It is octagonal in shape and houses statues of the eight wise men of the world, including Buddha, Confucius, Socrates and ... Jesus Christ!'

We were speechless. No mathematical gymnastics or manipulation could have helped us to obtain this result: hail, 8, Japan, Eight Large Islands.

Now David grabbed the Hebrew alphabet and rushed to the blackboard. Slowly he wrote:

$$\text{Hiroshima} = 566 = 5 + 6 + 6 = 17 = 8$$

He turned towards us. His face was ashen ... 'Any thoughts?'

I was the only one who replied. In a strangled voice I said: 'The attack on Hiroshima took place at … eight o'clock in the morning …' As I was saying this I suddenly remembered a book I had read a few years ago. A series of images suddenly came flooding into my head. I went to get the book[14] from the library and located the passage in question:

Eight o'clock in the morning … The first atomic tragedy of the world took place at that precise instant … A flash of lightning, white. It looked as if the sun was exploding. It blinded 300,000 people all at once. It filled the sky with such intensity that houses, hills, streets and shadows disappeared immediately. Only a devouring light remained on the retina of people's eyes. Instinctively they held out their hands as they felt their way slowly towards pain and suffering.

The first steps made by humanity in that thermic instant were taken in a whitish nothingness ['like the colour of hail']. It must have been the same at the beginning of creation. One ten-thousandth of a second, that was the length of the first event.

… In this gestating world that came straight from the first pages of the Bible, the explosion could be heard 40 or 50 kilometres away.

… A wind rose, its opposing currents unfurling over Hiroshima at the very instant that the bomb exploded. It was like a series of punches knocking out all 300,000 inhabitants at the same time, tearing their clothes from their bodies, including their underwear, and hurling them to the ground while showers of broken glass and pointed pieces of bamboo rained upon them.

… It was at that moment that large rain drops began to fall ['and there came hail and fire'].They fell heavily on Hiroshima, leaving behind everywhere the outline of their shape everywhere. They were black, full of soot, dust and ash. As soon they touched the ground they evaporated again. The inhabitants believed they were seeing a miracle and they looked up at the sky, to which their guardian gods seemed to have returned. They implored them for mercy, and were about to thank them for this rain that was going to save them. But in vain. Salvation did not come from above. It did not come at all. On the contrary, the five minutes of rain that fell on the city were the most deadly. Every drop created by the giant atomic mushroom 9,000 metres high was the bearer of radioactive elements that gave the Hiroshima cataclysm its apocalyptic colour.

I looked up at the blackboard where words were flashing before my eyes like lightning:

Hail = 206 or 8
The earth = 296 or 8
Fire mixed with blood = 665 or 8
The trees = 215 or 8
Atomic bomb = 8
Hiroshima = 8
Japan = Eight Large Islands

The number 8 yet again! Death – Meth = 440 = 4 + 4 = 8 – ever present … I muttered as if thinking aloud: 'But no reference to Nagasaki … '

Jean-Pierre replied: 'Yes, there is one … ' And I would go even further. Beyond Hiroshima and Nagasaki. I am in fact convinced that the crucial events of the two conflicts, the one in the past and the other in the future, are contained in chapter 8, in verses 6 to 12:

Now the seven angels who had the seven trumpets made ready to blow them.

The first angel blew his trumpet, and there came hail and fire, mixed with blood, and they were hurled to the earth; and a third of the earth was burned up, and a third of the trees were burned up, and all green grass was burned up.

The second angel blew his trumpet, and something like a great mountain, burning with fire, was thrown into the sea. A third of the sea became blood, a third of the living creatures in the sea died, and a third of the ships were destroyed.

The third angel blew his trumpet, and a great star fell from heaven, blazing like a torch, and it fell on a third of the rivers and on the springs of water. The name of the star is Wormwood. A third of the waters became wormwood, and many died from the water, because it was made bitter.

The fourth angel blew his trumpet, and a third of the sun was struck, and a third of the moon, and a third of the stars, so that a third of their light was darkened; and a third of the day was kept from shining, and likewise the night.

'Now we know that the first angel is announcing Hiroshima. The second one is announcing Nagasaki. I may be wrong, but in my opinion the expressions "like a great mountain, burning with fire" and "the sea became blood" symbolize the consequences of the second nuclear attack.'

He wrote under the name Nagasaki:

Like a great mountain, burning with fire = 689 or 5
Nuclear bombing = 1,013 = 5

And below that:

> The sea became blood = 234 or 9
> Nagasaki = 225 or 9

He turned towards us: 'What do you think?'

At first there was no reaction. Then, very soon, objections began to fly.

'I do not agree,' cried out Dimitri. 'It's too vague. Too imprecise.'

And David went even further, adding: 'Also, you are using two different expressions. For Hiroshima we used the term "atomic bomb". But you used "nuclear bomb". You are only doing this because it gives you the same numerical value as "like a great mountain, burning with fire". There is a lack of intellectual rigour here.'

Jean-Pierre protested: 'What difference is there between an atomic and a nuclear bomb? Why should the apostle not use the two expressions in turn? I would also like to remind you that Nagasaki is a harbour surrounded by mountains. And ... '

'Don't insist,' interrupted David. 'This interpretation is not really at all convincing. I am sure there must be another interpretation in the verse.'

Jean-Pierre shrugged his shoulders and looked resigned: 'As you wish ... '

He turned towards me as if looking for support. But I could not give it to him as I firmly agreed with my two other friends. 'I find the discovery of Hiroshima amazing enough. To push the interpretation further would only reduce its credibility.'

After the events that had blinded them and crushed their hearts, the inhabitants of Hiroshima searched for the road to salvation. Over 200,000 never found it, not on that day or any other. And 9,000 survivors are still vainly looking today.

The reality engraved in the book of the visionary of Patmos was indeed a much more haunting reality than any possible dream.

15 The second revelation

A time to kill, and a time to heal; a time to break down,
and a time to build up.

Ecclesiastes 3:3

THE ATMOSPHERE ON Mount Athos is impossible to describe; it no doubt emanates from the tranquil contemplation taking place within the monasteries. The atmosphere of a landscape in prayer was further emphasized by the heat of July and leaden heaviness of the sky. After three years of investigation I felt I absolutely had to see Father Alexander.

I found an emaciated man, gaunt faced and of uncertain gait.

'Age, my friend … Age is God's punishment for a pedantic youth. And it is right that it should be so.'

He dropped into the armchair and leant forward towards the file I had brought him, the result of all our work. He invited me to sit down and buried himself in the notes I had just handed him.

From the window, I could see the steely blue of the sea. The horizon was perfect. The light had that unique quality so typical of Greece.

When Father Alexander closed the file, there was something inexpressible in his eyes. He remained silent for a long time before murmuring as he stared into the distance: 'In the beginning was the Word, and the Word was with God, and the Word was God … '[1]

Then he continued: 'This is excellent, very commendable work. What else is there to say? When three years ago we spoke about the Book of Revelation, I did not realize that the text was so full of meaning.

But the most terrible thing is that centuries have passed since it was first written, and no one has been able to change the course of history. This observation raises a tragic question: is what was foreseen in the past our inexorable fate, or is it possible for us to influence the course of events?'

'Does that mean that if we had been better informed earlier we might have been able to avoid all those years of war, Nazism, the millions of victims, the Shoah?'

The priest looked pensive. 'That is indeed the question I am asking myself ... Is there an inexorable fatality written into the genes of humanity or do we have a choice? That is the real question.'

'And if others before us had been able to discover the date, day and time of the Second World War, if they had been able to warn the world against all the atrocities that might happen, would anybody have believed them? They would have been treated like cranks, like charlatans.'

'That is all too likely.' A painful expression crossed his wrinkled face. 'And yet we had been warned,' he continued, 'so many times! These illuminati were none other than Daniel, Isaiah, Ezekiel, Jesus ... "For nation will rise against nation, and kingdom against kingdom, and there will be famines and earthquakes in various places: all this is but the beginning of the birth pangs."[2] As if man's fate was to die in order to be born again, worthier, greater, more noble.' He took a deep breath: 'And now ... There is tomorrow ... '

I looked at him, perplexed.

'Yes,' he continued. 'You have delved into the past but what about the future? You would be making a serious mistake if you did not pursue your investigations of John's writings. You have implied quite clearly, in fact, that there are not two Revelations merged into a single text with one a repetition of the other, but two Revelations happening at two different times, represented by the two beasts, the dragon and Satan, who play a constant part in both. Don't you think it would be more useful to look at the future now?'

'More useful? In what sense?'

'It is very likely that what you will find will exceed, and by far, what you have already discovered. All you need to do is to look at the verses you have not yet studied to realize this.'

'But what would be the use of that? Why would you want to … '

'Because it is your duty.' He gave the ghost of a smile. 'Unless you fear being seen as a crank. If, by the grace of God, a handful of good men were to take note of your work – who knows? – perhaps this fatality we are talking about might finally be overcome. As you know, you do not have to be numerous to modify the course of history. A single being is sufficient. Moses, Jesus, Mohammed and Gandhi did not have armies, nor did Martin Luther King. I tell you, a single being can be enough: a single individual can be the grain of sand capable of bringing the most powerful, most sophisticated machine to a grinding halt. It would be wonderful to think that one man will stand up after reading about the fate of future generations … just one man.'

'Forgive me, Father Alexander, but your reasoning is double-edged. If we really discovered something terrible, would we have the right to disclose the information to the public at large? Although our discoveries might be considered meaningless trifles in the eyes of some, others might be destabilized by them and lose all hope. Because, let us be honest, everything leads one to believe that the destruction caused by this second Revelation will exceed all the calamities humanity has ever known.'

'That is more than likely. And I admit that you have there a problem of conscience. The choice is yours … '

I reflected for a while on Father Alexander's words: 'The future … Where is it in the apostle's writings? Where shall I find it?'

'Start at the beginning. If a new era of disasters is about to strike humanity, you can be sure that John will give us the day, month and definitely the year.' He stood up with some difficulty and shook my hand: 'Forgive me, my friend, I must rest now. Tomorrow I am leaving for Athens where those modern apothecaries known as doctors await me. According to them I must undergo a series of tests to determine what is ailing me.'

He laughed quietly: 'I am sure they will find out what the illness is, but will they be able to cure it? That is another story. Goodbye, my friend, keep me informed of your discoveries.'

I watched him as he walked to the door with difficulty. It was the last time I was to see Father Alexander.

Towards the middle of July, all five us met up in a little village in Chalcidicum called Vourvourou, on the coast not far from Salonika. We had rented two houses to contain all the members of our respective families, but far from the noise and madness of the Greek summer.

Start at the beginning ...

'The beginning or the end?' Dimitri joked. He pointed at chapter 20:

20:2 He seized the dragon, that ancient serpent, who is the Devil and Satan, and bound him for a thousand years.
20:3 and threw him into the abyss, and locked and sealed it over him, so that he would deceive the nations no more, until the thousand years were ended. *After that he must be let out for a little while.*

'Clearly, the answer lies in the expression "until the thousand years were ended", since the verses indicate at the same time the end of the rule of the dragon-fascism – "He seized the dragon" – and the timespan that separates us from his return: "and locked and sealed it over him ...

▲ *Gérard Bodson, scholar, researcher and theologian, who, working with an international team of experts, cracked the Apocalypse code.*

▶ *St John the Evangelist at Patmos. The practice of gematria was extremely widespread in the time of St John and he himself refers frequently to this method of coding*

◄ *Hitler – the first beast of the Apocalypse. The second beast who will rule in the twenty-first century will be like him in character, sharing his thirst for violence and hunger for global supremacy.*

▼ *US President Franklin D Roosevelt addressing the nation on the neutrality, October 1939. According to the Apocalypse code, his destiny has been sealed in the Book of Revelation since the dawn of time, representing the absolute duality of the struggle of opposites.*

▶ The seven-headed serpent from the Book of Revelation, representing an uneasy coalition of seven nations on the side of the Third Reich.

▼ Hitler's Minister of Propaganda Joseph Goebbels (right) saluting a Nazi rally. He is referred to in the Book of Revelation as the false prophet.

▲ Panzer tank units of the
German Army pass through
a blazing Russian village:
the Panzers are the armoured
locusts of the first Apocalypse.

◄ Allied might at a Normandy
beachhead – the D-day
landings at six o'clock on the
sixth day of the sixth month:
'I will send fire on Magog and
on those who live securely in
the coastlands' . . .

Five of the chief Nazis or 'twenty-four elders' in the dock during the final stages of the Nuremberg trial. From front left to right, the photograph shows Hermann Goering, Rudolf Hess, Joachim von Ribbentrop and Wilhelm Keitel. Baldur von Schirach and Fritz Sauckel are seated behind them, the third and fourth from the left respectively.

▲ Field Marshal Erwin Rommel, Dwight Eisenhower's dark counterpart in the Apocalypse of the first Revelation.

▲ Neville Chamberlain
addressing the crowd on his
return from Munich, 30
September 1938. With
Daladier, he had signed an
agreement that annexed
11,000 square miles of
Czechoslovakia to Germany
in an attempt to prevent the
outbreak of war.

▶ The Four Horsemen of the
Apocalypse – the code words
for America leading the
armies of God, fascism,
North Korea and global
starvation.

Abraham Lincoln (right) and J F Kennedy (below) were caught
up together in one of the cycles of history. Lincoln was elected to
congress in 1846 and to the presidency in 1860; Kennedy followed
in his footsteps exactly one hundred years later. There are many
other coincidences between them, underscoring the time-scale
used to forecast the events of the two Revelations.

'The first angel blew his trumpet and there came hail and fire, mixed with blood': the first atomic explosion over Hiroshima, Japan. Japan is also predicted to be the first victim of the second Apocalypse.

▼ A lone protester confronts tanks in Beijing, China, 1989. Could the 'scarlet beast' represent the awakening power of China?

until the thousand years were ended".'

'A thousand years ... ,' said Jean-Pierre. 'But why a thousand years and not two thousand or five thousand? What do the scholars say on the subject?'

Dimitri immediately joined in and explained: 'As always, contradictions abound. In the early days of Christianity, most of the Church Fathers firmly believed in the year 1000 AD as the prophetic date. It was only in the fourth century that St Augustine changed this conception by explaining that the resurrection described in chapter 20, verses 1–6 was a spiritual one, referring in fact to the conversion of Christians after the coming of Christ. For Augustine only a spiritual resurrection could precede the coming of the Apocalypse. Many centuries later, some experts claimed that the millennium corresponded to the awakening of the Church under Constantine. Others compared it to an antechamber of the resurrection for the souls of the believers after death.[3] As you can see, no one version has ever been accepted unanimously.'

'If we were to take St John's text literally ... from when would we start the thousand years?'

'I would say from Hitler's death, 30 April 1945.'

'That's plausible.

'1945 ... 2945.'

Myriam objected: 'Your choice of date is debatable. We could just as well work from the date of the Führer's birth rather than that of his death.

'1889?'

She nodded in agreement.

I replied: 'Impossible. For two reasons. St John says "He seized the dragon". One seizes someone who is guilty of one or more reprehensible deeds ... not a new-born baby. Moreover, the apostle continues: "and threw him into the abyss". Well, we know how Hitler died: he died "underground", having committed suicide in his bunker, in his "abyss". That is why we opt for his date of death: 1945.'

Curiously, without openly admitting to it, we all felt that none of us was really very keen on that interpretation, probably because we were not used to getting results so easily. There must be trap, a code within the code.

'Are we not contradicting ourselves?' Jean-Pierre suddenly said.

'What do you mean?'

'Do you remember chapter 13, verse 5: "*and it was allowed to exercise authority for forty-two months*". Based on this sentence, we have established that the long series of the Führer's military victories, his "power to act", had ended in the snows of Stalingrad. That was in 1943. The two years that followed saw Germany's descent into the underworld. If we want to remain consistent in our approach, we should take 1943 as the date of departure for the one thousand years, and not 1945.

'He's right,' I said. 'And that takes us to 2943.'

Dimitri laughed wryly: '2943! Praise be to God … We shall be far away by then. And my children too, and my grandchildren. I … '

Myriam interrupted him: 'I doubt that,' she said with surprising seriousness. 'Your children, my children – if I have any – may very well witness the Apocalypse.'

'In 2943? My dear, I know that life expectancy is constantly increasing, but do you not think that this is going too far? My son is six today. You cannot really believe he is going to live to the ripe old age of nine hundred years!'

She thought for a moment: 'When the next war breaks out your son will be fifty-one.'

Dimitri nearly choked. 'Have you really decided to frighten me to death?'

'I am sharing your fear … I have just turned thirty. God willing, I shall be seventy-five when the next war breaks out. Not quite Methuselah … but still hoping to live a few more years … '

I could not accept her interpretation: 'Myriam, can you explain? What year?'

The young woman merely quoted: '"For a thousand years in your sight are like yesterday when it is past, or like a watch in the night." Psalm 90, verse 4. "For a thousand years in your sight are like yesterday when it is past, or like a watch in the night."'

'Which means?"

'"A thousand years" is symbolic here … It implies "many years" but not necessarily a thousand. If I go by the gematria I would say that a thousand years in fact represents one hundred.'

'How do you arrive at that figure?'

'God, the absolute truth, is represented by the figure 10. Satan, on the other hand, is represented by the figure 2. Why? because in the Hebraic tradition, the figure 2 personifies the two spirits of evil: the Leviathan, the beast of the sea, and the Behemoth, the beast of the earth. It is no coincidence that John should mention the four synonyms of evil (dragon, serpent, Devil, Satan) in chapter 20 (value 2) and in verse 2.'

'What are you driving at?' David asked impatiently.

'Since God is worth 10 and Satan only 1, we can conclude that the time of the Devil is one tenth of God's time. In other words, one hundred years. But the number 2,943 also contains an element that I would define as "grammatical". Two is equal to the letter beth (בסוף), or *at the end*, 40 is equal to the letter mem (מוות), or *death*, and 3 is equal to the letter guimel (נידונם), or *the underworld*: the end, death, the underworld.'

David looked sceptical: 'An interval of one hundred years? 1943 to 2043.'

Dimitri was backing Myriam: 'It would not surprise me ... There are indeed such cycles in the history of humanity. It would not be the first time. Do you know when Abraham Lincoln was elected to Congress?' And without waiting for an answer, he continued: 'In 1846. And to the presidency? In 1860.' He was silent for a moment then continued: 'Do you know when Kennedy was elected to Congress? Precisely one hundred years later: 'In 1946. And to the presidency? In 1960. The names of these two presidents have seven letters. Now, does any one know the name of Abraham Lincoln's successor?'

None of us knew.

'Johnson. Andrew Johnson. Born in 1808. And Kennedy's successor? Johnson, Lyndon Johnson, born ... one hundred years later, in 1908. Their names and first names together consist of thirteen letters. Lincoln's murderer was John Wilkes Booth. He was born in 1839. Kennedy's assassin was, as I am sure you know, Lee Harvey Oswald. Born one hundred years later, in 1939. The two presidents were killed by a bullet in the head in the presence of their wife, and their murderers were both killed before they were tried. Their triple names have fifteen letters. But we are only halfway there.'

He waved his forefinger in the air to emphasize the importance of what he was saying: 'Lincoln's killer committed his act of murder in a theatre, then took refuge in a warehouse. Kennedy's killer shot his victim from a warehouse, then hid in a theatre. Lincoln was assassinated in the Ford Theater, while Kennedy was killed in a Ford motorcar ... a Lincoln. Shall I go on? Lincoln's secretary was called Kennedy. Kennedy's secretary was called Lincoln. Lincoln's secretary had asked Lincoln not to go to the theatre, while Kennedy's secretary had begged Kennedy not to go to Dallas. And finally, the two presidents were murdered on a Friday. And all that happened after an interval of one hundred years.'

There was a moment's silence.

'Do you still believe that it is unreasonable to assume that one thousand years for God are equivalent to one hundred years for the Devil? As far as I am concerned I believe that the date of 2043 is extremely plausible.'

We did not know what to think any more. We immersed ourselves in the text again in search of a further argument which would support our analysis, until one of us – Dimitri again – pointed to verse 15 in chapter 9.

So the four angels were released, who had been held ready for the hour, the day, the month, and the year, to kill a third of humankind.

'"The hour, the day, the month, and the year ... " If there is an answer we shall surely find it in this verse.'

'But how?'

'Only by using a logical approach. Take the first word, "the "hour".'

'The apostle does not provide any more information on the subject.'

'Not in this verse. But we all know that we are dealing here with a puzzle whose pieces are scattered all over the place. In which other places is the word "hour" mentioned?'

David consulted his computer: 'It occurs eleven times ... Would you like to have a print-out of the verses in question?'

'Yes, please ...'

A few minutes later, we had the verses in front of us. We started by making a first selection, then a second, each time eliminating the sentences in which the word "hour" seemed repetitive or without any particular interest. In the end, we were left with just two verses:

17:12 And the ten horns that you saw are ten kings who have not yet received a kingdom, but they are to receive authority as kings for one hour, *together with the beast.*
18:10 they will stand far off, in fear of her torment and say, 'Alas, alas, the great city, Babylon, the mighty city! For in one hour your judgement has come.'

At the end of a lively debate, we agreed that the verse in chapter 18 was no different from the one in chapter 17, apart from a slight difference: verse 12 mentioned the gathering of *ten kings* who were given royal power. But then we found ourselves in a dilemma once more.

We gave up in despair and decided to look for the second word in the passage of St John, 'the day'. Again we proceeded by elimination until we were left with only one verse:

11:9 For three and a half days *members of the peoples and tribes and languages and nations will gaze at their dead bodies and refuse to let them be placed in a tomb;*

But here too we found ourselves going round in circles. We therefore decided to investigate the last word in the passage: 'month'. This word appeared easier to investigate. It occurred only six times, and of those six verses, only two seemed likely to contain a clue, the others referring to a reign of 'forty-two months'.

9:5 They were allowed to torture them for five months, but not to kill them.
9:10 They have tails like scorpions, with stings, and in their tails is their power to harm people for five months.

'Five months? The fifth month?' Jean-Pierre asked. 'Could it be the month of May?'

'Too easy,' said Myriam. 'It's a waste of time.'

Bursting with frustration, Dimitri leapt up and shouted: 'I'm fed up! I'm going for a walk on the beach.'

We all joined him.

16 The hour, the day, the month and the year

So when you see the desolating sacrilege
standing in the holyplace, as was spoken of by
the prophet Daniel (let the reader understand) ...
Matthew 24:15

THE FOLLOWING MORNING, as the sun was rising above the sea, I was
enjoying my first cup of coffee of the day and reflecting on the infinite
complexity of this second Revelation that we had just started to
investigate. In particular I thought about the handful of verses that had
suddenly become completely impervious, as if to take revenge
for some imagined offence. It occurred to me that we had arrived at
a line of demarcation that we were forbidden to cross – unless, of course,
it was just that we were hampered by our own weaknesses.

I tried to take stock of the situation.

He seized the dragon, that ancient serpent, who is the Devil and Satan,
and bound him for a thousand years.

So the four angels were released, who been held ready for the hour,
the day, the month and the year.

We had concluded that the countdown of the thousand years (reduced
to one hundred) started in 1943, with the defeat of Stalingrad. But, on
reflection, this defeat did not take place in a single day. I looked through

history books to try and reconstruct the events of that period. At what precise moment might it be said that the battle was lost for the German divisions? What were the stages that led to their surrender?

- On 12 December, the troops of von Manstein were still winning a few victories.
- On about the 20th, the Russians counter-attacked. Manstein retreated.
- On 8 January 1943, General von Paulus, who was surrounded, refused the ultimatum that offered him an honourable surrender.
- On 24 January, he went back on his decision and asked Hitler for permission to surrender. It was refused.
- On 26 January, a new Russian attack was launched.
- On 27 January, pockets of German resistance were liquidated.
- On 31 January, German resistance was finallly broken.
- On 2 February, the Germans surrendered. 2,500 officers, 24 generals, and von Paulus himself were taken prisoner.

The end of the reign of the beast could therefore be situated somewhere between 31 January and 2 February. The 'months' mentioned by St John would therefore correspond to January or February. It was possible, but which of the two?

I was deep in thought when Myriam and Jean-Pierre joined me on the balcony. I told them my early morning thoughts and deductions.

'They definitely have some interesting points,' Jean-Pierre conceded, 'but as you yourself remarked, we are straddling two months, without any point of reference. January or February? How can we know?'

We continued sipping our coffee while staring at the sea. A light breeze was carrying the voices of the last fishermen returning to the little port of Aghios Nicolaos.

Suddenly Myriam's voice rose above the humming of their engines: 'We are betraying St John.'

'Betraying him?'

'Let's go back a little. What principle is our method of work based on?'

'What do you mean?'

'When we started working together we agreed one thing. Since it was an established fact that we were dealing with a work written in Greek by a Jew, there was only one conclusion. In order to decode its system of symbols, the work had to be interpreted in the language in which John conceived it, that is, in Hebrew, and not the Greek in which it was written.'

'That's right. That is indeed what we have been doing.'

'So why this sudden change in our method of work? John was a Jew. The calendar he was using was the Hebrew calendar which – in its present form – dates back to the fourth century AD. This ignores an earlier attempt to establish a chronology by rabbi Yosé ben Halafta in the second century AD. I shall spare you the details, but suffice it to say that the Hebrew calendar starts in 3762 BC, which is the accepted date of the Creation; the Jewish year 1 starts in year 1 of the Creation. Apart from the fact that there were many co-existing ways of calculating time from the time of antiquity to the Middle Ages, it was only in the early nineteenth century that there were thoughts of a possible reform of the universally recognized Gregorian calendar. So we must not look there for a solution. In looking for confirmation of the month when hostilities will start, we must find it in the Hebrew calendar and nowhere else.'

We could not disagree with her. I asked her to continue her line of argument. She got up, disappeared briefly and returned with a pencil and notebook.

'Listen carefully. There are twelve Jewish months in non-leap years: Tichri, Hechvan, Kislev, Tèvet, *Chevat*, Adar, Nissan, Iyyar, Sivan, Tammouz, Av and Eloul. In leap years there are thirteen months, because the month of Adar is repeated. Now take the verse of the apostle that speaks of the month:

9:10 They have tails like scorpions, with stings, and in their tails is their power to harm people for five months.

'The fifth month of the Jewish calendar is the month of Chevat. In 2043, it will start on 12 January and end on 10 February.'

Jean-Pierre let out a cry of surprise: 'You mean that it too straddles January and February, which coincides with the end of the reign of the beast: 31 January/2 February?'

'That is not my interpretation of the text; it is John himself who says this. Fifth month = Chevat = January/February.'

I exclaimed: 'But in that case, we must take the date of 2 February as the basis for our calculations, because that is the date when von Paulus surrendered at Stalingrad.'

She shook her head. 'True and false. According to John it would be 5 February.'

I stared at her, completely nonplussed.

She explained: 'Verse 9, chapter 11: " ... For *three and a half days* members of the peoples and tribes and languages and nations will gaze at their dead bodies and refuse to let them be placed in a tomb." If we interpret the text literally, we must add three and a half days.'

'2 February plus three and a half days ... '

'Takes us to 5 February at ... midday.'

It was at this moment that Dimitri and David joined us on the balcony. Before they had time to understand what was happening they were met with a flood of information. Like boxers reeling under a hail of punches, they stood still, trying to digest it all.

'So,' said Dimitri hesitantly, 'the next conflict would start at midday on *5 February 2043*.'

I agreed, as I put all the relevant verses of the chapters onto one page. 'Read it again!'

He seized the dragon, that ancient serpent, who is the Devil and Satan, and bound him for a thousand years.

'1943 plus 100 = 2043. (One thousand is equivalent to 100.)'

... For three and a half days *members of the peoples and tribes and languages and nations will gaze at their dead bodies and refuse to let them be placed in a tomb.*

The hour and the day: 2 February plus three and a half days = 5 February at midday.'

9:5 They were allowed to torture them for five months ...

'Confirmation of the month of February = *Chevat*, fifth month of the Hebraic calendar – 12 January/10 February, in the year 2043'.

There was jubilation in the air. Our heads were in a whirl and we decided 'to let our findings rest' and spend the rest of the day out on the sea.

At the end of the afternoon we were still lying on the deck of one of those little boats that take you on excursions round the islands. We were living a paradoxical moment. A few hours ago we had discovered that a new conflict might set the world ablaze in less than fifty years, that is, almost tomorrow, and here we were relaxing in the sun without a care, as if the earth and humanity were no longer part of our family.

Was this unconscious? An instinctive desire to rid ourselves of the latent terror that had taken hold of us? Absolutely. Because we knew ...

'A flash of lightning, white. It looked as if the sun was exploding. It blinded 300,000 people all at once. It filled the sky with such intensity that houses, hills, streets and shadows disappeared immediately.'

We could no longer dissociate the wonderful sun over the dark blue sea from the flash of lightning that had destroyed the retinas of those hundreds of thousands of unfortunates first in Hiroshima, then in Nagasaki ... 'That consuming light.'

Lost in thought, I suddenly heard Jean-Pierre's voice as if in a nightmare: 'And when you think that all this will take just one hour ... '

And with a calmness that sent cold shivers down the spine he quoted two verses that we had not looked at again:

And the ten horns that you saw are ten kings who have not yet
received a kingdom, but they are to receive authority as kings for
one hour, *together with the beast.*[1]

'Alas, alas, the great city, Babylon, the mighty city!
For in one hour *your judgment has come.'*[2]

A single hour ... To destroy Hiroshima, one ten-thousandth of a second had been enough. How many 'ten-thousandths of a second' in one hour? How many targets? How many children?

17 A scarlet beast

THE HOLIDAYS WERE over and we went back to Paris. It was the end of July and it was pouring with rain in the capital; it was as if the sun had decided to stay behind, a prisoner in Chalcidicum. We resumed work the day after we got back.

We had one date: 5 February 2043 at midday. Our next task was to discover the most important element of this second Revelation: the identity of the second beast. Who could it be? As expected, this task was very much harder. Nothing distinguished the second beast from the first beast – Adolf Hitler – in the verse where it was mentioned. Nothing, apart from the information given by the apostle in his description 'scarlet beast'.

So he carried me away in the spirit into a wilderness, and I saw a woman sitting on a scarlet beast that was full of blasphemous names, and it had seven heads and ten horns.[1]

Why did John think it so important to add that detail: 'scarlet' beast?

Jean-Pierre suddenly interjected: 'It is only a supposition, but this qualifying adjective is very much like a deliberate metaphor: the beast returns, draped in red, red with the blood of its past victims.'

'That is certainly possible. However, for the Second World War the apostle gave us a key: the number 666. That is what enabled us to discover Adolf Hitler's personality. But here?'

'Remember: "That is where you need shrewdness!" There must be a second key.'

'In that case, let's go back to the Second World War. Who were the protagonists? Who represented them?'

David replied with hesitation: 'Gog and Magog. Magog represented Germany and the Axis powers, and Gog, America.'

'Perfect. What does John tell us when he mentions the return of the second beast? Chapter 20, verses 7 and 8:

When the thousand years are ended, Satan will be released from his prison and will come out to deceive the nations at the four corners of the earth, Gog and Magog, in order to gather them for battle.

'As you can see, Gog and Magog are again involved.'

'That seems quite unthinkable ... if not impossible. Who these days could imagine another war between Germany and the other countries of Europe, or the United States?'

'Quite so.' But suddenly I had a worrying thought. 'Tell me, David, all the information we have gathered over these past months, is it all on a hard disk?'

He replied that it was, slightly surprised by my question.

'Have you thought of making a back-up copy?'

He looked quite shocked as if I had said something blasphemous. 'Of course I have! I always copy everything from my laptop. Why?'

'I have been told that computers – like human beings – can some-times "crash" for no apparent reason. If we were to lose all our work because of some electronic failure ... '

'Don't worry. I have taken all the necessary precautions.'

'Speaking of the computer,' said Myriam, 'why don't we try and see whether it might help us?'

David's eyes lit up. 'What would you like to find?'

'Key in the words "scarlet beast" in Hebrew and let's see whether their numerical value helps at all.'

'And what is their numerical value?

'84. Or 3.'

The computer specialist began tapping on the keyboard. After a while, he suddenly cried out: 'Gog!'

'Gog?'

'Absolutely. The computer refers me back to Gog. And with good reason: "scarlet beast" equals 3, "Gog" equals 12 or 3.'

'That's strange,' said Jean-Pierre. 'I seem to remember that Gog was worth 5. And that it represented America.'

It was Dimitri who answered: 'You are right. But we obtained that figure on the basis of Greek numeration. Gog (Γω γ) = 806. But here the computer's calculations are based on the Hebraic numeration, because that is the only one you had programmed.'

Without realizing it we had inverted the process. When decoding the Second World War, we had effectively assessed the values of Gog and Magog in Greek. Here, we worked from the Hebrew.

'So,' I said thoughtfully, 'once again we are in front of a mirror.'

'What do you mean?'

I explained: 'More than once the apostle has shown us the face of good immediately followed by that of evil … ' I leant towards Myriam: 'Wasn't it you who said about the twenty-four elders: "Why not look for an inverted interpretation, one that is diametrically opposed to that provided by religious scholars?" And when I expressed surprise, you added: "A mirror image. Did not John help us establish that Lilith was none other than Eve's negative twin? Would it not be possible to imagine that the twenty-four elders who represent good would also have their evil doubles?" And you concluded by taking Solomon's seal as an example: "You find this duality suggested by John in the Maggen David. Good is the the reverse of evil. On one side is darkness, on the other light. As the Apocalypse unrolls, the Devil uses the same weapons as God, and the Antichrist transforms Christ's agreements into evil instruments."'

The young woman agreed. 'But in this present case?'

'It's easy. Evil becomes good, and good becomes evil. Truth becomes falsehood and falsehood becomes truth. Gog who represented Europe's saviour (America) during the Second World War will become the symbol of falsehood in the next conflict.'

She jumped. 'You mean that in 2043 the United States will have become fascist? You don't … '

I interrupted her: 'Not at all! You have not understood what I was saying. I simply said that the hostile country that will declare war will represent Gog. And conversely, the countries that will rise against it will be Magog.'

Myriam nodded: 'Referring to the studies of some cabbalists, this inversion appears to be possible. Because actually the identities of Gog and Magog do not really matter, although they are described as characters or countries. They represent virtual functions that may be attributed to a people, a state or an individual according to the merits of the situation.'

There was a moment of silence.

'The scarlet beast … Gog … Value 3 … ' The words were going round in our minds, like panicking bats in search of an exit.

'We have a solution!' Dimitri suddenly cried out. He grabbed David by the arm and dragged him to the computer. 'Listen. Since Gog equals 3, would it not be possible to find which country has the same value?'

David frowned. 'Do you know how many countries there are in the world?'

'I don't care. The main thing is to discover which one has the same number as Gog.'

David roared with laughter: 'You must be dreaming, my friend. I do not need my computer to answer your question. There must be at least a dozen, if not more!'

'I suppose so. But it is also possible that there is only one country with a value of 3 that fulfils all the necessary conditions to play the part in 2043 that Germany played in 1940. We are looking for a growing power. A power that would be capable of challenging the world.'

David sat down at his computer and began to work. He looked extremely sceptical. A series of names appeared on the screen. None of them could ever be thought to represent a powerful nation as our Greek friend had suggested. None, that is, until one ... Dimitri asked us to come and have a look at the screen.

'Look,' he said hoarsely. The name of a country with the same value as Gog had just appeared on the screen in black letters on a blue background.

CHINA

Myriam confirmed the computer's figures: 'China (סין), value 120 or 12. The same number as Gog.'

Someone whispered: 'The scarlet beast ... Value 3.'

Even in the distant past, in the time of Genghis Khan, the terrified Europeans had placed the people of 'Gog and Magog' in this mysterious region, the ancient 'Cathay'. Suddenly a torrent of words came into my head: the Yangtze river, the 'red waters', the Red Basin of Sichuan, the 'red' army. How could we not believe the accuracy of this result?

Almost immediately we remembered the famous warning given almost two centuries ago by Emperor Napoleon Bonaparte: 'When China awakens, the world will tremble.'[2] How was China doing today? We spent the next few days consulting all the statistics[3] we could find to discover more about the country:

- In 2050, according to the United Nations, the population of the world will have increased to between 8 and 9. 5 billion people. The population of the European Union will not increase and the population in the rest of the continent will even decrease slightly. On the other hand, the population of China (between 1.4 and 1.5 billion inhabitants) will (with India) be greater than that of all the developed countries together.
- China's budget for scientific research increased from $15 million in 1995 to $100 million one year later.
- At 3 pm on 16 October 1964, China exploded its first atomic bomb at the Lop Nor base in the province of Xinjiang. Technically the equivalent of that which was dropped on Hiroshima, it contained an explosive charge of 200 kilotonnes.[4]
- Between 1965 and 1979, more than half the funds for research and military development were allocated to the nuclear armament programme.[5]
- On 17 June 1967 China carried out its first unilateral test, (one year before France).
- Almost $10 billion a year are allocated to military expenditure.

The Chinese army is thought to number approximately 3 million men, 1 million more than all of NATO's forces together.[6]

- In 1987 China tested its multiple-head intercontinental ballistic missile.
- In 1989 the Chinese government announced an increase in its military budget, presented as a result of the country's economic growth. Between 1989 and 1993, China's military budget doubled.
- In spite of the fact that the Cold War has ended and there is an international desire to reduce armaments, China has never ceased to update its nuclear arsenal.
- Four more nuclear power stations are presently under construction to the south of Guangdong, near Hong Kong.
- All experts are unanimous in recognizing that China is becoming an increasingly powerful nation and that its position and role in the world in the next few years is one of the great questions of the moment.
- In general, China practises a policy of secrecy regarding its nuclear arsenal. Based on Western assessments, China has a number of DF-5 intercontinental missiles with a range of 12,000km, between 10 and 20 DF-4s (range about 5,000km), over 50 DF-2s (2,700km) and 36 DF-21 mobile missiles (1,800km). China also has many DF-15 tactical missiles, capable of carrying a nuclear load and with a range of 600km.[7]

In 1967, Suharto's Indonesia, Malaysia, Thailand, Singapore and the Philippines, all anti-communist countries, joined forces to form the Association of South-East Asian Nations, ASEAN. In 1994, twenty-seven years later, ASEAN had to adapt to a very different and more fluid world order. The Soviet Union no longer existed, the Cold War had ended, and the only remaining great power was the United States. However, the decline of US military influence in Asia was thought to be unavoidable in the long term (US bases in the Philippines were closed down at the end of 1992), while the as yet ill-defined regional ambitions of Japan and China were causing concern so far as the balance of power was concerned.

China has tried to calm international fears by denying all expansionist or imperialist intentions. But China's rapid growth in economic and military power (its defence budget for 1994 was 34 per cent more than that of 1993) is a grave concern to its neighbours.

David pointed out: 'We have established that the expression "fascism" represents the negation of man on a more global scale. In this light, it seems to me that we can safely apply it to the Chinese regime. How else could one describe a country with 8-10 million prisoners condemned to forced labour; a nation where about 500,000 people are tried every year and about 500,000 people are sent to "re-education camps"? There are more than 1,200 in these camps and 50 million people have passed through them since 1949.'

He grabbed other documents giving further information:

- Although China has since 1984 displayed a vigorous policy of reform that seemed to open the way for significant democratic developments, the events of 1989 brutally crushed the hopes of a large part of the population. Provoked by the death of Hu Yaobang, the reformist leader who had been dismissed in 1987, from 15 April many demonstrations in support of the principles of democracy were organized in Tiananmen Square in Peking, uniting over 1 million people. The students who started the movement were soon supported and joined by civil servants, journalists and workers – the latter threatening the monopoly of the Chinese Communist Party (CCP) by creating a free trade union. Martial law was declared on 17 May. On 4 June, the People's Liberation Army (PLA) brutally intervened in Beijing, after several failures and attempts at fraternization between some units and the capital's population. Over 150,000 soldiers were sent in to take part in the repression, and although it is difficult to give precise figures, it is thought that there were at least 700 dead among the demonstrators and several thousand wounded.

- After these events, Zhao Ziyang's resignation signalled a change in the political attitude of China's leaders, who were worried by the political developments in the USSR and Central Europe. The demonstrations of April/May 1989 were denounced by Deng Xiaoping on 9 June as "a counter-revolutionary conspiracy", and in the capital alone over 50,000 party members were the victim of purges in a campaign against liberal ideas.

- In addition, the regime's constant use of aggressive nationalist rhetoric reflected the change in China's initially defensive position, based on the massive mobilization of large forces, to a more offensive strategy, centred on China's claims to maritime zones in the South China and East China Seas.

- This increasing power of a China no longer threatened by the Soviet Union was worrying to Beijing's neighbours. Also, the country's amazing economic growth has enabled it to update on a continuous basis the naval forces it needs to achieve its ambitions.

- Since the end of the 1980s, Beijing has one by one seized several small islands in the South China Seas, thus further alarming its neighbours about its ability to integrate itself harmoniously into the regional system.

- The fourteenth Congress of the CCP took place on 12 October 1992. The leading role of the party was emphasized and all political liberalization was excluded.
- On 6 February 1994, Li Peng signed two decrees regulating religious practices more strictly.
- On 10 March 1994, Chinese intellectuals sent a petition to the People's Congress whose annual session was just starting. In it they asked that repression and infringement of freedom of thought be ended. Their requests were in vain.
- On 8 March 1996 Beijing launched an exercise using unarmed missiles in the high seas off Taiwan – the third in eight months. It simulated a siege of the two major ports of the nationalist island.
- On 12 March 1996, China's air and sea manoeuvres with real ammunition in the Formosa Straits sufficiently worried the United States to prompt them to send two aircraft carriers to the region. Tension subsided after Taiwan's presidential election on 23 March.
- On 10 June 1996, China carried out nuclear tests although other atomic powers had been observing an informal moratorium since 1992.
- On 25 August 1996, the United States announced economic sanctions against China, accusing it of having supplied parts for M-11 missiles to Pakistan. This crisis clearly illustrated the worsening of Sino-American relations. Nevertheless, the United States and most democratic countries now no longer required China's observance of human rights as a precondition for bilateral relations such as commercial agreements.
- From 15 to 18 November 1996, the American Secretary of State paid his first visit to China since the 1989 repression. He failed to

obtain any concessions on human rights, the export of military material, or the North Korean nuclear threat.

- In April 1997, France, backed by Germany, Italy and Spain, encouraged the countries of the European Union to tone down their protests against Beijing's regime.[8]
- Some Russian strategists denounce Russian arms dealers for contributing to the rising, possibly uncontrollable, power of the Chinese armed forces.
- In spite of apparently normal Sino-Indian relations, mutual suspicion still exists. The visit of the Indian Prime Minister, Narasimha Rao, to Beijing in 1993 helped reduce military tension at the borders, but was unable to solve the power struggle between these two increasingly powerful nations.
- In May 1997, a wire from Agence France Presse revealed: 'The *Washington Times* has just reported that by the year 2000 China will have new mobile strategic missiles capable of striking American forces in the Pacific and certain parts of the United States. Referring to a secret report of the American Air Force, the newspaper observed that this new generation of Chinese missiles would reduce the gap that exists between Chinese, American and Russian missile systems. The report drawn up by the American Air Force's information agency said that the striking power of the Dong Feng 31 might be hard to counteract. The document said that the missile was in the final stage of development.'[9]

In the light of all this information, Gog representing China was no longer a hypothesis without foundation. Now we had to try and discover as soon as possible who Magog was ...

That is what we decided to do on that Sunday in early August in a wonderfully deserted Paris. The only clue we had was Magog's value: 52.

'There is a solution staring us in the face,' Jean-Pierre said all of a sudden. '52 is simply the number of countries forming a coalition, like the one formed by the Allies during the Second World War.'

Myriam could not hide her irritation. 'We have been slogging over this text for months now. Every letter is like a steep mountain. Every sentence is a labyrinth. Do you really think that in a moment of exhaustion John would suddenly decide to give us plain, uncoded words?'

'She's right,' David replied. 'As far as I am concerned I would lean towards an almost hereditary enemy of China: the United States'

'And how can you prove it?'

'Magog equals 52, doesn't it?'

'Yes' …

'And how many American states are there?'

I cried out: 'Fifty, of course!'

The computer specialist shook his head: 'Fifty-two.'

'Are you joking?

He insisted: 'Fifty-two if we include the District of Columbia and the associated state of Puerto Rico.'

His proposal caused a general outcry of indignation. I almost yelled: 'To think of Puerto Rico as an American state is not only a serious error but also an insult to Puerto Ricans!'

David replied angrily: 'Go back to school! Although Puerto Rico is part of the Caribbean Islands, it is United States territory.'

'I am sorry, but constitutionally it is not a state! Everything puts this island in opposition to the continental United States. On 9 February 1989, a few days after moving into the White House, President George Bush announced that he was personally in favour of Puerto Rico becoming the fifty-first state in the Union. He proposed a referendum to allow the 3.5 million inhabitants to "determine their own future". What was the reaction of the Puerto Rican government to this proposal? Well, it was extremely hostile, and it re-asserted the island's Hispanic cultural roots, and it repeated its refusal in 1993.'[10]

I repeated, stressing each word: 'Puerto Rico is not an American state. And I'm sure it never will be!'

'And as far as the District of Columbia is concerned,' Dimitri joined in, 'the idea of a state is even further removed, not to say non-existent. In 1791 the question was raised of where to establish the American capital without giving an advantage or disadvantage to any one of the states in the Union. Until then the capital had been itinerant, from Annapolis to Philadelphia and New York. Washington, Jefferson and Madison decided to choose a central location, between North and South, on the lower Potomac, straddling the states of Virginia and Maryland. Each of the two states gave up part of its territory: that is how the District of Columbia came into being, placed under the sole responsibility of Congress. It does not remotely resemble a state.'

David gave up and withdrew to a corner, looking disappointed.

'Shall we get back to Gog and Magog?' Myriam proposed. 'There is something interesting about these words. Look at them closely and tell me what you notice?' She stood up and wrote the two words on the board, one above the other:

GOG

MAGOG

'There are no vowels among the twenty-two letters that make up the Hebrew alphabet. They are all consonants. The vowels are represented by mekoudots, dots placed under the letters. This means that in the word "Magog" we can ignore the "false" vowel (A) that, like the letters E, I, O and U, has no numerical value,

She wrote again:

MGOG

'The only letter that differentiates the two words is the letter M.'

'Yes, I can see that', said Jean-Pierre. 'But what then?'

The young woman turned to Dimitri: 'What is the Greek value of M?

'40.'

'40 ... Exactly the same as in Hebrew. But we know we can ignore the zero, which gives us 40 and thus 4. It is the same in the two languages, which is not without interest.'

Turning to me, she asked: 'Could you read us the verse mentioning Gog and Magog?'

I read:

20:7 When the thousand years are ended, Satan will be released from his prison and will come out to deceive the nations at the four corners of the earth, Gog and Magog, in order to gather them for battle.

Myriam immediately pointed out: ' "The four corners of the earth." Do you see? Number 4 is indeed there.'

'And what do you deduce from this?'

'That the enemies of China consist of forty nations grouped together – forty countries that for various reasons have decided to unite against China.'

'It is hard to believe that countries like the United States or European countries would not be part of this coalition, if only for historical reasons, and because of military alliances such as NATO for instance.'

But there were several questions that remained unanswered. Verses 3, 12, 13 and 16 in chapter 17 stipulated:

And I saw a woman sitting on a scarlet beast … and it had seven heads and ten horns … And the ten horns that you saw are ten kings … but they are to receive authority as kings … They are united in yielding their power and authority to the beast … they will hate the whore.

'Ten kings' …

What could these ten kings represent if not the ten nations that would back China? Eleven on one side, forty on the other. Not one of us believed for one moment that the next war would be a conventional war, a 'real' war, to use the expression that had its hour of glory some time in the past and that remained engraved in the exploded entrails of Iraqi children.

David joined in: 'Do you remember what Einstein wrote in the 1950s? "Today man finds himself facing the most terrible danger he has ever had to confront. The poisoning of the atmosphere by radioactivity and, as a result, the destruction of all life on earth (short of the total disintegration of matter itself) are within the realm of technical possibilities. It is an apparently inevitable process in this sinister course of events. Each step forward seems to be the unavoidable consequence of what has preceded it. At the end of the road, the spectre of total annihilation becomes increasingly possible."[11]

But who were these ten kings following in China's footsteps on this road to 'total annihilation'?

18 Ten kings

Then two great dragons came forward,
both ready to fight, and they roared terribly.
At their roaring every nation prepared for war,
to fight against the righteous nation. It was a day of darkness and gloom,
tribulation and distress, affliction and great tumult on the earth.

Addition A to the Book of Esther

WHEN WE MET together as usual some ten days later, one of us was missing. David. Had we not known of his customary reliability, we would probably not have worried. But his punctuality was legendary. I called him at home, but his answering machine was on. At around ten o'clock that evening our curiosity turned into fear. Something serious must have happened to him. A car accident? The most frustrating thing was that we were not able to contact any close friends or relatives. They all lived in England. David was a confirmed bachelor, almost a misogynist, and he lived alone. Not surprisingly, our meeting was short.

The next morning, I telephoned his office. I was told that he had rung to say that he was not well and would not be coming in. Later that afternoon, Jean-Pierre suggested that we go to David's house and check for ourselves. I went with him.

No one answered the intercom. I rang the concierge's doorbell. He confirmed that our computer specialist was indeed upstairs in his flat. He had delivered a parcel to him just a few minutes earlier. We did not hesitate any longer.

We had to use every trick of diplomacy before David finally agreed to open the door to us. He was in his dressing gown, unshaven, with black circles under his eyes. With great reluctance he asked us to sit down. After a while he announced in a hollow voice: 'I am giving up, and I advise you to do the same.'

I looked at him in utter consternation.

'Yes, you heard correctly. I have thought about it at great length. We have been playing around for three years. I refuse to continue.'

I was trying to understand: 'It is your right to do so. But I don't understand your reasons.'

'I am stopping. That's all there is to it.' He stared at each of us in turn. 'Anyway, I have erased all the data from the computer ... '

Jean-Pierre leapt up from his armchair, beside himself: 'You have done what?'

'Initialized. Erased ... you know what that means? It's very simple. You press a key and then ... It's all gone! Nothing. The disk is completely blank as it was at the beginning. Nothing! Nothing! All finished!'

'You mean to say there is nothing left of our work? All the work we've done these past three years – all gone?'

'You've got it in one.'

Jean-Pierre grabbed David by the shoulders and began shaking him. It must be said that physically the Englishman was very light indeed. Rather short and flabby, there was nothing Rambo-like about him. I managed to separate them with great difficulty, and asked David for a double whisky.

I waited for a moment until we had all calmed down a little before questioning David further. 'Perhaps I am rather stupid, but I still do not see what motivated your action.'

He answered in a slightly calmer tone of voice: 'I am a scientist, and by nature a scientist is a man who practises the art of knowledge. Knowledge is not something evanescent or ethereal. What a scientist proposes, he must also prove, and prove "concretely".Only proven truths can be accepted. If this is not the case, it is called charlatanism.'

I refrained from interrupting him and let him finish.

'I have come to the point where the scientist does not want to follow the man any longer. Is that clear?'

'Not really. But I shall try and put into words what you may be thinking. Because you are unable to prove the information we have decoded in the Book of Revelation "scientifically", you'd rather resign than be considered a charlatan by your colleagues.'

His face turned purple with indignation. 'Wrong! Absolutely wrong. I do not care about my colleagues. I am the problem. I could give you a long list of scientists who have been insulted and dragged in the mud, simply because they had put forward a theory that did not conform with the spirit of their time. I really do not care what my colleagues think. No, that is not the problem. It's all to do with me and me only. I am betraying myself and all my beliefs. We are working with the super-natural, whereas the main principle of science is to disregard the supernatural.'

A heavy silence fell on the room. I tried to think of an answer but could find none.

'So, you're pulling out,' Jean-Pierre said, 'you are leaving in midstream.'

'I am not pulling out, I have decided to stick to reality.'

'And your state of mind is allowing you to destroy the work of an entire team. You are deciding for all of us.'

'You haven't lost anything; in fact, I am sparing you great humiliation. You should be thanking me.'

'Thanking you?'

Jean-Pierre's voice was trembling with anger. I feared the worst. Curiously, it was with a tense but controlled voice that the semiologist continued: 'Do you know what your real problem is, David? You're big-headed!'

'Say that again.'

This time Jean-Pierre really exploded: 'What are you thinking? That science is the absolute, immovable, transcendental, definitive truth? That one must prove the existence of God with an equation? That love can be declined to the square of the hypoteneuse? For millions of years you have been hitting your head against the walls of the Universe to explain "scientifically" where we are coming from, why and how, only to suffer cosmic migraines. Every time you make a step forward, the mysteries of the Universe make fun of you and recede further. Every time you think you have reached the boundaries of the Universe they melt away and you are left staring into nothingness. Everything disappears and you start again. But believe it or not, I too consider myself a scientist. I am infinitely respectful of science, but I do not allow it to censure my dreams and my innocent soul. From the moment a person is forbidden to dream, he loses his ability to progress.'

He caught his breath and continued in a more neutral tone: 'So, you are accusing us of not producing "rigorously scientific" work. You should realise that this is an absurd accusation. What are we working on? Laboratory mice? A newly identified virus? A tumour? An atom? No, my dear chap, wake up. We are working on ancient writings, thousands of years old, of which we know nothing or almost nothing. Look at the New Testament with a "scientific" eye. It is a mixture of history and literature, and to separate one from the other, to decide what is legend and what is truth, is purely hypothetical. We do not have the birth certificate of the man known as Christ, or the minutes of his trial, or his death certificate. The four Gospels also vary on the date of the crucifixion. No one can say with any certainty when the Gospels were written, where, by whom or for what purpose. And as far as the Old Testament is concerned, I have never seen a photograph of the garden of Eden, nor of Adam or Eve. I have never seen Cain's photograph in a police station, appealing for witnesses. I have seen nothing, apart from a few scraps of Noah's Ark; I have never had the pleasure of dining with Sarah, Esther or Judith. And Moses has never given me a photocopy of the Ten Commandments. What would science be doing here?'

He paused while he gathered his thoughts. 'In this case, how could you imagine for a moment that we might be able to prove "scientifically" discoveries which we are making in a completely "unscientific" text. Any intellectual who studies the Bible is faced with a dilemma: either he rejects all the stories it contains because they are all made up, or he takes them seriously and consequently has to abandon the word "science". Faith is as incompatible with this word as water is with fire. We have accepted John's text as an authoritative work. We are convinced that there is a "second reading" concealed behind the apparent syntax. That is all. There are no test tubes, no microscopes, no blind testing. Conviction, that's what has guided us all these months. If you no longer have that conviction, let's forget about it.'

And without another word, Jean-Pierre dragged me to the door. A moment later we were in the street. So all our work had been destroyed, reduced to dust, to nothing. We felt completely annihilated. Of course, we could have started all over again, rebuilding what we had lost. But our hearts were no longer in it.

A week went by. Then suddenly we heard from David. Had perhaps Jean-Pierre's words helped him to see the light? Had he perhaps become aware of the unproductiveness and, above all, the unfairness of his behaviour? He was – and is still – the only one who knows the answer to this. He telephoned to say that he had found the back-up of our work, which had always been kept in a safe place, and that he was willing to continue working on the project – that is, if we were still prepared to have him. You can imagine how relieved we were. The thought that all our sleepless nights had been wasted was unbearable. It would have been such a terrible loss.

We started again where we had left off, with the question of who these ten kings were who were likely to join forces with China in 2043.

> *17:12* And the ten horns that you saw are ten kings *who have not yet received a kingdom, but they are to receive authority as kings for one hour, together with the beast.*

'Since time immemorial, horns have symbolized power,' Jean-Pierre explained. 'Alexander the Great chose the ram's horns as his emblem, and the Gauls used to wear helmets with horns. They are also a symbol of virility. And – forgive me this triviality – in Italian slang, the penis is called *corno* (horn). Hence the supreme insult: *cornuto* (cuckold). In Judeo-Christian tradition, horns also represent strength and symbolize a ray of light, lightning. The following description can be found in Exodus:

> *34:29 Moses came down from Mount Sinai. As he came down from the mountain with the two tablets of the covenant in his hand, Moses did not know that the skin of his face shone because he had been talking with God.*

34:30 When Aaron and all the Israelites saw Moses, the skin of
his face was shining, *and they were afraid to come near him.*
34:35 The Israelites would see the face of Moses, that the skin of
his face was shining …

'That is why artists in the Middle Ages represented the prophet with
horns on the top of his head. But there is also another interpretation
that I believe to be closer to our investigation. In contemporary analysis,
horns are considered an image of divergence representing regressive
forces: is not the devil too represented with horns? The ten kings –
whoever they are – would therefore be serving evil. Or Satan … '

In spite of all our efforts, we could find no other solution.

Then, in desperation, Dimitri made a suggestion: 'Why don't we try
and find out what the two other horses mentioned by St John represent?
Do you remember, there are four:

6:2 I looked, and there was a white horse! …
6:4 And out came another horse, bright red …
6:5 … and there was a black horse …
6:8 I looked and there was a pale green horse!

'We know that the white horse represents America and the green horse
Germany. But we don't know what the other two – the red and the
black – represent. Let's calculate their respective values.'

David consulted his computer: '"Black horse" equals 640 or 1.
"Red horse" equals 177 or 6.'

I asked our computer specialist: 'Would it be possible to make a list
of the most important Asian countries and their numerical values?"

'Important on what basis? Size? Population? Military power?

Strategically?"

'I would say the last."

David replied: 'It is possible but it will take some time. Let's say forty-eight hours.'

'That's perfect.'

'What are you hoping to discover?

'A country with the same numerical value as the red or black horse. This would enable us to follow a different route. A route which would lead us to the ten kings. But in the meantime, we could try and find elements to support the hypothesis we put forward at our last meeting. Without being able to prove it, we concluded that if China started the next war, a coalition would immediately be formed to stand up to the aggressor. On the basis of the letter M of Magog, we established that this coalition would be made up of forty countries. We also deduced that the United States and European countries would be part of it. But without any cross-checking.'

'That's true,' David agreed. 'But where can we find the proof we are looking for?'

'Let's get back to the verse which mentions the "scarlet beast".

So he carried me away in the spirit into a wilderness, and I saw a woman sitting on a scarlet beast that was full of blasphemous names, and it had seven heads and ten horns.[1]

'What do the next verses say?

Dimitri began to read them out:

The woman was clothed in purple and scarlet, and adorned with gold and jewels and pearls, holding in her hand a golden cup full of abominations and the impurities of her fornication; and on her forehead was written a name, a mystery: 'Babylon the great, mother of whores and of earth's abominations.[2]

I went to the blackboard: 'Let's apply our usual method. Which words in these verses seem to be "carriers"?'

Dimitri immediately replied: 'Undoubtedly the words "a woman" and "the whore".'

Jean-Pierre added: 'I would also include "Babylon".'

'But we already know what this word represents: the symbol of evil.'

'Of course. But what have we got to lose?'

I agreed and wrote on the blackboard:

A WOMAN

THE WHORE

BABYLON

I asked David: 'Can you tell us their numerical values?'

He came back with the answer: 'A woman = 316 or 1. The whore = 73 or 1. Babylon = 34 or 7.'

'So we already have a first concordance between the woman and the whore.'

'And Babylon?'

Dimitri joined me in front of the blackboard: 'Let's think. To the apostle, Babylon represents evil. Falsehood. Betrayal. So, strangely enough, it is against Babylon that Gog – that is, China and her allies – will fight in the next war. If Gog represents China, and … '

He suddenly stopped. 'We must be stupid! Magog is Babylon!'

He quickly wrote down:

Babylon = 7

Magog = 52 or 7

'We have one side represented by Gog and one represented by Magog. On one side China and her ten allies and on the other, as we expected, America and Europe.'

'Where is the proof?' I asked.

It was David who replied: 'Europe = 302 or 5. America = 356 or 5. The two together add up to 10. Or 1.'

He too got up and wrote on the blackboard:

A woman = 1

The whore = 1

Europe + America = 1

'I don't think there's any doubt about it. It will be the West against Asia.'

Jean-Pierre nodded gravely: 'And everything leads us to believe that it will be a terrifying conflict. Listen to what John says about it:

And the ten horns that you saw, they and the beast will hate the whore; they will make her desolate and naked; they will devour her flesh and burn her up with fire.[3]

'If we gave free rein to our imagination, we would still be far from imagining what would really happen, which will be unthinkably terrible.'

'What escapes me is why,' said David. 'Why this sudden hatred towards the West, towards America? Why this reversal of symbols? The absolute image of evil is now attributed to those who fought against Nazism, the first beast. I don't understand.'

We were unable to reply. But something inside me told me that there was one man who knew why: a sick man, far away, on Mount Athos …

19 Rider of the red horse

FATHER ALEXANDER'S VOICE was clear and firm, and for the moment it seemed as though he had overcome his health problems.

'My friend, do you really believe that the world is immutable? That feelings are frozen in time and that data cannot be inverted? You seem surprised that those who were good yesterday can become bad tomorrow. Do not be offended, but I find your surprise rather childish. Have you forgotten that human beings are extraordinarily versatile? Look around you. What has become of our brilliant Western civilization? What has happened to its humanism and its hard-fought idealism? Man is crushed by his inventions; science, ever more feverish, is going crazy with its own inventions. Wherever we look, what do we see? A civilization squandering the earth's riches; societies which annihilate individuality in favour of the group that governs us; an evolution guided by a selection based on power and domination. What deserves to be saved in all this?'

He took a deep breath before continuing: 'And the third world is slowly dying. It is a commonplace, I know, and we are watching its agony with the benevolent attention of a spectator sitting comfortably in the first row in the theatre. Eight out of ten sufferers from AIDS are African. That too is a commonplace. Our nuclear shelters are made up of our commonplaces and the banalization of commonplaces. The

Sudan, Ethiopia, Sahel … Whole generations have been beheaded. It appears not to matter since the West has the means to contain the cataclysm within its walls! For centuries we have looked down on Asia, the East and Africa from the platform of science. Centuries of technological progress enable us to impose our laws and their humiliations. What else do you want me to say? You might think my words are the exaggerations of a sick old man or, worse, that I am being melodramatic. Too bad. I shall tell you a few more things. Did you know that between 1945 and 1965, almost 20 million Chinese died of hunger? That over a third of the population in developing countries, 800 million people, are in "extreme poverty"? That 600 million of them suffer permanently from malnutrition? That in the year 1981 alone, 17 million children died of hunger?[1] And do you really think that this will remain unchanged forever?'

I heard him sighing at the other end of the telephone line.

'The cult of the golden calf, my friend. The race for material goods at any cost still exists because we are mad enough to pay the highest price for them, that of happiness and dignity. St John's definition is eloquent: "The woman was clothed in purple and scarlet, and adorned with gold and jewels and pearls, holding in her hand a golden cup." And this gold blinds us and deprives us of the essential because it bans us from the vision of God. I suddenly thought of the remark made by your Jewish theologian regarding the word "Emeth", which means truth. If you take away the first letter, the meaning changes, and Emeth becomes Meth – that is, "death". Nothingness. Alas, I fear that our civilization is on the brink of committing that fatal error: removing that letter which would enable it to survive. Is it therefore so surprising that we should be punished? What does it matter if it is China who does the punishing? Nuclear disaster is no longer an undeserved punishment but the expected end of a civilization that wants to disappear, like the pistol that a desperate person points at his temple. Regarding fascism … why bother to mention it? To quote one of your politicians, it is a mere detail. Just remember that it did not die in a bunker one evening in April 1945. It only fell asleep. Once risen from its lethargy, it changed its name. That's all.'

'Forgive me, but listening to you, I have the impression that you find it quite normal that the West should pay the price of its economic progress and comfort.'

'I do not find anything normal, my friend. I am the first to deplore this self-destructive process in which we are caught up. However, allow me to compare this situation with a bullfight. Killing a bull because it is maddened is called self-defence; but driving a bull mad to kill him, that is murder. Well, that's what we have been doing for centuries. We have driven mad an animal called Asia, the Third World. We have not killed it but it is nearly as bad. So we had better be prepared when he enters the arena.'

I did not sleep much that night. There was something disconcerting about the thought that China – an atheist country – could become God's secular arm. But what if it was true?'

Two days later, a new piece of information arrived which clearly supported Father Alexander's claims.

David arrived with a series of notes. He gave each one of us a copy. 'You asked me to draw up a list of Asian countries according to their military or strategic importance, and also to check whether any of them had the same numerical value as the red horse (6) or the black horse (1). I have found just one which meets both criteria, and it is completely unexpected. Look at this.' He showed us the paper on which he had written:

Korea = 312 or 6

Red horse = 6

I spoke: 'Korea? But which Korea? North or South Korea?'

'As you can imagine, that was also the first question I asked myself. Here is the answer.'

Pyongyang = 213 or 6

'The capital of North Korea; and again the number of the Beast: 666.'

Dimitri looked perplexed: 'How has Korea got involved?'

I replied slightly reproachfully: 'Is that the historian speaking? If I had to suggest the name of the country most likely to side with China it would definitely be North Korea.'

David in turn had a question: 'Would you be more explicit?'

'The explanation lies in the past. I apologize in advance if my explanation is a bit long, but here it is.

'On 2 September 1945, the surrender of Japan was signed, and on the same day the Supreme Allied Commander announced that Korea would be divided into two almost equal parts, one to be occupied by the United States and the other by the USSR.

'In 1947, the General Assembly of the United Nations adopted a resolution by which a single form of government would be created by organizing general elections throughout the entire territory, to be supervised by a commission. The commission was unable to operate in the north, so on 10 May 1948 elections took place only in the south. Syngman Rhee's party won the elections and the American military government was replaced by the Republic of Korea, proclaimed on 15 August 1948 and recognized by the United Nations.

'Ten days later, in response to what had happened in the south, the north organized its own elections. On 18 September, the People's Republic of Korea was proclaimed, before becoming shortly afterwards the People's Democratic Republic of Korea. It was immediately recognized by the USSR and its allies, and by the People's Republic of China.

'After the creation of the two republics, the Soviet and American armies evacuated their respective zones of occupation in 1949.

'A year later, in June, North Korea launched a general attack on the south. Seoul was captured by the north on 28 June. Thereafter the communist troops continued to advance southwards.

'On 28 June, President Truman ordered the American Navy and Air Force to support the south and protect Formosa. Three days later, he brought in American ground forces to provide further support and authorized the air force to attack the north. This war lasted three years and its course was changed when 850,000 Chinese "volunteers" joined in. They were in fact the regular units of the prestigious Fourth People's Army, led by Lin Piao. The southern troops and United Nations withdrew towards the south. Faced with this situation, Truman declared that "the use of the nuclear bomb is still being considered", but this did not stop the communist forces pushing south to recapture Pyongyang on 4 December.

'Finally, on 27 July 1953, an armistice was signed between representatives of the United Nations' forces on one side, and the Chinese and North Korean forces on the other.

'The total loss in human life during this war (dead, disappeared and wounded) was over 2 million. This terrible war solved nothing so far as reunification was concerned. Its sequels are still felt today. There, now you know everything, or nearly ...'[2]

'What is the situation today?' David asked.

'Let's say that since 1993, because of the failure of his policy of self-sufficiency, President Kim Il-Sung's regime has been trying to attract foreign capital. But his intransigence regarding nuclear power has driven away potential outside help. Meanwhile the country has carried out its first – successful – nuclear test of a Rodong-I missile, capable of carrying a nuclear load as far as Japan.

'On 4 February 1994 four of the five permanent members of the United Nations Security Council – the United States, France, Great Britain and Russia – threatened to impose economic sanctions on North Korea if it did not authorize the inspection of its nuclear sites. An agreement was reached but it was soon flouted.

'On 21 March 1996, the American President Bill Clinton announced the deployment within forty-five days of Patriot anti-missile missiles in South Korea, where 37,000 US soldiers were stationed. North Korea immediately declared that it considered this deployment an act of aggression. On 31 March the United Nations Security Council unanimously adopted an undemanding declaration simply requiring North Korea to allow experts to complete their inspections. The text of this declaration was the result of a compromise between China, North Korea's ally, and the United States.

'On 17 December, an American military helicopter was shot down north of the demarcation line between the two Koreas. One pilot was killed. Washington claimed that the helicopter was off course due to a navigational error, but Pyongyang claimed that it was spying.

'From 5 to 7 April 1996, after the warlike declarations from Pyongyang, North Korean troops made incursions inside the demilitarized zone between the two Koreas, along the 38th parallel, thus violating the armistice agreement signed in 1953. This renewed tension between the two countries was reflected in the beaching of a North

Korean submarine on the South Korean coast in September 1996.

'As you can see, that North Korea should side with China in the next conflict is more than a hypothesis, it is a certainty.'

'You know what that would mean ... Japan would be in the front line.'

'There is no doubt about that,' Dimitri agreed, 'and the rest of the world would follow.'

'If we are right, the confirmation must be somewhere in the text.'

'Absolutely,' said David. 'As I mentioned before, the main events of the two conflicts are in chapter 8, verses 6 to 12.

Now the seven angels who had the seven trumpets made ready to blow them.

The first angel blew his trumpet, and there came hail and fire, mixed with blood, and they were hurled to the earth; and a third of the earth was burned up, and a third of the trees were burned up, and all green grass was burned up.

The second angel blew his trumpet, and something like a great mountain, burning with fire, was thrown into the sea. A third of the sea became blood, a third of the living creatures in the sea died, and a third of the ships were destroyed.

The third angel blew his trumpet, and a great star fell from heaven, blazing like a torch, and it fell on a third of the rivers and on the springs of water.

The name of the star is Wormwood. A third of the waters became wormwood, and many died from the water, because it was made bitter.

The fourth angel blew his trumpet, and a third of the sun was struck, and a third of the moon, and a third of the stars, so that a third of their light was darkened; a third of the day was kept from shining, and likewise the night.

'The first angel symbolizes Hiroshima. And I remain convinced that, in spite of your reticence, the second angel represents Nagasaki. The third and fourth angels definitely refer to the coming war. And because all the pieces of this puzzle are scattered around everywhere, I believe that the four angels also symbolize the countries or regions that will be involved in 2043.'

I remarked: 'Unless they refer only to the ten nations that will be China's allies. I also point out that we still have not discovered who the "ten kings" are, mentioned by John in chapter 17, verse 12: "And the ten horns that you saw are *ten kings* … "'

'But we have identified one of the ten countries: North Korea.'

'That's true, but … '

David interrupted: 'Come on. Let's stick to the point. Let's go back to chapter 8. If you look more closely at the verses, you will notice that one word recurs many times: a "third".'

> A third *of the earth was burned up, and a* third *of the trees was burned up … A* third *of the sea became blood, a* third *of the living creatures in the sea died, and a* third *of the ships were destroyed.*
> *… and it fell on a* third *of the rivers and on the springs of water.*
> A third *of the waters became wormwood.*
> *… a* third *of the sun was struck, and a* third *of the moon, and a* third *of the stars, so that a* third *of their light was darkened; a* third *of the day was kept from shining, and likewise the night.*

'The word occurs twelve times … or 3 (1+2).'

'Would that be a clue?' asked Dimitri.

'Probably.'

I joined in: 'But a clue that would lead where?'

David got up and grabbed a piece of chalk: 'What must we keep? Which expressions? The third of the trees? Of the sea? Of the creatures?'

After a pause, Dimitri remarked: 'All things considered, three words stand out from the others.'

'Which ones?

'Read the last verse again:

... a third of the sun was struck, and a third of the moon, and a third of the stars, so that a third of their light was darkened; and a third of the day was kept from shining, and likewise the night.

'It is the only one out of the seven verses that mentions the astral bodies: "sun, moon, stars". The others evoke more general elements like trees, forests or creatures.'

'True. So what do you suggest?'

'Well, we must start by calculating their numerical value. And I am sure we shall see ... '

Without waiting, David typed the three words on the computer. The answer appeared on the screen almost immediately.

Sun = 640 or 1
Moon = 218 or 2
Stars = 98 or 8

'I cannot see where these numbers are leading.'

I suggested: 'What if, with these astral bodies, St John was referring to several countries and one religion at the same time?'

My question further increased my friends' confusion.

'You'll soon understand. Can we assume that the sun would be Japan's emblem?'

'Because of its flag?'

I nodded.

'And the moon is the symbol of Islam, isn't it?'

'And the stars ... '

David interrupted me: 'You are thinking here of the United States. The stars and stripes.'

'It is only a hypothesis.'

'Which we could easily confirm or invalidate ... '

David calculated the numerical values of the two nations and the religion referred to and wrote the results down on the blackboard:

Japan = 140 or 5

Islam = 141 or 6

United States = 208 or 1

America = 356 or 5

It was obvious that nothing corresponded to my theory. We spent some time reflecting on these numbers but were unable to draw any conclusion whatsoever.

I suggested: 'Why don't we include the word "third"? After all, it is part of the expression. Let's enter it in again.'

David typed in:

Third of the sun = 1325 or 2

Third of the moon = 903 or 2

Third of the stars = 783 or 9

Total: 3011 or 5

The result was still just as disappointing.

'So where do go from here?' Dimitri sighed. 'Where?

'Since we are looking for the identity of the nine missing kings,' David proposed, 'or the nine countries, let us check whether there are three countries that might have a value similar to a third of the sun, the moon or the stars.'

I protested: 'That's absurd! First, from a purely statistical point of view, there is every chance we shall find at least three. Secondly, discovering them will not prove anything. Whereas for North Korea, we have a triple confirmation – red horse (6), Pyongyang (6), Korea (6) – this time we have nothing on which to base our conclusions.'

The ease with which David allowed himself to be persuaded made me think that he too felt that he was on the wrong track.

'I give up,' he said, looking discouraged. 'I don't know any more.'

It was obvious that we were all growing increasingly despondent. Dimitri suddenly suggested: 'And what if the expressions were referring to continents?'

I could not understand: 'But there are only three expressions … '

'What does it matter? Perhaps only three continents will be involved in the war.'

Indifferent to my lack of conviction, Dimitri continued, but he addressed himself to David: 'Could you calculate the value of each of the continents and add them up?'

A few moments later, the five numbers were written on the blackboard:

Asia = 76 or 4
Africa = 396 or 9
America = 356 or 5
Europe = 302 or 5
Oceania = 192 or 3
Total = 1322 or 8

Looking at the results I could not help pointing out: 'As you can see, we are going round in circles.'

Furious, David turned off his computer. Dimitri put his notes away. Jean-Pierre did the same. As for myself, I was so exhausted emotionally that I just stood there for a very long time after my friends had left, staring blankly at what we had written.

I cannot remember when I decided to call Myriam. Something was telling me we should start with a clean slate.

Two days later I received Myriam's e-mail:

Shalom!

You were not far from the solution. I must admit that I too nearly missed it. It does indeed refer to the continents, but with one difference: Oceania is not part of it, and for good reason. Oceania consists only of a series of archipelagos and small islands, and although there are many of them, these represent represent a tiny surface area compared with the continents. In fact, it is difficult to see what part they would play – at least directly – in any major conflict. In any case, if you had even the slightest doubt, the result below should completely reassure you.

Third of the sun (שליש מהשמש) = 1325
Third of the moon (שליש מהירח) = 903
Third of the stars (שליש מהכוכבים) = 783
Total = 3011 or 5

Asia (אסיה) = 76
Africa (אפריקה) = 396
America (אמריקה) = 356

Europe (אירופה) = 302

Total = 1130 or 5

Nuclear bombardment = 1013 or 5

Note – and this is very important – that the three numbers are made up of exactly the same digits: 3011, 1130 and 1013. This is proof that we are right.

So to conclude, everything leads us to believe that on 5 February 2043 at midday, these four continents will become involved in the next conflict. But allow me to add here that the expression 'third' should not be taken literally. One doesn't have to be a prophet to realize that the damage caused by a nuclear world war would affect far more than a third of the world. We shall not be dealing with forest fires, but fires on a planetary scale.

20 The Alpha and the Omega

KNOWING WHEN IT will all end makes one lose the will to act; it creates a truly inhuman atmosphere. We still did not know the identity of the nine kings or the nine countries who would side with China, but that hardly seemed to matter in the knowledge of what was going to happen to us.

But was it believable? Was it possible that the end of the world, or of a world, had been described in a two thousand-year-old document written on an isolated Greek island by a man called John?

I was looking at the date: *5 February 2043 at midday*. The name of the second beast: *China*. The identity of China's ally, or at least its alibi: *North Korea* and its capital. Four continents: *Europe, Africa, Asia* and *America*, which would all be destroyed.

Does fatalism exist? For some time now I had been reflecting on something that an Oriental friend of mine once said to me, which I had thought rather naive at the time. What he had said was: 'You see, my friend, in the East we believe in certain things. Things that you in the West think rather absurd or even ridiculous. Like the evil eye, for instance, but also, more importantly, predestination. We are convinced that everything is written in the Great Book of stars: our joys, suffering, loves, the time of our birth and our death. Rejecting this philosophy, you prefer using words like providence, coincidence or fate when faced with extraordinary events.'

I still found the idea of predestination hard to accept, and I preferred Romain Rolland's definition and explanation: 'Fatalism is the excuse of souls without willpower.'

And yet … The first beast, Goebbels, Roosevelt, Hiroshima had all been mentioned by John. So why not China in the future? There was only one way to answer this question: to continue our investigations, to discover other clues, to go like speliologists ever deeper into the cave of the visionary of Patmos.

It was late November 1997. Myriam was with us again. We had only just started our meeting when she suddenly changed the direction of the debate: 'For some time now I have been reflecting on the fundamental meaning of the Book of Revelation. I feel that the text contains more than a prophetic vision: it contains a warning. I am sure of that. It is almost certain that chapter 8 contains the fundamental information: namely, Hiroshima, Nagasaki, the future. There are three sentences in which this warning is clearly expressed:

> 'I am the Alpha and the Omega,' says the Lord God, who is and who was and who is to come, the Almighty.
> Then he said to me, 'It is done! I am the Alpha and the Omega, the beginning and the end.'
> 'I am the Alpha and the Omega, the first and the Last, the beginning and the end.'

'What attracted my attention is the position of these verses in the text: 1:8, 21:6, 22:13. Which gives us 9, 9 and 8. Do you remember what

I told you about the word "Emeth", worth 441 or 9? I told you that since Adam's sin, the most perfect being could never obtain more than 9. On the other hand, God, absolute truth, was the only one with a value of 10. I also explained that in this word Emeth, the figure 1 placed at the end represented Omega (the end). By adding alpha – the beginning – (1) at the start of the number, we obtained 1441 or 10, the absolute truth. Do you remember?'

I remembered it all the better because Father Alexander had mentioned the same example a few weeks earlier.

Myriam continued: 'Note the numerology of the three verses: 9, 9, 8. Here we have a configuration that re-unites the past and the future.'

'How?' David wondered.

'The first 9 represents the man, Adam (45) with his weaknesses and his part of divinity. The 8 symbolizes Alpha, the first step towards self-destruction: Japan, or "Eight Large Islands", and also Hiroshima.'

'And the second 9?' asked Jean-Pierre.

She had no problem answering the question. We had all guessed that this last figure represented the end and the new beginning. Japan would be a martyr again: on 5 February 2043 at midday $(2 + 4 + 3 = 9)$.

'It would be mad,' Dimitri muttered, 'but if it really is Korea and China who are going to start the next war, it would indeed be possible.'

'We could check it,' I said rather uneasily. 'Let's look again at the verses linked to the third angel.'

I wrote on the blackboard in large letters:

The third angel blew his trumpet and a great star fell from heaven, blazing like a torch, and it fell on a third of the rivers and on the springs of water. The name of the star is Wormwood. A third of the waters became wormwood, and many died from the water, because it was made bitter.

'Which words do you suggest we concentrate on?'

There were various suggestions, but finally we selected three that we thought contained the essential of the two verses. Myriam joined me and wrote the numerical value next to each expression:

Wormwood star (כּוֹכב לענה) = 203 or 5

Third of the rivers (שְׁלִישׁ מהנהרוֹת) = 1346 or 5

The springs (המעינוֹת) = 581 or 5

There was a pause, then David said: 'If Myriam's reasoning is correct, we have a choice: either we go straight to the target and we prove it, or we go the long way round using side roads.'

'Try and explain yourself,' said Myriam.

'If I understand you correctly, Japan was, and will be again, the first target. "The Alpha and the Omega".'

'That's right.'

'In this case, two words – and two words only – will confirm your theory.'

'Which ones?

'Japan and Tokyo. Anything else would only be a digression or fiction.'

Myriam agreed with David's suggestion. She wrote on the blackboard:

Japan = 140 or 5

Tokyo (טוֹקיוֹ) = 131 or 5

'We are convinced that everything is written down in advance in the Great Book of stars ... '

The words of my Oriental friend flooded back into my head like a torrent. 'Fatalism? Predestination?' A strange thought suddenly entered my mind and I tossed it out as a kind of challenge, as trying to find fault with St John's text. 'As we know, "wormwood" in Ukrainian is "chernobyl". What is its value?'

'155 or 2,' Myriam replied.

'Perfect. Now compare it with the word "radioactivity!" '

The young woman hesitated for a moment, then she answered: '758 … also 2.'

I felt as if the ground was giving way under my feet.

'What are you trying to prove?'

How could I explain? How could I tell her that I was suddenly trying deliberately to put an end to what was becoming a nightmare? This story was impossible! How could a man of flesh and blood, a mortal man now turned to dust, how had he read in the stars, in the face of God, 2,000 years ahead of time: how could he have known terms like 'radioactivity'? He was not to know that these terms would have the same numerical value as 'wormwood' and that 'wormwood' was called 'chernobyl' in Ukrainian!

I was filled with anger: 'The verse speaks of waters having become bitter! Give me the numerical value of "bitter waters"!'

My friends looked at me as if I had become a total stranger. Myriam did as I had asked and her hand slowly, deliberately wrote down on the blackboard:

Bitter waters (מים מרים) = 380 or 2

I became dizzy.

Wormwood star = 203 or 5
Third of the rivers = 1346 or 5
The springs = 581 or 5
Japan = 140 or 5
Tokyo = 131 or 5

Bitter waters = 380 or 2
Wormwood (לענה) = 155 or 2
Radioactivity (רדיו אקטיביות) = 758 or 2

In *Prometheus Bound*, Aeschylus foresaw that God had created in man a fearful adversary capable of overthrowing him, because man would one day invent 'a fire compared to which lightning would be laughable and whose noise would be louder than that of thunder'.

'Stop,' I said. 'We shall continue later.'

During the following week, I was very tempted to put an end to our investigations. For completely different reasons from those which had provoked David's sudden crisis of conscience, I felt that I no longer had the strength to continue. David had wanted to abandon the whole project because of his scruples as a scientist; I wanted to do the same, but because of a crisis of faith. I could not accept that this God in whom I believed with all my heart would have been capable of conceiving such a destiny for his creatures. If the Lord knew, then why? What was the purpose of it all in that case? Could a father give birth to a child, knowing that this child would spread death before annihilating itself? Auschwitz, Treblinka, Hiroshima ... I needed to understand, so I picked up the telephone and called the monastery at Mount Athos. 'Father Alexander, please.'

There was a slight pause at the other end. Someone answered in halting French: 'Father Alexander – unfortunately he is no longer with us.'

I felt as if I had been punched in the face.

'When?'

'Two days ago. Are you a friend?'

I muttered a very bewildered 'yes'.

'Your name?'

'Bodson, Gérard Bodson.'

'Ah, Monsieur Bodson.'

It suddenly sounded as if he had been waiting for my call.

'Father Alexander ... he had written you a letter. He was going to post it. I was going to ... '

'No need. Could you read it to me?'

'My French is not ... '

'Don't worry. This is very important, I beg of you.'

I heard the receiver being put down. I waited for what felt like an eternity.

'Monsieur Bodson?'

'You have the letter?'

'Yes.'

I could hear the rustling of paper.

'Forgive me if my reading ... '

'It does not matter ... I am listening.'

The voice started to read: 'My very dear friend, since our last conversation I have been overcome by remorse. I am angry with myself because I was so strict in my judgement and so harsh in my conclusions. I also blame myself for having painted such a desperate portrait of man and his future. I told you these terrible words, among other things: "Nuclear disaster is no longer an undeserved punishment but the expected end

219

of a civilization that wants to disappear, like the pistol that a desperate person points at his temple". It is an unforgivable statement because it implies a suicidal world, a world abandoned by its creator, left to its folly. This is a thought that I very much reject. You see, if man has been able in a few centuries to develop the means to annihilate himself, he can also annihilate these means. God wanted us free. Free to choose. The freedom he gave us is the most important expression of his love. What would you say of a father who spends his time pursuing his child, punishing him every time he behaves badly, even into adulthood and beyond? Such a child would have been driven mad and ready to be locked up. I am sure you have read that wonderful book by George Orwell, *1984*. God is not "Big Brother", an omnipresent computer managing people's lives, their thoughts, their actions, the way they move, love and breathe. I am telling you, if God behaved like that, we would all be in the madhouse. He has created us free. Free, do you understand? He conceived the universe with its infinite beauties like a brilliant architect creates a house. He installed us in it, then threw the key into the abyss of the cosmos so as not to be tempted to intervene.'

He paused for a moment. For a fraction of a second, I had the feeling that he was praying.

'This kind of language spoken by a priest may surprise you. However, it is my faith and my faith alone that prompts me to say these words. No, nothing is pre-determined. All that St John does in his Book of Revelation is to warn us. He showed us Cain's fate knowing that there is an Abel present in all of us, who may take over at any time. Man's destruction is not ineluctable. The choice to live or die is man's.'

There was another moment of silence, then:

'No, my friend. Do not make God responsible for our mistakes. He spent his youth sending us messengers such as Moses, Daniel and Jesus;

he has warned us a hundred or a thousand times. The Holy Scripture is nothing other than a series of letters sent from heaven. Now it is up to us to read them again and to find the strength in them to overcome the beast, to prevent the infernal machine from getting out of control. Have you not established for yourself that the beast and the Lamb are one and the same person? In other words, man. If man wishes to do so, he can destroy this ill-fated double character that is dormant within him. He has the power to do so, and this power was given to man by God the Father who is in heaven, who gave it to him the day he made him from clay. Affectionately … '

As soon as I put the phone down, I felt that a light was flowing through my entire body, illuminating even the darkest corners. By sending me this message from the other world, the priest had given me back my strength, but above all, he was giving me hope. So, everything was not lost. More than ever, I wanted to continue deciphering the mysteries of the Book of Revelation – not for reasons of voyeurism or from morbid curiosity, but to pass on everything there is to know about it so that one day, who knows, someone will appear who will stop the wheel of disaster turning.

21 A black horse

There will be great earthquakes, and in various places famines and plagues; and there will be dreadful portents and great signs from heaven ...

Luke 21:11

DAVID WAS SPEAKING. 'So, the scenario could be summed up as follows. In 2043, a man will be ruling China, a man who is already among us. His character will be like that of the first beast, Adolf Hitler, with probably the same feelings of violence and longing for supremacy. For reasons we do not yet know, this man, in alliance with North Korea, will launch a nuclear attack on Japan. If we take into account the progress that has been achieved since 1945, the fire resulting from this attack will be of such violence that Tokyo and the whole of Japan will be completely destroyed. "The third angel blew his trumpet, and a great star fell from heaven, blazing like a torch." It is more than likely that the United States and its Western allies will respond by launching a counter-attack, not a conventional kind but a nuclear attack like that launched by the aggressor. In whose camp will the Russians be? It is impossible to say. But they will take part in the conflict in one camp or the other, and raging fires will destroy our countries.'

He picked up a document and read from it:

'"A hydrogen bomb is ten thousand times more powerful than the atomic bomb that destroyed Hiroshima. Ten thousand times ... In 1961, when the Russians tested a thermo-nuclear warhead of approx-

imately 80 megatons, the shock wave went round the world three times."
It is interesting to compare some of John's verses describing the effects
caused by an experiment of this type. Look for instance at verses 13
and 14 in chapter 6: " … and the stars of the sky fell to the earth as
the fig tree drops its winter fruit when shaken by a gale. The sky vanished
like a scroll rolling itself up, and every mountain and island was removed
from its place." If we translate these words into the language of today,
they would read as follows: "the shock wave consists of highly pres-
surized gas at a very high temperature, accompanied by an extremely
violent wind sweeping up everything in its way and transforming the
smallest object into a deadly projectile." With an excess pressure of 0.35
bars[1] – which corresponds to the point at which the eardrums rupture
– the wind can reach a maximum speed of 250 km/h. With an excess
pressure of 2 bars, the wind can reach a speed of over 1,000 km/h. It
is a terrifying thought when one realizes that the wind in the most deadly
hurricanes rarely exceeds 200 km/h.'

He paused for a moment and then quoted another verse: ' " … and
a great star fell from heaven, blazing like a torch."[2] In today's language,
"the energy produced during a thermo-nuclear explosion will raise the
temperature by several million degrees, while during a traditional explosion it does not exceed 5000° Celsius. In less than one millionth of a
second, an unimaginably large quantity of energy is released. A fireball
consisting of a mass of air and gaseous residues, more brilliant than the
sun, will dilate and cool down in a few seconds, thereby creating a
thermic flux capable of burning everything in its path to a cinder.' "

David gulped down some coffee before continuing: 'Now read chapter
8 verse 12 again: " … and a third of the sun was struck, and a third of
the moon, and a third of the stars, so that a third of their light was darkened; a third of the day was kept from shining, and likewise the night."

Suppose we assume that during the next conflict 10,000 megatons – or only half the present stock of nuclear weapons – were used as follows: 90 per cent on Europe, Asia and North America; 10 per cent on South America. This would result in the extermination of one in two of the earth's inhabitants – over 3 billion people. All infrastructures would be destroyed. Epidemics caused by the putrefaction of several million corpses would be impossible to control, let alone the billions of insects more resistant to radiation than man. And then nuclear winter would follow.'

'Nuclear winter,' Myriam asked in a tone of surprise. 'What does that mean?'

David put his hand on the Book of Revelation: 'St John. It is all there in the verse I have just read to you. The explosions and fires will cause gigantic whirlwinds of dust and toxic fumes in the stratosphere, which will conceal the sun: " … so that a third of their light was darkened; a third of the day was kept from shining, and likewise the night." This will result in a drop in temperature. In addition, the ozone layer will be very largely destroyed, and we know what that means. Without its protective shield, the earth will be literally bombarded by ultraviolet rays. No more marine plankton, no more seeds, and no more harvests. Even worse, our retinas will be carbonized. We would be left as groups of blind survivors, feeling our way as we roamed the countryside, like blind ghosts among the ruins.'

We listened, quite unable to react.

'Today, eight countries have the capability of unleashing this cataclysm: the United States, Russia, France, Great Britain, China, India, Israel and Pakistan. There are six countries likely to acquire nuclear weapons by 2043: Iran, the two Koreas, Brazil, Argentina and possibly Iraq. But there are other countries who could also develop their own nuclear bombs using the radioactive waste from nuclear power stations throughout the world, countries such as Algeria and Libya (both, strangely enough, with China's help), Germany, Australia, Austria, Belgium; the list is endless. I would also like to add the following.

He grabbed a sheet of paper and looked at it briefly: 'A physicist friend of mine told me something yesterday that I did not know. Beyond the atom, there exists an intermediate particle of mass, between the electron and the proton: the meson. This was discovered in 1935 by a Japanese research scientist, Professor Yukawa, and confirmed in 1948 by a Brazilian scientist, Professor Lattès. Today we are able to produce these mesons in a laboratory. Without going into technical detail, suffice it to say that a few kilograms could develop the power of 10,000 hydrogen bombs in a single explosion. Compared to such destructive power, the Hiroshima bomb is like a drop of water falling into the Niagara Falls. It is true that for the moment we are unable to check the disintegration time of these particles, their lifespan being extremely ephemeral. Nevertheless, can we be certain that such a weapon will not be created before 2043? And in the hands of the beast … '

By now dusk had fallen, throwing threatening shadows on the walls. We were sitting in absolute silence as if to protect ourselves from we knew not what.

At last someone spoke. It was Dimitri. 'Asia, Africa, Europe, America. But what about the Middle East? It has not been mentioned at all in our discussions. Don't you think that is strange?'

It was Myriam who answered: 'The fact that we have not noticed it does not mean that it is not mentioned somewhere in the twenty-two chapters. Perhaps we shall discover it. But first I would like to return to David's description of events. Although I agree with his conclusions, I do not believe that the verses on which he has based them are the right ones. The information regarding these two catastrophes is to found in chapter 9, verses 1 and 2:

> *And the fifth angel blew his trumpet, and I saw a star that had fallen from heaven to earth, and he was given the key to the shaft of the abyss … and from the shaft rose smoke like the smoke of a great furnace, and the sun and the atmosphere were darkened with the smoke from the shaft.'*

Myriam stood up and walked to the blackboard: 'Look at the text … What do you notice when you read it for the first time?'

I remarked immediately: 'Everything is there: the star, which could be translated by warhead or missile. The smoke that darkened the air and the sun are signs heralding the coming of the nuclear winter.'

The young woman smiled. 'But this is still all theoretical … '

'You're right,' said Dimitri. 'Moreover, you must have noticed that the word "atmosphere" is not a good translation. It is an anachronism. The Greek text says "air".'

'That is true, but it doesn't change the basic meaning of the verse. As I said, this is all still theoretical. Until now we have always tried to prove our interpretations through gematria, because we cannot merely describe an event in a subjective manner and according to what strikes our imagination. Moreover …'

David interrupted her. 'I presume that you have an idea.'

'Yes,' she said. 'It was the word "abyss" that gave me the idea. You see, it occurs approximately forty times, in the Torah and in the New Testament. And most of the time it does not have the meaning one thinks it has. What is an "abyss" if it is not a void hollowed out of the earth? And yet … '

She went through her notes and continued: 'Here are a few examples: Genesis, chapter 1, verse 2:

The earth was a formless void and darkness covered the face of the abyss, *while a wind from God swept over the face of the waters.*

'Proverbs 8:27:

When he established the heavens, I was there, when he drew a circle on the face of the abyss.

'But it is in the Psalms that I have found the strangest verses:[3]

You set the earth on its foundations, *so that it shall never be shaken.* You cover it with the abyss as with a garment; *the waters stood above the mountains.*

'As you can see, in any of these verses the word "abyss" does not have the meaning usually given to it. Let's take Genesis. Can darkness "cover the abyss" in a "formless void"? And in Proverbs, God "established the heavens" and "drew a circle on the face of the abyss". Would the "abyss" therefore be above the earth? And in the extract from the Psalms, does it not seem surprising that God creates the earth, then "covers it with the abyss as with a garment"?'

'What conclusion do you draw from this?'

'When John wrote: "he opened the shaft of the abyss", he implies that the angel tears open "the garment of the earth".'

'So the ozone layer … '

Myriam wrote on the blackboard:

The ozone layer (שיכבת האוזון) = 807 or 6
The air (אוירה) = 222 or 6

'We could extrapolate further by replacing the word "fumes" with "toxic gases".

Fumes (עשן) = 420 or 6

Toxic gases (גזים רעילים) = 420 or 6

'Two perfectly equal numbers.' The young woman turned towards David: 'That only reinforces your deductions. But we can go even further in the confirmation of your scenario. Let's have a quick look at chapter 6, verse 12:

When he opened the sixth seal, I looked, and there came a great earthquake; the sun became black as sackcloth, the full moon became like blood …

'There is here an inconsistency that is quite striking. How can these two stars be there at the same time? If it was an eclipse of the sun there would be no sun; and conversely, if it was an eclipse of the moon, there would be no moon. Therefore, we must be dealing here with a metaphor. The sun being the star of the day, one could replace the word "sun" by the word "day" and "moon" by the word "night". So in other words we could read that at the height of the conflict "the day will become night".

Dimitri joined in and added: 'Remember that for the Greeks, Chaos was the personification of the primordial void that preceded creation, at a time when order had not yet been imposed on the elements. This notion corresponds to the confusion and "formless" earth of Genesis, reflecting desert and emptiness. And, still according to Greek mythology, it was Chaos that created night. So St John's expression clearly means that after the chaos and cataclysms we shall enter darkness.'

'The nuclear winter that David described a moment ago. Yet more elements proving that it will be a total nuclear war that will strike the world on 5 February 2043 at midday. Seen in this light, the interpretation of the missing symbol appears perfectly clear.'

'What symbol?'

'The fourth horse. We have proved that the white horse represents the United States. The greenish horse is the 'brown pest' or fascism. The red horse is North Korea and, indirectly, her ally, China. The only horse we have not deciphered is the black one:

When he opened the third seal, I heard the third living creature call out, 'Come!' I looked, and there was a black horse! Its rider held a pair of scales in his hand, and I heard what seemed to be a voice in the midst of the four living creatures saying, 'A quart of wheat for a day's pay, and three quarts of barley for a day's pay, but do not damage the olive oil and the wine!'[4]

'No other words better express the meaning of this metaphor as used in this verse than those of a certain Kadinsky. I found them again recently: "The black is like a nothing without possibilities, a nothing that dies after the death of the sun, like an eternal silence, without future or even any hope of a future."

'Black is the definitive destruction, the fall without return, into nothingness. It represents the obscurity of origins: "The earth was a formless void and darkness covered the face of the abyss."[5] The planet will experience the destruction of climatic convulsions that defy the imagination: hurricanes, radioactive rain, fires, darkened sun, destruction of the ozone layer …

'The black horse can therefore only represent the end and hunger – famine. What does the rider of the black horse hold in his hand? Scales. He has been ordered to weigh the wheat, barley, oil and wine, thus restricting the earth's harvest. In other words, the black horse is the consequence of the three others. In fact, he is invited to attend the opening of the third seal. And we know that the number three represents – among other things – indissolubility.

'In the Cabbala, the number three is the acting principle. It is also the action of this subject and the verb, and finally also the object of this action, and its result. The black horse and the third seal reflect this ensemble: the famine and nothingness will be the outcome of a deregulation of pure thought, of moral and physical order. The black horse is the ultimate blow to humanity. I wonder how those who escape the nuclear strikes will survive without water and food.'

'Survivors,' murmured Dimitri. 'Will there be any?'

22 With one seated on the throne ...

Immediately after the suffering of those days the sun will be darkened, and the moon will not give its light; the stars will fall from heaven, and the powers of heaven will be shaken.

Matthew 24:29

There was a dirt track over the mountains, but he could never reach that summit in time. The dawn would be coming very soon and he wanted to see it and look into the east. There was Mecca. Faye raced his car until its light chassis quivered like a bird whose wings are clipped, giving all of himself to the task, looking for the peace which comes from curious contests, the ice-cream-eating derby, the public-speaker's symposium, the apple-polisher's jubilee.

He made the rise in time to see the sun lift out of the table of the east, and he stared into that direction, far far out, a hundred miles he hoped. Somewhere in the distance across the state line was one of the great gambling cities of the South-west, and Faye remembered a time he gambled round the clock, not even pausing at dawn when a great white light, no more than a shadow of the original blast somewhere further in the desert, had dazzled the gaming rooms and lit with an illumination colder than the neon tube above the green roulette cloth the harsh dead faces of the gamblers who had worn their way through the night.

Even now, there were factories out there, out somewhere in the desert, and the tons of ore in all the freight cars were being shuttled into the great mouth, and the factory laboured, it laboured like a gambler for twenty-four hours of the day, reducing the mountain of earth to a cup of destruction, and it was even possible that at this moment soldiers were filing into trenches a few miles from a loaded tower, and there they would wait, cowering in the dawn, while army officers explained their purpose in the words of newspaper stories, for the words belonged to the slobs, and the slobs hid the world with words.

So let it come, Faye thought, let this explosion come, and then another, and all the others, until the Sun God burned the earth. Let it come, he thought looking into the east at Mecca where the bombs ticked while he stood on a tiny rise of ground trying to see one hundred, two hundred, three hundred miles across the desert. Let it come, Faye begged, like a man praying for rain, let it come and clear the rot and the stench and the stink, let it come for all of everywhere, just so it comes and the world stands clear in the white dead dawn.

I closed the book which I had been reading – *The Deer Park* by Norman Mailer – and stared thoughtfully into space. Was such despair possible? If indeed it was, it could probably be experienced only by a few isolated individuals. But if, in February 2043, John's predictions were to come true, then this despair would spread like those green marks that appear on decomposing corpses. Survivors would be filled with despair and death would no longer appear like a plague but like a deliverance.

The survivors … I picked up the Book of Revelation again and tried to find something – a sign, a word – that brought hope. For some days

I had been dwelling on a few verses of chapter 7 that kept coming back into my head. If there was a light, this was where I would find it.

> 7:3 'Do not damage the earth or the sea or the trees, until we have marked the servants of our God with a seal on their foreheads.'
> 7:4 And I heard the number of those who were sealed, one hundred and forty-four thousand, sealed out of every tribe of the people of Israel:
> 7:5 From the tribe of Judah twelve thousand sealed, from the tribe of Reuben twelve thousand sealed, from the tribe of Gad twelve thousand sealed
> 7:6 from the tribe of Asher twelve thousand, from the tribe of Naphtali twelve thousand, from the tribe of Manasseh twelve thousand,
> 7:7 from the tribe of Simeon twelve thousand, from the tribe of Levi twelve thousand, from the tribe of Issachar twelve thousand,
> 7:8 from the tribe of Zebulun twelve thousand, from the tribe of Joseph twelve thousand, from the tribe of Benjamin twelve thousand sealed.

Indeed. What else could this mean but that the Creator had decided to save a few souls?

> And I heard the number of those who were sealed, one hundred and forty-four thousand, sealed out of every tribe of the people of Israel.

But why 144,000? Was it a symbolic number? If so, why? And what had these people done to deserve salvation?

Although no meeting had been planned for the immediate future, I decided to submit my findings to my friends as soon as possible.

Because of work we were only able to meet two months later, in the middle of January 1998; there were just four of us, Dimitri having returned to Greece for family reasons. As soon as the meeting started David handed each one of us a page with notes from his computer. This is what it said:

Judah = 12,000 = 3
Reuben = 12,000 = 3
Gad = 12,000 = 3
Asher = 12,000 = 3
Naphtali = 12,000 = 3
Manasseh = 12,000 = 3
Simeon = 12,000 = 3
Levi = 12,000 = 3
Issachar = 12,000 = 3
Zebulun = 12,000 = 3
Joseph = 12,000 = 3
Benjamin = 12,000 = 3
Total = 144,000 = 36 or 9

'The Seventh Day Adventists were convinced that this passage and this number referred to them. Meanwhile Jehovah's Witnesses used to preach to all those who were prepared to listen that the world would end when they had 144,000 members. However, they had to change their story when the 144,001st member joined.'

Myriam noted: 'In my opinion, only one number matters: number 9.'

'Why?'

'It sums up the human condition based on the example of the word "Emeth", Truth.'

'Which has a value of 9.'

'Precisely, as does the first man, Adam. Remember; divine truth equals 10. But since the original sin, human beings are unable to go beyond the ninth degree. To me, the number 144,000 does not refer to the actual number of survivors but has a symbolic value. John is only trying to convey the fact that there will be survivors, but they will all be the "servants of God". In other words, men of goodwill, men who are as close as possible to the absolute truth, and thus of the figure 9 that represents it. How many survivors will there be? No one can tell.'

David was smiling: 'You have always insisted that we prove what we put forward: where is the proof?'

Myriam remained unperturbed: 'Precisely in the number 144,000 and in its direct correspondence with the word "Emeth". Emeth equals 441. You can see that the word is there but inverted in the number 144. In Emeth, God is at the end of the word; he is Omega. In 144, God is at the beginning of the word; he is Alpha. In short, we have Adam (9), and thus the man, and we have the word "truth", which is confirmed twice. This seems rather convincing to me. I repeat, only men of goodwill who have lived an exemplary life will be spared.'

'Do you realize the consequences of this statement? It means there will be a kind of last judgement. On one side the chosen, on the other the damned.'

Myriam quoted verse 8 in chapter 21:

But as for the cowardly, the faithless, the polluted, the murderers,
the fornicators, the sorcerers, the idolaters, and all liars ...

Then she added: 'On one side truth, on the other falsehood. Evil and good. The last act in the fight of man against man, of the Lamb against the beast. The ultimate face-off between God and the Devil.'

'But then,' Jean-Pierre asked, rather surprised, 'where is this famous "Celestial Jerusalem" predicted by John? I quote:

> And in the spirit he carried me away to a great, high mountain and showed me the holy city Jerusalem coming down out of heaven from God. It has the glory of God and a radiance like a very rare jewel, like jasper, clear as crystal.

'In fact, John describes it with geometrical precision:

> It has a great, high wall with twelve gates, and at the gates twelve angels, and on the gates are inscribed the names of the twelve tribes of the Israelites; on the east three gates, on the north three gates, on the south three gates, and on the west three gates. And the wall of the city has twelve foundations, and on them are the twelve names of the twelve apostles of the Lamb.
>
> The angel who talked to me had a measuring rod of gold to measure the city and its gates and walls. The city lies foursquare, its length the same as its width; and he measured the city with his rod, fifteen hundred miles; its length and width and height are equal. He also measured its wall, one hundred and forty-four cubits by human measurement, which the angel was using.'[1]

Myriam looked up as if to call on heaven as her witness and cried out: 'Forgive them, Lord, they have eyes and they do not see; they have ears and do not hear.' Leaning towards David, she whispered: 'There is no "Celestial Jerusalem".' She stood up and walked to the blackboard. 'Let's look at the verse again:

12 doors
12 angels
12 tribes
Total? 36 or 9!

3 gates to the east
3 gates to the north
3 gates to the south
3 gates to the west
12 foundations
12 apostles
Total? 36 or 9!

'Let's go on:

12,000 stadia in length
12,000 stadia in width
12,000 stadia in height
Total? 36 or 9!

'And furthermore:

A rampart of 144 cubits
1 + 4 + 4 = 9

'And to conclude, I shall take the liberty of reminding you that the West Wall or Wailing Wall that was part of terrestrial Jerusalem stands 18 metres high, or ... 9! In addition, as if he feared we might not understand, St John tries to clarify it further by adding: "The angel measured by human measurement"! That can only mean that the measure every man must try and achieve is 9. The Truth! Always and again Truth! There is no salvation for those who do not follow this path. In fact, the word "rampart" gives a definitive confirmation:

The rampart (החומה) = 64 or 10

'In this case the rampart is none other than God. It is very clear. This Jerusalem has nothing celestial about it. It is yet again a metaphor used by the apostle to try and make us understand that it is up to us to create our own terrestrial Jerusalem, which will rise upward to the Eternal. Because it is not up to God to come down to the level of his creature; rather it is up to the creature to rise towards God. God cannot inhabit an impure city, inhabited by impure people. The Jerusalem described by John is that which his heart was hankering after. A Jerusalem cleansed of all evil. The Jerusalem that God had promised to enter even before the creation of the "Celestial Jerusalem". But ... ' She did not finish her sentence, as if something was worrying her.

I asked what was wrong.

'It's nothing,' she said evasively.

'Come on, Myriam, what's going on?'

She finally replied: 'After reading this text every day for months I have come to know it by heart, as you all do as well. But every time I read it, I find something strange, something new, a clue which had escaped me the day before. For instance ... ' She hesitated for a moment then wrote:

At once I was in the spirit, and there in heaven stood a throne,
with one seated on the throne.[2]

'I have analyzed this verse from every angle. It fascinated me. And do you know why?'

David was the first to answer: 'Yes, I know; I myself have wondered about it a lot.' He said slowly: 'One ... '

Myriam nodded in agreement: 'Quite. One. Why does St John use such a vague expression? He mentions elders, the dragon, the beasts, the woman, the Lamb, he mentions the number of gates, of stadia and then suddenly "one".'

It is true that there was something imperfect in this formula.

Myriam continued: 'I have also calculated the value of the word. The result did not answer my question.'

'What is its value?'

'361.

'10!'

'Absolutely. 10, the symbol of the Almighty ... '

'So it would be God sitting on that throne?

The young woman suddenly looked rather uneasy. She added rather uncertainly: 'Or Jesus ... '

I could not believe my ears. I cried out: 'Jesus?'

'Same numerical value as "one" ... (מישהו) Jesus (ישׁי) 316. There again, the symbol of divine truth.'

I repeated unconsciously: '361 and 316 ... '

'Strange, isn't it?'

I agreed and said: 'Not for a Christian ... In all objectivity, I am convinced that Jesus – in spite of the status ascribed to him by various people – had definitely reached a higher level of knowledge and divine truth.'

Myriam smiled rather cheekily: 'Unless it is not God or Jesus on the throne but only ... some "one".'

23 The seventh seal

STARING AT HIS computer, David whispered: 'One hour. Just one hour and over 4 billion dead. It's completely mad.'

'And yet … It could happen.' I stood up and looked distractedly out of the window. It was night-time. The street was deserted. It was three weeks since our last meeting. Myriam had returned to Israel. Dimitri and Jean-Pierre were getting ready to go on holiday for the festive season.

I wandered back towards David, looked over his shoulder and read the list that he had drawn up two days before. It consisted of a series of verses, between chapters 8 and 20, that all mentioned some aspects of this end of the world. I read the list for the third time, as if to convince myself of I do not know what:

Then God's temple in heaven was opened, and the ark of his covenant was seen within his temple; and there were flashes of lightning, rumblings, peals of thunder, an earthquake, and heavy hail.[1]

Then the angel took the censer and filled it with fire from the altar and threw it on the earth; and there were peals of thunder, rumblings, flashes of lightning, and an earthquake.[2]

And there came flashes of lightning, rumblings, peals of thunder, and a violent earthquake, such as had not occurred since people were upon the earth, so violent was that earthquake.[3]

And huge hailstones, each weighing about a hundred pounds, dropped from heaven on people, until they cursed God for the plague of the hail, so fearful was that plague.[4]

And every island fled away, and no mountains were to be found.[5]

... and it became like the blood of a corpse, and every living thing in the sea died.[6]

And on another page, David had drawn another list, consisting of contemporary terms that could have corresponded to the apostle's descriptions by virtue of their numerical value:

Lightning = 357 or 6
Nuclear missiles = 492 or 6

Voices = 542 or 2
Howling = 704 or 2

Thunder = 360 or 9
Bombs = 666 or 9

Earthquake = 734 or 5
Bombing = 671 or 5

Hail = 211 or 4
Atomic explosion = 1,543 or 4

Large hailstones = 525 or 3
Nuclear warheads = 1,002 or 3

Yes, indeed, this list was quite random and obviously subjective, but it was nevertheless eloquent. I turned to Dimitri and then to Jean-Pierre: 'What do you think of all this?'

'As far as I am concerned,' said Dimitri, 'I do not agree with it. I see it as a random mixture.'

'I feel the same,' said Jean-Pierre. 'Furthermore, I do not see the value of trying to confirm what we know already: that there will be a nuclear war that will be devastating. But we still do not know the outcome.'

'The outcome?' David asked in a surprised voice. 'But we do know the outcome: a devastated planet, a handful of survivors ... '

In response, Jean-Pierre opened the Book of Revelation at chapter 20 and read:

> *When the thousand years are ended, Satan will be released from his prison and will come out to deceive the nations at the four corners of the earth, Gog and Magog, in order to gather them for battle; they are as numerous as the sands of the sea. They marched up over the breadth of the earth and surrounded the camp of the saints and the beloved city.[7]*

'Did you hear? "Gog and Magog" who are now allies in the war ... will lay siege to the "beloved City". I find it quite incomprehensible. How should Gog (China and their allies) join forces with Magog (the United States and their allies) – because it is indeed an alliance – to conquer the "beloved city", which is obviously Jerusalem? Two enemies who have fought to a state of complete exhaustion and who yet find the strength to turn against Israel after having joined forces. You must admit that it is very strange.'

Dimitri agreed: 'All the more so because they are already very weak.'

'Whatever their military weakness, why turn against Israel?'

It was difficult to make this piece fit into the puzzle of the general conflict.

'And then,' Jean-Pierre continued, 'there is also the first verse of chapter 14:

Then I looked, and there was the Lamb, standing on Mount Zion!
And with him were one hundred and forty-four thousand who had
his name and his Father's name written on their foreheads.

'The survivors, the hundred and forty-four thousand, will therefore be gathered in Israel?'

No one seemed able to find a solution to this imbroglio. Gog and Magog allies? Israel their joint target? How could we unravel all the intricacies of this puzzle? Something was telling us that we were close to the final resolution of this Apocalypse, but it still escaped us.

Around midnight I had a sudden thought, which I immediately conveyed to my friends: 'And what if it was not Israel?'

'What do you mean?'

'If Israel was only a symbol … like the "beloved city" and Zion.'

'I agree that it is indeed possible. But the symbol of what?'

'Of a region … the Middle East for instance. If the final battle … '

I stopped suddenly. 'Yes, yes … That is the proof!' I grabbed my notes. 'Listen:

16:11 … and cursed the God of heaven because of their pains and
sores, and they did not repent of their deeds.
16:12 The sixth angel poured his bowl on the great river Euphrates,
and its water was dried up in order to prepare the way for the kings
from the east.

16:15 'See, I am coming like a thief! Blessed is the one who stays awake and is clothed, not going about naked and exposed to shame.'
16:16 And they assembled them at the place that in Hebrew is called Armageddon.

'Everything seems to point to the Middle East: the Euphrates, the kings from the East, Armageddon! Armageddon ... the final battle!'

I suddenly had a thought that made me very excited and I asked David to find the numerical value of the words Middle East, the beloved City, the camp of the saints, and Zion. This was the result:

Middle East = 741 or 3
The beloved City = 309 or 3
The camp of the Saints = 903 or 3
Zion = 156 or 3

I was jubilant: 'So I was right, it was the Middle East! That is where the last act will take place.'

My friends tried to calm me down a little.

'You are obviously right,' Dimitri said. 'But I still cannot understand the motive. What strategic interest can there be? The Middle East may have been spared during the conflict but its destruction is inevitable. Driven by the winds, the radioactivity that will poison the atmosphere will eventually arrive in the Middle East. The destruction of the ozone layer will also affect it. But how can you explain that China and its former enemies should suddenly become accomplices?'

The arguments put forward by the Greek were perfectly logical. There was a fault in my reasoning.

'Moreover,' Jean-Pierre said, 'we also know that this part of the world has been the scene of conflicts for half a century. On one side we have the Israelis, on the other the Arab countries. It is difficult to imagine them joining forces against a common enemy, even China. They will certainly choose sides as soon as the conflict starts. So who are these "kings of the east" mentioned by St John?'

We were groping in the dark yet again. We had no other choice but to send Myriam a resumé of our hypotheses. We did this in the hope that she might have some explanation. We only had two days left before we all went our separate ways on holiday.

The day before our departure we received an e-mail from our friend.

Dear friends,

I could not find any answer to your question, except the one that I submit to you now and that will surprise you, I think. After a while, I became interested in another verse, in another chapter:

21:1 Then I saw a new heaven, and a new earth; for the first heaven and the first earth had passed away, and the sea was no more.

This verse naturally reminded me of Israel and its history.

The reign of King Saul, the first king of Israel, lasted from 1035 to 1015 or twenty years. That of King David lasted from 1015 to 975 or forty years. If we add up these two reigns we get sixty years. Now, these two kings were first and foremost warrior kings who spent most of the time warring with their neighbours in order to consolidate the borders of their kingdom. We have to wait until King Solomon's arrival before witnessing peace and harmony and prosperity in the region.

If we take 1948 of our era, the date when the state of Israel was created, and we add the number of years that Saul and David reigned (sixty years) it is possible to envisage – history is always repeating itself – that *peace in the Middle East will only become a reality in 2008.* Not before.

In the light of this verse, from this date onward the sons of Abraham and Ishmael and all the Christians in the region will be part of one and the same camp: that of fraternity and peace. Not another drop of blood will be shed. Not another life will be taken from this land through violence. If you calculate the numerical value of 'new land' you will get 608 or 5.

Compare this expression with 'united land' and you will get 509 or 5.

Strangely enough, the word 'sea', which has a value of 50 or 5, has the same numerical value as 'nationality', 77 or 5.

Consequently, what should we conclude when John writes: 'and the sea was no more'?

But knowing your scepticism, I have searched for a confirmation of this theory. I found it in verse 9 of chapter 17:

'This calls for a mind that has wisdom: the seven heads are seven mountains on which the woman is seated; also, they are seven kings ... '

So, show some wisdom – as John asks us to:

Hills = 481 or 4
Land = 697 or 4
Seven kings = 517 or 4
The Middle East = 751 or 4

I believe the message is clear. We have confirmed it – as did Father Alexander before us: the West has dominated Asia, the Third World and the East for centuries. We have seen that this seated woman, this whore, Babylon, is none other than Magog and that she represents the West in this new war.

That is why I interpret the verse in the following manner: The seven heads are none other than the seven countries on which the woman (the West) is seated, but they also symbolize the East in general. In fact, if you have any doubt, you only need to read verse 15 of chapter 17 to find confirmation of what I am saying:

' ... *The waters that you saw, where the whore is seated,*
are peoples and multitudes and nations and languages ... '

Note the words: peoples, multitudes, nations, languages ...

And finally, a final argument, which emphasizes the apostle's statement:

5:6 Then I saw ... a Lamb ... as if it had been slaughtered,
having seven horns and seven eyes ...

Do you know how many countries surround Israel? Six. Lebanon, Egypt, Syria, Jordan, Iraq and Saudi Arabia. And with Israel we get seven, like the seven-branched candlestick. I leave you to draw your own conclusions ...

Best wishes, Myriam.

We spent the evening reading the document over and over again. If Myriam's interpretation was correct – and everything led us to believe that it was – there were still two questions that remained unanswered: Why did Gog and Magog move from the enemy camp to that of the allies? And why did they decide to fight a last battle in this region of the world?

Just as we were leaving, David suddenly asked me: 'Have you ever read *Paradise Lost* by Milton?

I replied that I had not.

'Lucifer says: "Better to reign in hell, than serve in heaven." I think that there are two reasons why the final battle will be fought in the Middle East. The first reason is to be found in this sentence of Lucifer's. We know that the second beast, he who will rule over China, will be a portrait of the first beast, Adolf Hitler. Like him, he will quench his thirst with the blood of men. Like him, he will pursue the same aim: to rule the planet. Like him, he will throw himself into a mindless policy of scorched earth. Like him, he will cry out among the ruins as he laments China's betrayal: "The army has betrayed me! My generals are good for nothing. It's finished. The country is lost, but it was not quite ready or strong enough for the mission I had entrusted to it. Since the war is lost, the people must be lost too. There is no need to worry about what they will do to survive. On the contrary, it is better they should all be annihilated because our country proved to be the weakest. Anyway, only the weakest have survived." This is the speech the beast will make, but with one exception: unlike his predecessor, he will have vanquished Magog, or what will be left of it, and Magog will be forced to obey him and follow him to the site of the last battle – to Armageddon. Contrary to what we thought, they will not be accomplices but one will domi-nate the other and be forced to follow him into the flames of the ultimate fire. As John's verse specifies: " … and cursed the God of heaven because of their pains and sores, and they did not repent of their deeds."'

Still confused, I asked: 'But why the Middle East?'

'For two reasons. A madman would not allow one small island to survive. Even if the days of that small island are numbered. He would pursue his mad mission to the bitter end. To the very limit: "Better to rule in hell than serve in heaven." The second reason is purely strategic. At the end of this hour of hell man will have regressed almost to the stone age. And the only place in the world were there will still be a source of energy – the oldest kind – will be the Middle East: petrol. The beast will do anything to lay his hands on it. And this means destroying the towns that have survived, but this time with conventional weapons.'

I swallowed with difficulty and remained silent until we entered the station. 'David … From the very beginning when we started this adventure I have been obsessed by three verses … three obscure verses.'

He gave me a questioning look.

When the Lamb opened the seventh seal, there was silence in heaven for about half an hour.[8]

… And when he shouted , the seven thunders sounded. And when the seven thunders had sounded, I was about to write, but I heard a voice from heaven saying, 'Seal up what the seven thunders have said, and do not write it down'.[9]

'Why this silence of half an hour? What is the mystery of the seven thunders that John was not allowed to write down?'

David looked me in the eye: 'We are in 2043. In Armageddon. The two armies are facing each other. There is a half-hour silence. The mystery of the seven thunders is about to happen ... '

I muttered: 'I do not understand ... '

'I must go now. I shall miss my train.'

I saw him disappear into the carriage while I remained on the platform, motionless, waiting for I do not know what. As the train was leaving David's face appeared at the window.

He shouted: 'What did God tell the visionary of Patmos?'

That was all. I left, and walked away slowly ... In my head God's words tolled like a knell: 'Seal up what the seven thunders have said, and do not write it down.'

Epilogue

AT THE BEGINNING of this book I mentioned that we had not intended to publish the results of our work. I explained that an event that happened in September 1998 then made us question our decision not to publish. This is how *Le Monde* of Wednesday 2 September 1998 describes the circumstances surrounding that event.

North Korea launches ballistic missile over Japan
Japanese government holds crisis meeting

After the Pakistani and Indian atomic tests, the spectre of nuclear war reappeared over Asia on this 31 August. Launched by North Korea, an experimental ballistic missile – which would be capable of carrying nuclear warheads – flew over Japan before crashing into the Pacific. Did North Korea, the last communist dinosaur of the Cold War, risk war – as was claimed by a high official of the Japanese government – by carrying out without notice this missile launch over the Nipponese archipelago? The Japanese Prime Minister, Keizo Obuchi, admitted having been warned in advance about the preparation for this nuclear test, probably by his secret service because the government in Pyongyang had said nothing.

However, on 1 September, the Japanese government held an extraordinary meeting to discuss the 'management of the crisis'. No details are known about this meeting. But a government spokesman had already announced that Tokyo intended to 'protest strongly' to Pyongyang. Diplomatic relations do not exist between Japan and North Korea.

As a retaliatory measure, Japan and the other countries of the consortium charged with financing the construction of two nuclear reactors in North Korea have already suspended the signing of the agreement due to to take place on Monday. Four years ago, Pyongyang and Washington concluded an agreement whereby the North Korean nuclear programme for military purposes would be frozen, in exchange for two light-water cooled reactors built by a consortium that included the United States, South Korea and Japan. Washington had also made a commitment itself to supply North Korea with 500,000 tons of fuel per year, but Congress blocked the necessary funds because Pyongyang had supplied missiles to Pakistan. North Korea responded by implying that it might relaunch its nuclear programme.

Through its Secretary of State, Madeleine Albright, the United States, which protects Japan under its 'nuclear umbrella', expressed its 'concern' over this experimental launch, which was considered 'successful' but described as 'serious' though 'not completely surprising' by the Pentagon. In spite of this incident, American and North Korean representatives have resumed their discussions on nuclear questions in New York.

The missile is thought to have been a Taepo-Dong with a striking range of 1,500 to 2,000 kilometres. Tokyo is about 1,000 kilometres from North Korea and seems now within range of this new missile, which confuses the strategic data in the region. Besides the tactical Scud B and C missiles (with a striking range of 300 to 500 kilometres) that were acquired from the former USSR and that it tested in the 1980s, North Korea has already deployed Rodong 1 missiles whose range (approximately 1,000 kilometres) would enable them to reach some parts of Japan. In 1993, Pyongyang had already caused a big stir in Tokyo by testing a medium-range Rodong 1 missile in the sea off the Japanese coast, thus demonstrating that part of the west coast of Japan lies within its reach.

Today, North Korea is concentrating on the development of two longer-range missiles: the Taepo Dong 1 and the Taepo Dong 2, capable respectively of hitting targets 1,500 and 4,000 kilometres away and carrying traditional explosive charges of up to 1 tonne. The North Korean stock of armaments is thought to total 150 missiles of all kinds. North Korea is also suspected of having exported missiles – namely Scuds – to countries such as Iran and Syria.

Notes

PROLOGUE

1   See the complete text at the end of this book.
2   Luke 22:8; John 18:16; 20:2–10; 21:15–23; Acts 3:1–11; 4:13 and 19.
3   Acts 8.
4   *Historia*, December 1998.
5   A town in Cappadocia in Turkey.
6   A Jewish-Christian heretic who taught in Asia Minor at the end of the first century. To him, the world was the work of a power foreign to the supreme God, the unknown God. Jesus was a man only, born of Joseph and Mary; the Holy Spirit descended on him at his baptism in the River Jordan, but it left him before the Passion.
7   *Adversus haereses*, V, 33, 3.

CHAPTER 1   *The number of the beast*

1   13:17
2   13:18
3   Sharou Ken in Assyrian. King of Assyria.
4   The oral law.
5   Term derived from the root *dorash*, which in Biblical Hebrew means 'to search for', 'to examine'. At the time of the Second Temple it acquired the meaning of educating and study (see 2 Chronicles 13:22).
6   Plural of *Hassid*, pious man.
7   The term cabbala, literally 'tradition', describes the origin of a doctrinal tradition, based on the Bible (apart from the Pentateuch), and in particular the transmission, at first oral, then written, of teachings concerning the practice of religion. It was only in the eighth century that this term meant a particular doctrinal system and in the fourteenth century that the thinkers of this current were called 'cabbalists' in preference to any other designation.

8   See the table of the Hebrew alphabet and its corresponding numeration at the end of this book.
9   Sometimes translated 'I will be what I will be'.

CHAPTER 2   *A mind that has wisdom…*

1   All work in scientific or theological fields, and in order to respect and protect their professional lives, I will not reveal their true identities.
2   That which relates to eschatology, that is, the study of the end of mankind and of the world.
3   In the Book of Daniel.
4   The name 'Septuagint' given to that version comes from the fact that, on the orders of Ptolemy Philadelphus, seventy-two Israelite scholars translated the whole Hebrew Bible into Greek in seventy days.
5   To be precise, works from the Apocrypha of the Old Testament.
6   20:7–9 and Ezekiel 38 and 39.
7   Islam of course did not yet exist in the time of John. We use the word in the sense it was to acquire later.
8   13:18.
9   17:9.
10 11:7.
11 13:2.

CHAPTER 4   *Gog and Magog*

1   William L. Shirer, *The Rise and Fall of the Third Reich*, Arrow, London, 1991 edition.

CHAPTER 5   *The false prophet*

1   From Gregor Ziemmer, *Education for Death*, London and New York, 1941.
2   13:1.
3   17:3.
4   13:11.
5   John Toland, *Hitler*, Robert Laffont, 1976.
6   Plural of *amora*, name of the wise men who for several generations discussed doctrinal points.

CHAPTER 6   *Babylon the great, mother of whores*

1   The word Lamb-Gadia is the Aramaic term used in the time of Jesus, and which the Jews quote still in their liturgy of Pessah (Easter) when they recite a *Haggada* or *Hadgadia*.

2   Isaiah 13:19

CHAPTER 7   *The dragon*

1   Isaiah 27:1.

2   12:3, 12:4, 12:7, 12:9, 12:13, 12:16, 12:17, 13:2, 13:4, 16:13, 20:2.

3   This is the name by which Jehovah chose to reveal himself to Moses in the burning bush. See Father Alexander's explanation in chapter 1.

CHAPTER 8   *Two witnesses*

1   Revelation 11:3.

2   Numbers 35:30

3   William L. Shirer, *The Rise and Fall of the Third Reich*, Arrow, London, 1991 edition.

CHAPTER 9   *Twenty-four elders*

1   1 Chronicles 24:1–19.

CHAPTER 10   *A woman clothed in sun*

1   On 23 April 1945 Himmler met Count Bernadotte in Lubeck. He told him that he was taking over since Hitler was on the point of dying, and he was ready to negotiate Germany's surrender. Hitler found out about this and dismissed Himmler, who fled to Schleswig where he was arrested by the British. His suicide enabled him to escape the judgement of the International Military Tribunal at Nuremberg.

2   Heydrich was assassinated in Prague in 1942 by two Czech soldiers who had been trained in London and parachuted in to Czechoslovakia.

3   6:2.

CHAPTER 11 *Locusts*

1 6:8.
2 In contrast to the black shirts worn by the Italian Fascists under Mussolini.
3 Exodus 10:4, 10:12.
4 Judges 6:5.
5 Joel 1:6.
6 9:7, 9:8, 9:9.
7 *Le voyage de Patrice Périot*, 10.

CHAPTER 12 *Abaddon and Apollyon*

1 *Les grandes batailles de la seconde guerre mondiale*, Presse de la Cité. Paris 1981

CHAPTER 13 *Sands of the sea*

1 Gérald Messadié, *L'Homme qui devint Dieu*, Les Sources, Robert Laffont.
2 Surah 7:179, Al 'Araf.
3 Surah 101:1–5.
4 Surah 73:17–18.

CHAPTER 14 *Fire from heaven*

1 13:11.
2 13:12.
3 13:13.
4 See Chapter 5.
5 See Chapter 10.
6 See Chapter 13.
7 At the moment of the advance of the Soviet troops in 1945, von Braun, accompanied by his team, withdrew towards the American troops, to whom he surrendered with 300 of his fellow scientists and several examples of the V-2. He was taken to the United States,where he was assigned by the American army to repair the V-2 rockets brought over from Peenemünde, and then to develop the weapons derived from the V-2 such as the Viking, the Aerobee, the Redstone, etc. In 1955 he became an American citizen.

8   17:3.

9   Svetlana Alexievitch, *La Supplication: Tchernobyl, chroniques du monde après l'Apocalypse*, Editions J.-C. Lattès.

10   Ecclesiasticus, 39:29.

11   Psalm 148:8.

12   See (among others) Basil Hall Chamberlain, *Japanese Things*, Charles E Tuttle Co. Inc., 1971.

13   Politician, 1864–1948, previously a journalist in China and Korea. Became a Japanese member of parliament in 1902 and was re-elected fourteen times.

14   *Apocalypse de l'atome*, Fernand Gigon, Editions Del Duca.

CHAPTER 15   *The second Revelation*

1   John 1:1.

2   Matthew 24:7.

3   John H Alexander, *L'Apocalypse, La Maison de la Bible*, Geneva and Paris.

CHAPTER 16   *The hour, the day, the month and the year*

1   17:12.

2   18:10.

CHAPTER 17   *A scarlet beast*

1   17:3.

2   Napoleon said this in 1816 after reading *Journey to China and Tartary* by Lord Macartney, Britain's first ambassador to China.

3   *Encyclopedia Britannica, Encyclopedia Universalis* and *Quid*.

4   *Rélations internationales et stratégiques*, no. 21, Spring 1996.

5   E. Fouquoire-Brillet, 'La politique nucléaire de la Chine', *Relations Internationales*, no. 68, Winter 1991.

6   Quid, 1998, p. 972.

7   J-M Malik, 'Chinese Debate on Military Strategy, Trends & Portents', *Journal of Northeast Asian Studies*, Summer 1990, vol. 9, no. 2.

8   *Le Monde*, 9 April 1997.

9   *AFP*, no. 231924, May 1997.

10 When we were putting the finishing touches to this book, and for the third time in 30 years, by a referendum on 14 December 1998 the Puerto Ricans rejected the idea of becoming the 51st state of the Union. Compared with the count of 1993, it failed by a small amount: 50.6 per cent compared with 46.5 per cent. The independents received only 2.5 per cent of the vote.

11 See *Bulletin of Atomic Scientists*, July 1942, and *Le Figaro*, 14 February 1950.

CHAPTER 18   *Ten kings*
1   17:3.
2   17:4 and 5.
3   17:16.

CHAPTER 19   *Rider of the red horse*
1   Information confirmed by UNICEF.
2   Information taken from *Encyclopedia Britannica* and *Encyclopedia Universalis*.

CHAPTER 21   *A black horse*
1   Unit of measurement of pressure, used particularly in meteorology to measure atmospheric pressure.
2   8:10
3   Psalm 104:5–6.
4   6:5, 6:6.
5   Genesis 1:2.

CHAPTER 22   *With one seated on the throne*
1   21:12–17.
2   4:2.

CHAPTER 23 *The seventh seal*

1   11:19.
2   8:5.
3   16:18.
4   16:21.
5   16:20.
6   16:3.
7   20:7–9.
8   8:1.
9   10:3–4.

Numerical values of the Hebrew alphabet

1	א	Alef	30	ל	Lamed
2	ב	Beith	40	מ	Mem
3	ג	Guimel	50	נ	Noun
4	ד	Daleth	60	ס	Samekh
5	ה	Hé	70	ע	Ayin
6	ו	Vav	80	פ	Pé
7	ז	Zaïn	90	צ	Tsadé
8	ח	Heith	100	ק	Qof
9	ט	Teirh	200	ר	Reish
10	י	Yod	300	ש	Shin
20	כ	Kaf	400	ת	Tav

Appendix

Editor's Note: The text in this appendix is based upon the New Revised Standard Version of the Bible. There are, however, minor modifications in accordance with the author's own translation from the Greek and Hebrew.

THE REVELATION TO JOHN

1 The revelation of Jesus Christ, which God gave him to show his servants what must soon take place; he made it known by sending his angel to his servant John, 2 who testified to the word of God and to the testimony of Jesus Christ, even to all that he saw. 3 Blessed is the one who reads aloud the words of the prophecy, and blessed are those who hear and who keep what is written in it; for the time is near.

4 John to the seven churches that are in Asia: Grace to you and peace from him who is and who was and who is to come, and from the seven spirits who are before his throne, 5 and from Jesus Christ, the faithful witness, the firstborn of the dead, and the ruler of the kings of the earth. To him who loves us and freed us from our sins by his blood, 6 and made us to be a kingdom, priests serving his God and Father, to him be glory and dominion for ever and ever Amen.

7 Look! He is coming with the clouds; every eye will see him, even those who pierced him; and on his account all the tribes of the earth will wail. So it is to be. Amen.

8 'I am the Alpha and the Omega', says the Lord God, who is and who was and who is to come, the Almighty.

9 I, John, your brother who share with you in Jesus the persecution and the kingdom and the patient endurance, was on the island called Patmos because of the word of God and the testimony of Jesus. 10 I was in the spirit on the Lord's day, and I heard behind me a loud voice like a trumpet 11 saying, 'Write in a book what you see and send it to the seven churches, to Ephesus, to Smyrna, to Pergamum, to

Thyatira, to Sardis, to Philadelphia, and to Laodicea.' 12 Then I turned to see whose voice it was that spoke to me, and on turning I saw seven golden lampstands, 13 and in the midst of the lampstands I saw one like the Son of Man, clothed with a long robe and with a golden sash across his chest. 14 His head and his hair were white as white wool, white as snow; his eyes were like a flame of fire, 15 his feet were like burnished bronze, refined as in a furnace, and his voice was like the sound of many waters. 16 In his right hand he held seven stars, and from his mouth came a sharp, two-edged sword, and his face was like the sun shining with full force. 17 When I saw him, I fell at his feet as though dead. But he placed his right hand on me, saying, 'Do not be afraid; I am the first and the last, 18 and the living one. I was dead, and see, I am alive for ever and ever; and I have the keys of Death and of Hades. 19 Now write what you have seen, what is, and what is to take place after this. 20 As for the mystery of the seven stars that you saw in my right hand, and the seven golden lampstands: the seven stars are the angels of the seven churches.

2 'To the angel of the church in Ephesus write: These are the words of him who holds the seven stars in his right hand, who walks among the seven golden lampstands:
2 'I know your works, your toil and your patient endurance. I know that you cannot tolerate evildoers; you have tested those who claim to be apostles but are not, and have found them to be false. 3 I also know that you are enduring patiently and bearing up for the sake of my name, and that you have not grown weary. 4 But I have this against you, that you have abandoned the love you had at first. 5 Remember then from what you have fallen; repent, and do the works you did at first. If not, I will come to you and remove your lampstand from its place, unless you repent. 6 Yet this is to your credit: you hate the works of the Nicolaitans, which I also hate. 7 Let anyone who has an ear listen to what the Spirit is saying to the churches. To everyone who conquers, I will give permission to eat from the tree of life that is in the paradise of God.

8 'And to the angel of the church in Smyrna write: These are the words of the first and the last, who was dead and came to life:
9 'I know your affliction and your poverty, even though you are rich. I know the slander on the part of those who say that they are Jews and are not, but are a syna-

gogue of Satan. 10 Do not fear what you are about to suffer. Beware, the devil is about to throw some of you into prison so that you may be tested, and for ten days you will have affliction. Be faithful until death, and I will give you the crown of life. 11 Let anyone who has an ear listen to what the Spirit is saying to the churches. Whoever conquers will not be harmed by the second death.

12 'And to the angel of the church in Pergamum write: These are the words of him who has the sharp two-edged sword:
13 'I know where you are living, where Satan's throne is. Yet you are holding fast to my name,and you did not deny your faith in me even in the days of Antipas my witness, my faithful one, who was killed among you, where Satan lives. 14 But I have a few things against you: you have some there who hold to the teaching of Balaam, who taught Balak to put a stumbling-block before the people of Israel, so that they would eat food sacrificed to idols and practise fornication. 15 So you also have some who hold to the teaching of the Nicolaitans. 16 Repent then. If not, I will come to you soon and make war against them with the sword of my mouth. 17 Let anyone who has an ear listen to what the Spirit is saying to the churches. To everyone who conquers I will give a white stone, and on the white stone is written a new name that no one knows except the one who receives it.

18 'And to the angel of the church in Thyatira write: These are the words of the Son of God, who has eyes like a flame of fire, and whose feet are like burnished bronze:
19 'I know your works – your love, faith, service, and patient endurance. I know that your last works are greater than the first. 20 But I have this against you: you tolerate that woman Jezebel, who calls herself a prophet and is teaching and beguiling my servants to practise fornication and to eat food sacrificed to idols. 21 I gave her time to repent, but she refuses to repent of her fornication. 22 Beware, I am throwing her on a bed, and those who commit adultery with her I am throwing into great distress, unless they repent of her doings; 23 and I will strike her children dead. And all the churches will know that I am the one who searches minds and hearts, and I will give to each of you as your works deserve. 24 But to the rest of you in Thyatira, who do not hold this teaching, who have not learned what some call "the deep things of Satan", to you I say, I do not lay on you any other burden; 25 only hold fast to what you have until I come.

26 To everyone who conquers and continues to do my works to the end,

I will give authority over the nations;

27 to rule them with an iron rod, as when clay pots are shattered – 28 even as I also received authority from my Father. To the one who conquers I will also give the morning star. 29 Let anyone who has an ear listen to what the Spirit is saying to the churches.

3 'And to the angel of the church in Sardis write: These are the words of him who has the seven spirits of God and the seven stars:

'I know your works; you have a name for being alive, but you are dead. 2 Wake up, and strengthen what remains and is at the point of death, for I have not found your works perfect in the sight of my God. 3 Remember then what you received and heard; obey it, and repent. If you do not wake up, I will come like a thief, and you will not know at what hour I will come to you. 4 Yet you have still a few people in Sardis who have not soiled their clothes; they will walk with me, dressed in white, for they are worthy. 5 If you conquer, you will be clothed like them in white robes, and I will not blot your name out of the book of life; I will confess your name before my Father and before his angels. 6 Let anyone who has an ear listen to what the Spirit is saying to the churches.

7 And to the angel of the church in Philadelphia write:

These are the words of the holy one, the true one, who has the key of

David, who opens and no one will shut, who shuts and no one opens:

8 'I know your works. Look, I have set before you an open door, which no one is able to shut. I know that you have but little power, and yet you have kept my word and have not denied my name. 9 I will make those of the synagogue of Satan who say that they are Jews and are not, but are lying – I will make them come and bow down before your feet, and they will learn that I have loved you. 10 Because you have kept my word of patient endurance, I will keep you from the hour of trial that is coming on the whole world to test the inhabitants of the earth. 11 I am coming soon; hold fast to what you have, so that no one may seize your crown. 12 If you conquer, I will make you a pillar in the temple of my God; you will never go out of it. I will write on you the name of my God, the new Jerusalem that comes down from my God out of heaven, and my own new name. 13 Let anyone who has an ear listen to what the Spirit is saying to the churches.

14 'And to the angel of the church in Laodicea write: The words of the Amen, the faithful and true witness, the origin of God's creation: 15 'I know your works; you are neither cold nor hot. 16 So, because you are lukewarm, and neither cold nor hot, I am about to spit you out of my mouth. 17 For you say, "I am rich, I have prospered, and I need nothing." You do not realize that you are wretched, pitiable, poor, blind, and naked. 18 Therefore I counsel you to buy from me gold refined by fire so that you may be rich; and white robes to clothe you and to keep the shame of your nakedness from being seen; and salve to anoint your eyes so that you may see. 19 I reprove and discipline those whom I love. Be earnest, therefore, and repent. 20 Listen! I am standing at the door, knocking; if you hear my voice and open the door, I will come in to you and eat with you, and you with me. 21 To the one who conquers I will give a place with me on my throne, just as I myself conquered and sat down with my Father on his throne. 22 Let anyone who has an ear listen to what the Spirit is saying to the churches.'

4 After this I looked, and there in heaven a door stood open! And the first voice, which I had heard speaking to me like a trumpet, said, 'Come up here, and I will show you what must take place after this.' 2 At once I was in the spirit, and there in heaven stood a throne, with one seated on the throne! 3 And the one seated there looks like jasper and cornelian, and around the throne is a rainbow that looks like an emerald. 4 Around the throne are twenty-four thrones, and seated on the thrones are twenty-four elders, dressed in white robes, with golden crowns on their heads. 5 Coming from the throne are flashes of lightning, and rumblings and peals of thunder, and in front of the throne burn seven flaming torches, which are the seven spirits of God; 6 and in front of the throne there is something like a sea of glass, like crystal.

Around the throne, and on each side of the throne, are four living creatures, full of eyes in front and behind: 7 the first living creature like a lion, the second living creature like an ox, the third living creature with a face like a human face, and the fourth living creature like a flying eagle. 8 And the four living creatures, each of them with six wings, are full of eyes all around and inside. Day and night without ceasing they sing,

'Holy, holy, holy, the Lord God the Almighty, who was and is and is to come.'

9 And whenever the living creatures give glory and honour and thanks to the one

who is seated on the throne, who lives for ever and ever, 10 the twenty-four elders fall before the one who is seated on the throne and worship the one who lives for ever and ever; they cast their crowns before the throne, singing,

11 'You are worthy, our Lord and God, to receive glory and honour and power, for you created all things, and by your will they existed and were created.'

5 Then I saw in the right hand of the one seated on the throne a scroll written on the inside and on the back, sealed with seven seals; 2 and I saw a mighty angel proclaiming with a loud voice, 'Who is worthy to open the scroll and break its seals?' 3 And no one in heaven or on earth or under the earth was able to open the scroll or to look into it. 4 And I began to weep bitterly because no one was found worthy to open the scroll or to look into it. 5 Then one of the elders said to me, 'Do not weep. See, the Lion of the tribe of Judah, the Root of David, has conquered, so that he can open the scroll and its seven seals.'

6 Then I saw between the throne and the four living creatures and among the elders a Lamb standing as if it had been slaughtered, having seven horns and seven eyes, which are the seven spirits of God sent out into all the earth. 7 He went and took the scroll from the right hand of the one who was seated on the throne. 8 When he had taken the scroll, the four living creatures and the twenty-four elders fell before the Lamb, each holding a harp and golden bowls full of incense, which are the prayers of the saints. 9 They sing a new song:

'You are worthy to take the scroll and to open its seals, for you were
slaughtered and by your blood you ransomed for God saints from
every tribe and language and people and nation;
10 you have made them to be a kingdom and priests serving our God,
and they will reign on earth.'

11 Then I looked, and I heard the voice of many angels surrounding the throne and the living creatures and the elders; they numbered myriads of myriads and thousands and thousands, 12 singing with full voice,

'Worthy is the Lamb that was slaughtered to receive power and wealth
and wisdom and might and honour and glory and blessing!'

13 Then I heard every creature in heaven and on earth and under the earth and in the sea, and all that is in them, singing,

'To the one seated on the throne and to the Lamb be blessing and honour
and glory and might for ever and ever!'

14 And the four living creatures said, 'Amen!' And the elders fell down and worshipped.

6 Then I saw the Lamb open one of the seven seals, and I heard one of the four living creatures call out, as with a voice of thunder, 'Come!' 2 I looked, and there was a white horse! Its rider had a bow; a crown was given to him, and he came out conquering and to conquer.

3 When he opened the second seal, I heard the second living creature call out, 'Come!' 4 And out came another horse, bright red; its rider was permitted to take peace from the earth, so that people would slaughter one another; and he was given a great sword.

5 When he opened the third seal, I heard the third living creature call out, 'Come!' I looked, and there was a black horse! Its rider held a pair of scales in his hand, 6 and I heard what seemed to be a voice in the midst of the four living creatures saying, 'A quart of wheat for a day's pay, and three quarts of barley for a day's pay, but do not damage the olive oil and the wine!' 7 When he opened the fourth seal, I heard the voice of the fourth living creature call out, 'Come!' 8 I looked and there was a pale green horse! Its rider's name was Death, and Hades followed with him; they were given authority over a fourth of the earth, to kill with sword, famine, and pestilence, and by the wild animals of the earth. 9 When he opened the fifth seal, I saw under the altar the souls of those who had been slaughtered for the word of God and for the testimony they had given; 10 they cried out with a loud voice, 'Sovereign Lord, holy and true, how long will it be before you judge and avenge our blood on the inhabitants of the earth?' 11 They were each given a white robe and told to rest a little longer, until the number would be complete both of their fellow-servants and of their brothers and sisters, who were soon to be killed as they themselves had been killed. 12 When he opened the sixth seal, I looked, and there came a great earthquake; the sun became black as sackcloth, the full moon became like blood, 13 and the stars of the sky fell to the earth as the fig tree drops its winter fruit when shaken by a gale. 14 The sky vanished like a scroll rolling itself up, and every mountain and island was removed from its place. 15 Then the kings of the earth and the magnates and the generals and the rich and the powerful, and everyone, slave and free, hid in the caves and among the rocks of the mountains, 16 calling to the mountains and rocks, 'Fall on us and hide us from the face of the one seated on the throne and from the wrath of the Lamb; 17 for the great day of their wrath has come, and who is able to stand?'

7 After this I saw four angels standing at the four corners of the earth, holding back the four winds of the earth so that no wind could blow on earth or sea or against any tree. 2 I saw another angel ascending from the rising of the sun, having the seal of the living God, and he called with a loud voice to the four angels who had been given power to damage earth and sea, 3 saying, 'Do not damage the earth or the sea or the trees, until we have marked the servants of our God with a seal on their foreheads. 4 And I heard the number of those who were sealed, one hundred and forty-four thousand, sealed out of every tribe of the people of Israel:

5 From the tribe of Judah twelve thousand sealed
from the tribe of Reuben twelve thousand,
from the tribe of Gad twelve thousand,
6 from the tribe of Asher twelve thousand,
from the tribe of Naphtali twelve thousand,
from the tribe of Manasseh twelve thousand,
7 from the tribe of Simeon twelve thousand,
from the tribe of Levi twelve thousand,
from the tribe of Issachar twelve thousand,
8 from the tribe of Zebulun twelve thousand,
from the tribe of Joseph twelve thousand,
from the tribe of Benjamin twelve thousand sealed.

9 After this I looked, and there was a great multitude that no one could count, from every nation, from all tribes and peoples and languages, standing before the throne and before the Lamb, robed in white, with palm branches in their hands. 10 They cried out in a loud voice, saying,

'Salvation belongs to our God who is seated on the throne, and to
the Lamb!'

11 And all the angels stood around the throne and around the elders and the four living creatures, and they fell on their faces before the throne and worshipped God, 12 singing,

'Amen! Blessing and glory and wisdom
and thanksgiving and honour
and power and might
be to our God for ever and ever!
Amen.'

13 Then one of the elders addressed me, saying, 'Who are these, robed in white, and where have they come from?' 14 I said to him, 'Sir, you are the one that knows,' Then he said to me, 'These are they who have come out of the great ordeal; they have washed their robes and made them white in the blood of of the Lamb.

15 For this reason they are before the throne of God,and worship him day and night within his temple, and the one who is seated on the throne will shelter them.

16 They will hunger no more, and thirst no more; the sun will not strike them, nor any scorching heat;

17 for the Lamb at the centre of the throne will be their shepherd, and he will guide them to springs of the water of life and God will wipe away every tear from their eyes.'

8 When the Lamb opened the seventh seal, there was silence in heaven for about half an hour. 2 And I saw the seven angels who stand before God, and seven trumpets were given to them. 3 Another angel with a golden censer came and stood at the altar; he was given a great quantity of incense to offer with the prayers of all the saints on the golden altar that is before the throne.4 And the smoke of the incense, with the prayers of the saints, rose before God from the hand of the angel. 5 Then the angel took the censer and filled with fire from the altar and threw it on the earth; and there were peals of thunder, rumblings, flashes of lightning, and an earthquake.

6 Now the seven angels who had the seven trumpets made ready to blow them.

7 The first angel blew his trumpet, and there came hail and fire, mixed with blood, and they were hurled to the earth; and a third of the earth was burned up, and a third of the trees were burned up, and all green grass was burned up. 8 The second angel blew his trumpet, and something like a great mountain, burning with fire, was thrown into the sea. 9 A third of the sea became blood,a third of the living creatures in the sea died, and a third of the ships were destroyed.

10 The third angel blew his trumpet, and a great star fell from heaven, blazing like a torch, and it fell on a third of the rivers and on the springs of water. 11 The name of the star is Wormwood. A third of the waters became wormwood, and many died from the water, because it was made bitter.

12 The fourth angel blew his trumpet, and a third of the sun was struck, and a third of the moon, and a third of the stars, so that a third of their light was darkened; and a third of the day was kept from shining, and likewise the night. 13 Then I

looked, and I heard an eagle crying with a loud voice as it flew in mid-heaven, 'Woe, woe, woe to the inhabitants of the earth, at the blasts of the other trumpets that the three angels are about to blow!'

9 And the fifth angel blew his trumpet, and I saw a star that had fallen from heaven to earth, and he was given the key to the shaft of the abyss; 2 he opened the shaft of the abyss, and from the shaft rose smoke like the smoke of a great furnace, and the sun and the air were darkened with the smoke from the shaft. 3 Then from the smoke came locusts on the earth, and they were given authority like the authority of scorpions of the earth. 4 They were told not to damage the grass of the earth or any green growth or any tree, but only those people who do not have the seal of God on their foreheads. 5 They were allowed to torture them for five months, but not to kill them, and their torture was like the torture of a scorpion when it stings someone. 6 And in those days people will seek death but will not find it; they will long to die, but death will flee from them.

7 In appearance the locusts were like horses equipped for battle. On their heads were what looked like crowns of gold; their faces were like human faces, 8 their hair like women's hair, and their teeth like lions' teeth; 9 they had scales like iron breastplates, and the noise of their wings was like the noise of many chariots with horses rushing into battle. 10 They have tails like scorpions, with stings, and in their tails is their power to harm people for five months. 11 They have as king over them the angel of the abyss; his name in Hebrew is Abaddon, and in Greek he is called Apollyon.

12 The first woe has passed. There are still two woes to come.

13 Then the sixth angel blew his trumpet, and I heard a voice from the four horns of the golden altar before God, 14 saying to the sixth angel who had the trumpet, 'Release the four angels who are bound at the great river Euphrates.' 15 So the four angels were released, who had been held ready for the hour, the day, the month, the year, to kill a third of humankind. 16 The number of the troops of cavalry was two hundred million; I heard their number. 17 And this was how I saw the horses in my vision: the riders wore breastplates the colour of fire and of sapphire and of sulphur; the heads of the horses were like lions' heads, and fire and smoke and sulphur came out of their mouths. 18 By these three plagues a third of humankind was killed, by the fire and smoke and sulphur coming out of their mouths. 19 For the power of the horses is in their mouths and in their tails; their tails are like serpents, having heads; and with them they inflict harm.

20 The rest of humankind, who were not killed by these plagues, did not repent of the works of their hands or give up worshipping demons and idols of gold and silver and bronze and stone and wood, which cannot see or hear or walk. **21** And they did not repent of their murders or their sorceries or their fornication or their thefts.

10 And I saw another mighty angel coming down from heaven, wrapped in a cloud, with a rainbow over his head; his face was like the sun, and his legs like pillars of fire. **2** He held a little scroll open in his hand. Setting his right food on the sea and his left foot on the land, **3** he gave a great shout, like a lion roaring. And when he shouted, the seven thunders sounded. **4** And when the seven thunders had sounded, I was about to write, but I heard a voice from heaven saying, 'Seal up what the seven thunders have said, and do not write it down.' **5** Then the angel whom I saw standing on the sea and the land raised his right hand to heaven **6** and swore by him who lives for ever and ever, who created heaven and what is in it, the earth and what is in it, and the sea and what is in it: 'There will be no more delay, **7** but in the days when the seventh angel is to blow his trumpet, the mystery of God will be fulfilled, as he announced to his servants the prophets.'

8 Then the voice that I had heard from heaven spoke to me again, saying, 'Go, take the scroll that is open in the hand of the angel who is standing on the sea and on the land.' **9** So I went to the angel and told him to give me the little scroll; and he said to me, 'Take it, and eat it; it will be bitter to your stomach, but sweet as honey in your mouth.' **10** So I took the little scroll from the hand of the angel and ate it; it was sweet as honey in my mouth, but when I had eaten it, my stomach was made bitter. **11** Then they said to me, 'You must prophesy again about many peoples and nations and languages and kings.'

11 Then I was given a measuring rod like a staff, and I was told, 'Come and measure the temple of God and the altar and those who worship there, **2** but do not measure the court outside the temple; leave that out, for it is given over to the Gentiles and they will trample ove the holy city for forty-two months. **3** And I will grant my two witnesses authority to prophesy for one thousand two hundred and sixty days, wearing sackcloth.'

4 These are the two olive trees and the two lampstands that stand before the Lord of the earth. **5** And if anyone wants to harm them, fire pours from their mouth and consumes their foes; anyone who wants to harm them must be killed in this manner. 6 They have authority to shut the sky, so that no rain may fall during the days of their prophesying, and they have authority over the waters to turn them into blood, and to strike the earth with every kind of plague, as often as they desire. 7 When they have finished their testimony, the beast that comes up from the abyss will make war on them and conquer them and kill them, 8 and their dead bodies will lie in the street of the great city that is prophetically called Sodom and Egypt, where also their Lord was crucified. 9 For three and a half days members of the peoples and tribes and languages and nations will gaze at their dead bodies and refuse to let them be placed in a tomb; 10 and the inhabitants of the earth will gloat over them and celebrate and exchange presents, because these two prophets had been a torment to the inhabitants of the earth.

11 But after the three and a half days, the breath of life from God entered them, and they stood on their feet, and those who saw them were terrified. 12 Then they heard a loud voice from heaven saying to them, 'Come up here!' And they went up to heaven in a cloud while their enemies watched them. 13 At that moment there was a great earthquake, and a tenth of the city fell; seven thousand people were killed in the earthquake, and the rest were terrified and gave glory to the God of heaven.

14 The second woe has passed. The third woe is coming very soon.

15 Then the seventh angel blew his trumpet, and there were loud voices in heaven, saying,

> 'The kingdom of the world has become the kingdom of our Lord and
> of his Messiah, and he will reign for ever and ever.'

16 Then the twenty-four elders who sit on their thrones before God fell on their faces and worshipped God, 17 singing,

> 'We give you thanks, Lord God Almighty, who are and who were,
> for you have taken your great power and begun to reign.
> 18 The nations raged, but your wrath has come, and the time for judging the dead,
> for rewarding your servants, the prophets and saints and all who fear your name, both small and great,
> and for destroying those who destroy the earth.'

19 Then God's temple in heaven was opened, and the risk of his covenant was seen within his temple; and there were flashes of lightning, rumblings, peals of thunder, an earthquake, and heavy hail.

12 A great portent appeared in heaven: a woman clothed with the sun, with the moon under her feet, and on her head a crown of twelve stars.
2 She was pregnant and was crying out in birth pangs, in the agony of giving birth.
3 Then another portent appeared in heaven: a great red dragon, with seven heads and ten horns, and seven diadems on his heads. 4 His tail swept down a third of the stars of heaven and threw them to the earth. Then the dragon stood before the woman who was about to bear a child, so that he might devour her child as soon as it was born. 5 And she gave birth to a son, a male child, who is to rule all the nations with a rod of iron. But her child was snatched away and taken to God and to his throne; 6 and the woman fled into the wilderness, where she has a place prepared by God, so that there she can be nourished for one thousand two hundred and sixty days.
7 And war broke out in heaven; Michael and his angels fought against the dragon. The dragon and his angels fought back, 8 but they were defeated, and there was no longer any place for them in heaven. 9 The great dragon was thrown down, that ancient serpent, who is called the Devil and Satan, the deceiver of the whole world – he was thrown down to the earth, and his angels were thrown down with him.
10 Then I heard a loud voice in heaven, proclaiming,

'Now have come the salvation and the power and the kingdom of our God and the authority of his Messiah,
for the accuser of our comrades has been thrown down, who accuses them day and night before our God.
11 But they have conquered him by the blood of the Lamb and by the word of their testimony,
for they did not cling to life even in the face of death.
12 Rejoice then, you heavens and those who dwell in them!
But woe to the earth and the sea, for the devil has come down to you
with great wrath, because he knows that his time is short!'

13 So when the dragon saw that he had been thrown down to the earth, he pursued the woman who had given birth to the male child. 14 But the woman was given the two wings of the great eagle, so that she could fly from the serpent into the wilderness, to her place where she is nourished for a time, and times, and half a time. 15 Then from his mouth the serpent poured water like a river after the woman, to sweep her away with the flood. 16 But the earth came to the help of

the woman; it opened its mouth and swallowed the river that the dragon had poured from his mouth. 17 Then the dragon was angry with the woman, and went off to make war on the rest of her children, those who keep the commandments of God and hold the testimony of Jesus. 18 Then the dragon took his stand on the sand of the seashore.

13 And I saw a beast rising out of the sea, having ten horns and seven heads; and on its horns were ten diadems, and on its heads were blasphemous names. 2 And the beast that I saw was like a leopard, its feet were like a bear's, and its mouth was like a lion's mouth. And the dragon gave it his power and his throne and great authority. 3 One of its heads seemed to have received a death-blow, but its mortal wound had been healed. In amazement the whole earth followed the beast. 4 They worshipped the dragon, for he had given his authority to the beast, saying, 'Who is like the beast, and who can fight against it?' 5 The beast was given a mouth uttering haughty and blasphemous words, and it was allowed to exercise authority for forty-two months. 6 It opened its mouth to utter blasphemies against God, blaspheming his name and his dwelling, that is, those who dwell in heaven. 7 Also, it was allowed to make war on the saints and to conquer them. It was given authority over every tribe and people and language and nation, 8 and all the inhabitants of the earth will worship it, everyone whose name has not been written from the foundation of the world in the book of life of the Lamb that was slaughtered.

9 Let anyone who has an ear listen:

10 If you are to be taken captive, into captivity you go;

if you kill with the sword, with the sword you must be killed.

Here is a call for the endurance and faith of the saints.

11 Then I saw another beast that rose out of the earth; it had two horns like a lamb and it spoke like a dragon. 12 It exercises all the authority of the first beast, whose mortal wound had been healed. 13 It performs great signs, even making fire come down from heaven to earth in the sight of all; 14 and by the signs that it is allowed to perform on behalf of the beast, it deceives the inhabitants of earth, telling them to make an image for the beast that had been wounded by the sword and yet lived; 15 and it was allowed to give breath to the image of the beast, so that the image of the beast could even speak and cause those who would not worship the image of the beast to be killed. 16 Also it causes all, both small and great, both rich and

poor, both free and slave, to be marked on the right hand or the forehead, 17 so that no one can buy or sell who does not have the mark, that is, the name of the beast or the number of its name. 18 This calls for wisdom: let anyone with understanding calculate the number of the beast, for it is the number of a person. Its number is six hundred and sixty-six.

14 Then I looked, and there was the Lamb, standing on Mount Zion! And with him were one hundred and forty-four thousand who had his name and his Father's name written on their foreheads. 2 And I heard a voice from heaven like the sound of many waters and like the sound of loud thunder; the voice I heard was like the sound of harpists playing on their harps, 3 and they sing a new song before the throne and before the four living creatures and before the elders. No one could learn that song except the one hundred and forty-four thousand who have been redeemed from the earth. 4 It is these who have not defiled themselves with women, for they are virgins; these follow the Lamb wherever he goes. They have been redeemed from humankind as first fruits for God and the Lamb, 5 and in their mouth no lie was found; they are blameless.

6 Then I saw another angel flying in mid-heaven, with an eternal gospel to proclaim to those who live on the earth – to every nation and tribe and language and people. 7 He said in a loud voice, 'Fear God and give him glory, for the hour of his judgement has come; and worship him who made heaven and earth, the sea and the springs of water.'

8 Then another angel, a second, followed, saying, 'Fallen, fallen is Babylon the great! She has made all nations drink of the wine of the wrath of her fornication.' 9 Then another angel, a third, followed them, crying with a loud voice, 'Those who worship the beast and its image, and receive a mark on their forheads or on their hands, 10 they will also drink the wine of God's wrath, poured unmixed into the cup of his anger, and they will be tormented with fire and sulphur in the presence of the holy angels and in the presence of the Lamb. 11 And the smoke of their torment goes up for ever and ever. There is no rest day or night for those who worship the beast and its image and for anyone who receives the mark of its name.' 12 Here is a call for the endurance of the saints, those who keep the commandments of God and hold fast to the faith of Jesus.

13 And I heard a voice from heaven saying, 'Write this: Blessed are the dead who from now on die in the Lord.' 'Yes,' says the Spirit, 'they will rest from their labours, for their deeds follow them.'

14 Then I looked, and there was a white cloud, and seated on the cloud was one like the Son of Man, with a golden crown on his head, and sharp sickle in his hand! 15 Another angel came out of the temple, calling with a loud voice to the one who sat on the cloud, 'Use your sickle and reap, for the hour to reap has come, because the harvest of the earth is fully ripe.' 16 So the one who sat on the cloud swung his sickle over the earth, and the earth was reaped.

17 Then another angel came out of the temple in heaven, and he too had a sharp sickle. 18 Then another angel came out from the altar, the angel who has authority over fire, and he called with a loud voice to him who had the sharp sickle, 'Use your sharp sickle and gather the clusters of the vine of the earth, for its grapes are ripe.' 19 So the angel swung his sickle over the earth and gathered the vintage of the earth, and the threw it into the great wine press of the wrath of God. 20 And the wine press was trodden outside the city, and blood flowed from the wine press, as high as a horse's bridle, for a distance of about two hundred miles.

15 Then I saw another portent in heaven, great and amazing: seven angels with seven plagues, which are the last, for with them the wrath of God is ended.

2 And I saw what appeared to be a sea of glass mixed with fire, and those who had conquered the beast and its image and the number of its name standing beside the sea of glass with harps of God in their hands.

3 And they sing the song of Moses, the servant of God, and the song of the Lamb;
'Great and amazing are your deeds, Lord God the Almighty!
Just and true are your ways, King of nations!
4 Lord, who will not fear and glorify your name?
For you alone are holy. All nations will come and worship before you,
for your judgements have been revealed.'

5 After this I looked, and the temple of the tent of witness in heaven was opened, 6 and out of the temple came the seven angels with the seven plagues, robed in pure bright linen, with golden sashes across their chests. 7 Then one of the four living creatures gave the seven angels seven golden bowls full of the wrath of God, who lives for ever and ever; 8 and the temple was filled with smoke from the glory of God and from his power, and no one could enter the temple until the seven plagues of the seven angels were ended.

16 Then I heard a loud voice from the temple telling the seven angels, 'Go and pour out on the earth the seven bowls of the wrath of God.'

2 So the first angel went and poured his bowl on the earth, and a foul and painful sore came on those who had the mark of the beast and who worshipped its image. 3 The second angel poured his bowl into the sea, and it became like the blood of a corpse, and every living thing in the sea died. 4 The third angel poured his bowl into the rivers and the springs of water, and they became blood. 5 And I heard the angel of the waters say,

'You are just, O Holy One, who are and were, for you have judged these things;
6 because they shed the blood of saints and prophets, you have given them blood to drink.
It is what they deserve!'
7 And I heard the altar respond, 'Yes, O Lord God, the Almighty, your judgements are true and just!'

8 The fourth angel poured his bowl on the sun, and it was allowed to scorch people with fire; 9 they were scorched by the fierce heat, but they cursed the name of God, who had authority over these plagues, and they did not repent and give him glory.

10 The fifth angel poured his bowl on the throne of the beast, and its kingdom was plunged into darkness; people gnawed their tongues in agony, 11 and cursed the God of heaven because of their pains and sores, and they did not repent of their deeds.

12 The sixth angel poured his bowl on the great river Euphrates, and its water was dried up in order to prepare the way for the kings from the east. 13 And I saw three foul spirits like frogs coming from the mouth of the dragon, from the mouth of the beast, and from the mouth of the false prophet. 14 These are demonic spirits, performing signs, who go abroad to the kings of the whole world, to assemble them for battle on the great day of God the Almighty. 15 ('See, I am coming like a thief! Blessed is the one who stays awake and is clothed, not going about naked and exposed to shame.') 16 And they assembled them at the place that in Hebrew is called Armageddon.

17 The seventh angel poured his bowl into the air, and a loud voice came out of the temple, from the throne, saying, 'It is done!' 18 And there came flashes of lightning, rumblings, peals of thunder, and a violent earthquake, such as had not

occurred since people were upon the earth, so violent was that earthquake. 19 The great city was split into three parts, and the cities of the nations fell. God remembered great Babylon and gave her the wine-cup of the fury of this wrath. 20 And every island fled away, and no mountains were to be found; 21 and huge hailstones, each weighing about a hundred pounds, dropped from heaven on people, until they cursed God for the plague of the hail, so fearful was that plague.

17 Then one of the seven angels who had the seven bowls came and said to me, 'Come, I will show you the judgement of the great whore who is seated on many waters, 2 with whom the kings of the earth have committed fornication, and with the wine of whose fornication the inhabitants of the earth have become drunk.' 3 So he carried me away in the spirit into a wilderness, and I saw a woman sitting on a scarlet beast that was full of blasphemous names, and it had seven heads and ten horns. 4 The woman was clothed in purple and scarlet, and adorned with gold and jewels and pearls, holding in her hand a golden cup full of abominations and the impurities of her fornication; 5 and on her forehead was written a name, a mystery: 'Babylon the great, mother of whores and of earth's abominations.' 6 And I saw that the woman was drunk with the blood of the saints and the blood of the witnesses to Jesus.

When I saw her, I was greatly amazed. 7 But the angel said to me, 'Why are you so amazed? I will tell you the mystery of the woman, and of the beast with seven heads and ten horns that carries her. 8 The beast that you saw was, and is not, and is about to ascend from the abyss and go to destruction. And the inhabitants of the earth, whose names have not been written in the book of life from the foundation of the world, will be amazed when they see the beast, because it was and is not and is to come. 9 This calls for a mind that has wisdom: the seven heads are seven mountains on which the woman is seated; also, they are seven kings, 10 of whom five have fallen, one is living, and the other has not yet come; and when he comes, he must remain for only a little while. 11 As for the beast that was and is not, it is an eighth but it belongs to the seven, and it goes to destruction. 12 And the ten horns that you saw are ten kings who have not yet received a kingdom, but they are to receive authority as kings for one hour, together with the beast. 13 These are united in yielding their power and authority to the beast; 14 they will make war on the Lamb, and the Lamb will conquer them, for he his Lord of lords and King of kings, and those with him are called and chosen and faithful.'

15 And he said to me, 'The waters that you saw, where the whore is seated, are peoples and multitudes and nations and languages. 16 And the ten horns that you saw, they and the beast will hate the whore; they will devour her flesh and burn her up with fire. 17 For God has put it into their hearts to carry out his purpose by agreeing to give their kingdom to the beast, until the words of God will be fulfilled. 18 The woman you saw is the great city that rules over the kings of the earth.'

18 After this I saw another angel coming down from heaven, having great authority; and the earth was made bright with his splendour. 2 He called out with a mighty voice,

'Fallen, fallen is Babylon the great! It has become a dwelling-place of demons,
a haunt of every foul spirit, a haunt of every foul bird, a haunt of every foul and hateful beast.
3 For all the nations have drunk of the wine of the wrath of her fornication, and the kings of the earth have committed fornication with her, and the merchants of the earth have grown rich from the power of her luxury.'

4 Then I heard another voice from heaven saying,

'Come out of her, my people, so that you do not take part in her sins,
and so that you do not share in her plagues;
5 for her sins are heaped high as heaven, and God has remembered her iniquities.
6 Render to her as she herself has rendered, and repay her double for her deeds; mix a double draught for her in the cup she mixed.
7 As she glorified herself and lived luxuriously, so give her a like measure of torment and grief.
Since in her heart she says, "I rule as a queen;
I am no widow, and I will never see grief",
8 therefore her plagues will come in a single day – pestilence and mourning and famine –
and she will be burned with fire; for mighty is the Lord God who judges her.'

9 And the kings of the earth, who committed fornication and lived in luxury with her, will weep and wail over her when they see the smoke of her burning; 10 they will stand far off, in fear of her torment, and say, 'Alas, alas, the great city, Babylon, the mighty city!
For in one hour your judgement has come.'
11 And the merchants of the earth weep and mourn for her, since no one buys their cargo any more, 12 cargo of gold, silver, jewels and pearls, fine linen, purple, silk and scarlet, all kinds of scented wood, all articles of ivory, all articles of costly wood, bronze, iron, and marble, 13 cinnamon, spice, incense, myrrh, frankincense, wine, olive oil, choice flour and wheat, cattle and sheep, horses and chariots, slaves – and human lives.

14 'The fruit for which your soul longed has gone from you,
and all your dainties and your splendour are lost to you, never to be found again!'
15 The merchants of these wares, who gained wealth from her, will stand far off, in fear of her torment, weeping and mourning aloud,

16 'Alas, alas, the great city, clothed in fine linen, in purple and scarlet, adorned with gold, with jewels, and with pearls!
17 For in one hour all this wealth has been laid waste!'
And all shipmasters and seafarers, sailors and all whose trade is on the sea, stood far off 18 and cried out as they saw the smoke of her burning,

'What city was like the great city?"
19 And they threw dust on their heads, as they wept and mourned, crying out,
'Alas, alas, the great city, where all who had ships at sea grew rich by her wealth!
For in one hour she has been laid waste.'
20 Rejoice over her, O heaven, you saints and apostles and prophets! For God has given judgement for you against her. 21 Then a mighty angel took up a stone like a great millstone and threw it into the sea, saying,
'With such violence Babylon the great city will be thrown down, and will be found no more;
22 and the sound of harpists and minstrels and of flautists and trumpeters will be heard in you no more;
and an artisan of any trade will be found in you no more;
and the sound of the millstone will be heard in you no more;

23 and the light of a lamp will shine in you no more;

and the voice of bridegroom and bride will be heard in you no more;

for your merchants were the magnates of the earth, and all nations were deceived by your sorcery.

24 And in you was found the blood of prophets and of saints, and of all who have been slaughtered on earth.'

19 After this I heard what seemed to be the loud voice of a great multitude in heaven, saying,

'Hallelujah!

Salvation and glory and power to our God, 2 for his judgements are true and just;

he has judged the great whore who corrupted the earth with her fornication,

and he has avenged on her the blood of his servants.'

3 Once more they said,

'Hallelujah!

The smoke goes up from her for ever and ever.'

4 And the twenty-four elders and the four living creatures fell down and worshipped God who is seated on the throne, saying,

'Amen. Hallelujah!'

5 And from the throne came a voice saying,

'Praise our God, all you his servants,

and all who fear him, small and great.'

6 Then I heard what seemed to be the voice of a great multitude, like the sound of many waters and like the sound of mighty thunder-peals, crying out,

'Hallelujah!

For the Lord our God the Almighty reigns.

7 Let us rejoice and exult and give him the glory,

for the marriage of the Lamb has come, and his bride has made herself ready;

8 to her it has been granted to be clothed with fine linen, bright and pure; –

for the fine linen is the righteous deeds of the saints.' 9 And the angel said to me, 'Write this: Blessed are those who are invited to the marriage supper of the Lamb.'

And he said to me, 'These are true words of God.' 10 Then I fell down at his feet to worship him, but he said to me, 'You must not do that! I am a fellow-servant with you and your comrades who hold the testimony of Jesus. Worship God! For the testimony of Jesus is the spirit of prophecy.'

11 Then I saw heaven opened, and there was a white horse! Its rider is called Faithful and True, and in righteousness he judges and makes war. 12 His eyes are like a flame of fire, and on his head are many diadems; and he has a name inscribed that no one knows but himself. 13 He is clothed in a robe dipped in blood, and his name is called The Word of God. 14 And the armies of heaven, wearing fine linen, white and pure, were following him on white horses. 15 From his mouth comes a sharp sword with which to strike down the Gentiles, and he will rule them with a rod of iron; he will tread the wine press of the fury of the wrath of God the Almighty. 16 On his robe and on his thigh he has a name inscribed, 'King of kings and Lord of lords'.

17 Then I saw an angel standing in the sun, and with a loud voice he called to all the birds that fly in mid-heaven, 'Come, gather for the great supper of God, 18 to eat the flesh of kings, the flesh of captains, the flesh of the mighty, the flesh of horses and their riders – flesh of all, both free and slave, both small and great.'
19 Then I saw the beast and the kings of the earth with their armies gathered to make war against the rider on the horse and against his army. 20 And the beast was captured, and with it the false prophet who had performed in its presence the signs by which he deceived those who had received the mark of the beast and those who worshipped its image. These two were thrown alive into the lake of fire that burns with sulphur. 21 And the rest were killed by the sword of the rider on the horse, the sword that came from his mouth; and all the birds were gorged with their flesh.

20 Then I saw an angel coming down from heaven, holding in his hand the key to the abyss and a great chain. 2 He seized the dragon, that ancient serpent, who is the Devil and Satan, and bound him for a thousand years, 3 and threw him into the abyss, and locked and sealed it over him, so that he would deceive the Gentiles no more, until the thousand years were ended. After that he must be let out for a little while.
4 Then I saw thrones, and those seated on them were given authority to judge. I

also saw the souls of those who had been beheaded for their testimony to Jesus and for the word of God. They had not worshipped the beast or its image and had not received its mark on their foreheads or their hands. they came to life and reigned with Christ for a thousand years. 5 (The rest of the dead did not come to life until the thousand years were ended.) This is the first resurrection. 6 Blessed and holy are those who share in the first resurrection. Over these the second death has no power, but they will be priests of God and of Christ, and they will reign with him for a thousand years.

7 When the thousand years are ended, Satan will be released from his prison 8 and will come out to deceive the Gentiles at the four corners of the earth, Gog and Magog, in order to gather them for battle; they are as numerous as the sands of the sea. 9 They marched up over the breadth of the earth and surrounded the camp of the saints and the beloved city. And fire came down from heaven and consumed them. 10 And the devil who had deceived them was thrown into the lake of fire and sulphur, where the beast and the false prophet were, and they will be tormented day and night for ever and ever.

11 Then I saw a great white throne and the one who sat on it; the earth and the heaven fled from his presence, and no place was found for them. 12 And I saw the dead, great and small, standing before the throne, and books were opened. Also another book was opened, the book of life. And the dead were judged according to their works, as recorded in the books. 13 And the sea gave up the dead that were in it, Death and Hades gave up the dead that were in them, and all were judged according to what they had done. 14 Then Death and Hades were thrown into the lake of fire. This is the second death, the lake of fire; 15 and anyone whose name was not found written in the book of life was thrown into the lake of fire.

21 Then I saw a new heaven and a new earth; for the first heaven and the first earth had passed away, and the sea was no more. 2 And I saw the holy city, the new Jerusalem, coming down out of heaven from God, prepared as a bride adorned for her husband. 3 And I heard a loud voice from the throne saying,

'See, the home of God is among mortals.

He will dwell with them;

they will be his peoples,

and God himself will be with them;

4 he will wipe every tear from their eyes.

Death will be no more;

mourning and crying and pain will be no more,

for the first things have passed away.'

5 And the one who was seated on the throne said, 'See, I am making all things new.' Also he said, 'Write this, for these words are trustworthy and true.' 6 Then he said to me, 'It is done! I am the Alpha and the Omega, the beginning and the end. To the thirsty I will give water as a gift from the spring of the water of life. 7 Those who conquer will inherit these things, and I will be their God and they will be my children. 8 But as for the cowardly, the faithless, the polluted, the murderers, the fornicators, the sorcerers, the idolaters, and all liars, their place will be in the lake that burns with fire and sulphur, which is the second death.' 9 Then one of the seven angels who had the seven bowls full of the seven last plagues came and said to me, 'Come, I will show you the bride, the wife of the Lamb.' 10 And in the spirit he carried me away to a great, high mountain and showed me the holy city Jerusalem coming down out of heaven from God. 11 It has the glory of God and a radiance like a very rare jewel, like jasper, clear as crystal. 12 It has a great, high wall with twelve gates, and at the gates twelve angels, and on the gates are inscribed the names of the twelve tribes of the Israelites; 13 on the east three gates, on the north three gates, on the south three gates, and on the west three gates. 14 And the wall of the city has twelve foundations, and on them are the twelve names of the twelve apostles of the Lamb. 15 The angel who talked to me had a measuring rod of gold to measure the city and its gates and walls. 16 The city lies foursquare, its length the same as its width; and he measured the city with his rod, fifteen hundred miles; its length and width and height are equal. 17 He also measured its wall, one hundred and forty-four cubits by human measurement, which the angel was using. 18 The wall is built of jasper, while the city is pure gold, clear as glass. 19 The foundations of the wall of the city are adorned with every jewel; the first was jasper, the second sapphire, the third agate, the fourth emerald, 20 the fifth onyx, the sixth cornelian, the seventh chrysolite, the eighth beryl, the ninth topaz, the tenth chrysoprase, the eleventh jacinth, the twelfth amethyst. 21 And the twelve gates are twelve pearls, each of the gates is a single pearl, and the street of the city is pure gold, transparent as glass. 22 I saw no temple in the city, for its temple is the Lord God the Almighty and the Lamb. 23 And the city has no need of sun or moon to shine on it, for the glory of God is its light, and its lamp is the Lamb. 24 The nations will walk by its light, and the kings of

the earth will bring their glory into it. 25 Its gates will never be shut by day – and there will be no night there. 26 People will bring into it the glory and the honour of the Gentiles. 27 But nothing unclean will enter it, nor anyone who practises abomination or falsehood, but only those who are written in the Lamb's book of life.

22 Then the angel showed me the river of the water of life, bright as crystal, flowing from the throne of God and of the Lamb 2 through the middle of the street of the city. On either side of the river is the tree of life with its twelve kinds of fruit, producing its fruit each month; and the leaves of the tree are for the healing of the Gentiles. 3 Nothing accursed will be found there anymore. But the throne of God and of the Lamb will be in it, and his servants will worship him; 4 they will see his face, and his name will be on their foreheads. 5 And there will be no more night; they need no light of lamp or sun, for the Lord God will be their light, and they will reign for ever and ever.

6 And he said to me, 'These words are trustworthy and true, for the Lord, the God of the spirits of the prophets, has sent his angel to show his servants what must soon take place.'

7 'See, I am coming soon! Blessed is the one who keeps the words of the prophecy of this book.'

8 I, John, am the one who heard and saw these things. And when I heard and saw them, I fell down to worship at the feet of the angel who showed them to me; 9 but he said to me, 'You must not do that! I am a fellow-servant with you and your comrades the prophets, and with those who keep the words of this book. Worship God!'

10 And he said to me, 'Do not seal up the words of the prophecy of this book, for the time is near. 11 Let the evildoer still do evil, and the filthy still be filthy, and the righteous still do right, and the holy still be holy.'

12 'See, I am coming soon; my reward is with me, to repay according to everyone's work. 13 I am the Alpha and the Omega, the first and the last, the beginning and the end.'

14 Blessed are those who wash their robes, so that they will have the right to the tree of life and may enter the city by the gates. 15 Outside are the dogs and sorcerers and fornicators and murderers and idolators, and everyone who loves and practises falsehood.

16 'It is I, Jesus, who sent my angel to you with this testimony for the churches. I

am the root and the descendant of David, the bright morning star.'

17 The Spirit and the bride say, 'Come.'

And let everyone who hears say, 'Come.'

And let everyone who is thirsty come.

Let anyone who wishes take the water of life as a gift.

18 I warn everyone who hears the words of this prophecy of this book: if anyone adds to them, God will add to that person the plagues described in this book; 19 if anyone takes away from the words of the book of this prophecy, God will take away that person's share in the tree of life and in the holy city, which are described in this book.

20 The one who testifies to these things says, 'Surely I am coming soon.' Amen. Come, Lord Jesus!

21 The grace of the Lord Jesus be with all the saints. Amen.

Index